Other Neil Anderson titles published by Monarch Books:

The Bondage Breaker (with Study Guide)
Each New Day with Neil T. Anderson
Freedom from Fear
God's Power at Work in You
Higher Ground
Living Free In Christ
Radical Image
Righteous Pursuit
Set Free (Omnibus Edition)
Steps to Freedom in Christ

Available from Christian bookshops.

D0185237

Of the many things I appreciate about Neil Anderson's ministry, his commitment to God's Word tops my list. Neil goes to God's Word to demonstrate that resolution in life is found in the Word of life because it points us to the Lord of life.

Robert B. Bugh
Senior Pastor, Wheaton Bible Church
Wheaton, Illinois

Neil Anderson touches a nerve of vital need in the Body of Christ! His ministry in the arena of spiritual growth is sound-minded, trustworthy and — best of all — Christ-centered and Bible-based. I recommend him and his work.

Jack W. Hayford
President, The King's Seminary
Founding Pastor, The Church On The Way
Van Nuys, California

Dr. Neil Anderson has done a masterful job of taking a rather complex truth and making it plain enough for all to understand and practical enough for all to experience. The principles in *Victory over the Darkness* have helped us to disciple both old and new believers in our church. As a result, lives are being transformed by the power of God.

Gerald Martin
Pastor, Cornerstone Church and Ministries
Harrisonburg, Virginia

Victory over the Darkness is a much-needed book written for everyone who longs for spiritual growth and, even more, joyous spiritual victory in a dark world.

Robert L. Saucy
Talbot School of Theology
La Mirada, California

Victory
over
the Darkness

with Study Guide

Dr. Neil T. Anderson

MONARCH
BOOKS
Mill Hill, London

First published in the USA by Regal Books, a division
of GL Publications, Ventura, California, USA.
First British edition 1992.
Reprinted 1993, 1994, 1995, 1996, 1997.
New edition with study guide 1998.
Reprinted 1999, 2000.
Revised edition 2001.
Reprinted with Study Guide 2002.

ISBN 1 85424 572 4

British Library Cataloguing Data
A catalogue record for this book is available
from the British Library.

Book design and production for the publishers by
Bookprint Creative Services
P.O. Box 827, BN21 3YJ, England
Printed in Great Britain.

DEDICATION

To my wife, Joanne, who has been my faithful companion, ardent supporter, friend and lover through all it takes to be the person God wants me to be.

And to my children, Heidi and Karl, who have borne the brunt of being PKs. You are number one in my eyes, and I thank you for sharing many difficult years with me. You never asked for a father who was called into ministry, but I have never heard you complain about that. Thank you for being the great kids you are. I love you next to God.

CONTENTS

persons — new in relationship to God and new in themselves.'

ACKNOWLEDGMENTS

'Writing a book was a project I intended to do when I retired. I love the ministry, and interacting with people in teaching and counselling is my life. So when I attended a writers' conference at Biola University in anticipation of my first sabbatical as a seminary professor, I was probably the only one there who didn't want to write a book.'

I wrote those words 10 years ago when the first edition of this my first book went into print. More than 30 books, youth editions and study guides have come off the press these past 10 years. God obviously had other plans for my life. Ed Stewart assisted me in writing the first edition of this book, and a Talbot student named Carolina typed the first manuscript. I have done my own writing and typing ever since.

I am very grateful for the support of Gospel Light. Thank you for trusting me with the message of this book. I am delighted and surprised that 700,000 copies of the first edition have been sold and, hopefully, read, and for the many translations that have been distributed around the world. I am equally delighted that you asked me to do a second, 10-year anniversary edition. A lot of water has gone under the bridge since the first edition went into print. I have gained a lot of experience in writing and I have matured considerably myself. Consequently, I believe this second edition is a much better book than the first edition.

I am grateful for the excellent faculty at Biola University/

Talbot School of Theology, where I have had the privilege of teaching for 10 years. Special thanks to Dr. Robert Saucy, who has been my mentor, friend and favorite theologian. Bob, you have no idea how much I value your critical mind and your willingness to read what I produce.

Thanks to Mick Boersma and Gary McIntosh, my colleagues in the practical theology department at Talbot. I value you as friends and I enjoyed sharing in ministry with you. Your support was invaluable.

I am also thankful for the many Talbot students who challenged me to stay true to God's Word, and who allowed me to share my life with them.

None of this would be possible, however, without my parents, Marvin and Bertha Anderson. Thank you for my physical heritage that made it easy to enter into my spiritual heritage. Thousands of life illustrations have poured out of my messages from those early years on the farm in Minnesota. Thank you for faithfully taking me to church, and for the moral atmosphere in which I was raised.

It has been my privilege to witness thousands discover their identity in Christ and live victorious lives. The thought of many others being helped through the printed page is awesome, and I am grateful to all who made this opportunity possible.

INTRODUCTION
Lend Me Your Hope

Several years ago in my first pastorate, I committed myself to disciple a young man in my church. It was my first formal attempt at one-on-one discipling. Russ and I decided to meet early every Tuesday morning so I could lead him through an inductive Bible study on the topic of love. We both began with high hopes. Russ was looking forward to taking some major steps of growth as a Christian, and I was eager to help him develop into a mature believer.

Six months later we were still slogging through the same inductive Bible study on love. We weren't getting anywhere. For some reason, our Paul-and-Timothy relationship wasn't working. Russ didn't seem to be growing as a Christian. He felt defeated and I felt responsible for his defeat — but I didn't know what else to do. Our once high hopes for Russ's great strides toward maturity had gradually deflated like a balloon with a slow leak. We eventually stopped meeting together.

Two years later, after I had moved to another pastorate, Russ came to see me. He poured out the story of what had been going on in his life during our brief one-on-one relationship — a story that revealed a secret part of his life I never knew existed. Russ was deeply involved in sin and unwilling to share his struggle with me. I could sense that he wasn't free, but I had no clue why this was the case.

At that time, I had little experience with people in the bondage of sin and was determined to plough on. I thought the major problem was just his unwillingness to complete the material. Now, however, I am convinced that my attempts at discipling Russ failed for another reason.

The apostle Paul wrote, 'I gave you milk to drink, not solid food; for *you were not yet able to receive it.* Indeed, even now *you are not yet able*, for you are still fleshly. For since there is jealousy and strife among you, are you not fleshly, and are you not walking like mere men?' (1 Cor. 3:2,3, emphasis added). Apparently, because of unresolved conflicts in their lives, carnal Christians are not able to receive the solid food of God's Word.

That's when I began to discern that discipling people to Christian maturity involves much more than leading them through a step-by-step, 10-week Bible study. We live in a country glutted with biblical material, Christian books, radio and television, but many Christians are not moving on to spiritual maturity. Some are no more loving now than they were 20 years ago. We read in 1 Timothy, 'The goal of our instruction is love from a pure heart and a good conscience and a sincere faith' (1:5).

Since that time the focus of my ministry, both as a pastor and a seminary professor, has been the interrelated ministries of discipling and Christian counseling. I have been a discipler and a counselor of countless people. I have also taught discipleship and pastoral counseling at the seminary level and in churches and leadership conferences across the country and around the world. I have found one common denominator for all struggling Christians. They do not know who they are in Christ, nor do they understand what it means to be a child of God. Why not? If 'The Spirit Himself bears witness with our spirit that we are children of God' (Rom. 8:16), why weren't they sensing it?

As a pastor, I believed that Christ was the answer and truth would set people free, but I really didn't know how.

People at my church had problems for which I didn't have answers, but God did. When the Lord called me to teach at Talbot School of Theology, I was searching for answers myself. Slowly I began to understand how to help people resolve their personal and spiritual conflicts through genuine repentance by submitting to God and resisting the devil (see Jas. 4:7).

My seminary education had taught me about the kingdom of God, but not about the kingdom of darkness and that 'our struggle is not against flesh and blood, but against rulers, against the powers, against the world forces of this darkness, against the spiritual forces of wickedness in the heavenly places' (Eph. 6:12). Through countless hours of intense counseling with defeated Christians, I began to understand the battle for their minds and how they could be transformed by renewing their minds.

I am saddened by how we have separated the ministries of discipleship and counseling in our churches. Christian discipleship too often has become an impersonal program, although good theological material is being used. Christian counseling has been intensely personal, but often lacks good theology. I believe discipleship and counseling are biblically the same. If you were a good discipler you would be a good counselor and vice versa. Discipleship counseling is the process where two or more people meet together in the presence of Christ, learn how the truth of God's Word can set them free and thus are able to conform to the image of God as they walk by faith in the power of the Holy Spirit.

In the course of learning this, my family and I went through a very broken experience. For 15 months I didn't know whether my wife, Joanne, was going to live or die. We lost everything we had. God gave me something very dear to me that I could not fix. No matter what I did, nothing changed. God brought me to the end of my resources, so I could discover His. That was the birth of Freedom in Christ Ministries. Nobody reading this book knows any better than I do that I can't set anybody free; only God can do that. I can't bind up anybody's broken heart; only God can do that. He is the Wonderful Counselor. Brokenness is the key to effective ministry and the final ingredient for discipleship counseling. Message and method had come together.

Furthermore, it is my conviction that discipleship counseling must start where the Bible starts: We must have a true knowledge of God and know who we are as children of God. If we really knew God, our behavior would change radically and instantly. Whenever heaven opened to reveal the glory of God, individual witnesses in the Bible were immediately and profoundly changed. I believe that the greatest determinant of mental and spiritual health and spiritual freedom is a true understanding of God and a right relationship with Him. A good theology is an indispensable prerequisite to a good psychology.

Several weeks after one of my conferences, a friend shared with me the story of a dear Christian woman who had attended. She had lived in a deep depression for several years. She survived by leaning on her friends, three counseling sessions a week and a variety of prescription drugs.

During the conference this woman realized that her support system included everybody and everything but God. She had not cast her anxiety on Christ and she was anything but dependent on Him. She took her conference syllabus home and began focusing on her identity in Christ and expressing confidence in Him to meet her daily needs. She threw off all her other supports (a practice I do not recommend) and decided to trust in Christ alone to relieve her depression. She began living by faith and renewing her mind as the conference notes suggested. After one month she was a different person. Knowing God is indispensable to maturity and freedom.

Another point at which discipling and counseling intersect is in the area of individual responsibility. People who want to move forward in Christian maturity can certainly benefit from the counsel of others, and those who seek freedom from their past can also be helped by others. Ultimately, however, every Christian is responsible for his or her own maturity and freedom in Christ. Nobody can make you grow. That's your decision and daily responsibility. Nobody can solve your problems for you. You alone must initiate and follow through with that process. Thankfully, however, none of us walks through the disciplines of personal maturity and freedom alone. The indwelling Christ is eagerly willing to walk with us each step of the way.

This book is the first of two books I have written from my education and experience in discipling and counseling others. This book focuses on the foundational issues of living and maturing in Christ. You will discover who you are in Christ and how to live by faith. You will learn how to walk by the Spirit and be sensitive to His leading. The grace walk is living by faith in the power of the Holy Spirit.

In this book you will discover the nature of the battle for your mind and learn why your mind must be transformed so you can live by faith and grow spiritually. You will gain insight into how to manage your emotions and be set free from the emotional traumas of your past through faith and forgiveness.

In my second book, *The Bondage Breaker* (Harvest House Publishers), I focus on our freedom in Christ and the spiritual conflicts that affect Christians today. Being alive and free in Christ is an essential prerequisite for maturity in Christ. We cannot achieve instant maturity. It will take us the rest of our lives to renew our minds and conform to the image of God, but it doesn't take as long to realize our identity and freedom in Christ. The world, the flesh and the devil are enemies of our sanctification, but they have been and can be overcome in Christ.

I suggest that you complete this book first, learn about living and growing in Christ, then work through the subjects of spiritual conflicts and freedom by reading *The Bondage Breaker*.

Victory over the Darkness is arranged something like a New Testament Epistle. The first half of the book lays a doctrinal foundation and defines terms that are necessary for understanding and implementing the more practical chapters that follow. You may be tempted to skip over the first half because it seems less relevant to daily experience. It is critical, however, to discern your position and victory in Christ so you can implement the practices of growth in Him. You need to know what to believe before you can understand what to do.

I have talked to thousands of people like Russ, my first discipleship candidate. They are Christians, but they are not growing and they are not bearing fruit. They want to serve Christ, but they can't seem to get over the top and get on with their lives in a meaningful and productive way. They need to have their hope reestablished in Christ, as the following poem describes:

> Lend me your hope for awhile,
> > I seem to have mislaid mine.
> Lost and hopeless feelings accompany me daily,
> > pain and confusion are my companions.
> I know not where to turn;
> > looking ahead to future times does not bring forth
> > images of renewed hope.
> I see troubled times, pain-filled days, and more tragedy.
>
> Lend me your hope for awhile,
> > I seem to have mislaid mine.

Hold my hand and hug me;
>   listen to all my ramblings, recovery seems so far distant.
The road to healing seems like a long and lonely one.

Lend me your hope for awhile,
>   I seem to have mislaid mine.
Stand by me, offer me your presence, your heart and
>   your love.
Acknowledge my pain, it is so real and ever present.
I am overwhelmed with sad and conflicting thoughts.

Lend me your hope for awhile;
>   a time will come when I will heal,
>   and I will share my renewal,
>   hope and love with others.[1]

Do these words reflect your experience and echo your plea as a believer? Do you sometimes feel hemmed in by the world, the flesh and the devil to the point that you wonder if your Christianity is worth anything? Do you sometimes fear you will never be all God called you to be? Do you long to get on with your Christian maturity and experience the freedom God's Word promises?

I want to share my hope with you in the pages ahead. Your maturity is the product of time, pressure, trials, tribulations, the knowledge of God's Word, an understanding of who you are in Christ and the presence of the Holy Spirit in your life. You probably already have the first four elements in abundance; most Christians do. Let me add some generous doses of the last three ingredients. When Christians are alive and free in Christ, watch them grow!

Note

1. Adapted from the poem 'Lend Me Your Hope,' author unknown.

1
Who Are You?

I really enjoy asking people, 'Who are you?' It sounds like a simple question requiring a simple answer, but it really isn't. For example, if someone asked me, 'Who are you?' I might answer, 'Neil Anderson.'

'No, that's your name. Who are you?'

'Oh, I'm a seminary professor.'

'No, that's what you do.'

'I'm an American.'

'That's where you live.'

'I'm an evangelical.'

'That's your denominational preference.'

I could also say that I am five feet nine inches tall and a little over 150 pounds — actually *quite* a little over 150 pounds! My physical dimensions and appearance, however, aren't me either. If you chopped off my arms and legs would I still be me? If you transplanted my heart, kidneys or liver would I still be me? Of course! Now if you keep chopping you will get to me eventually because I am in here somewhere. Who I am, though, is far more than what you see on the outside.

The apostle Paul said, 'We recognize no man according to the flesh' (2 Cor. 5:16). Maybe the Early Church didn't, but generally we do. We tend to identify ourselves and each other primarily by what we look like (tall, short, stocky, slender) or what we do (plumber, carpenter, nurse, engineer, clerk). Furthermore, when we Christians are asked to identify ourselves in relation to our faith, we usually talk about our doctrinal position (Protestant, evangelical, Calvinist, charismatic), our denominational preference (Baptist,

Presbyterian, Methodist, Independent) or our role in the church (Sunday School teacher, choir member, deacon, usher).

Is who you are determined by what you do, or is what you do determined by who you are? That is an important question, especially as it relates to Christian maturity. I subscribe to the latter. I believe that your hope for growth, meaning and fulfillment as a Christian is based on understanding who you are — specifically, your identity in Christ as a child of God. Your understanding of who God is and who you are in relationship to Him is the critical foundation for your belief system and your behavior patterns as a Christian.

False Equations in the Search for Identity

Several years ago a 17-year-old girl drove a great distance to talk with me. I have never met a girl who had so much going for her. She was cover-girl pretty and had a wonderful figure. She was immaculately dressed. She had completed 12 years of school in 11 years and graduated near the top of her class. As a talented musician, she had received a full-ride music scholarship to a Christian university. She also drove a brand-new sports car her parents gave her for graduation. I was amazed that one person could have so much.

She talked with me for half an hour and I realized that what I saw on the outside wasn't matching what I was beginning to see on the inside.

'Mary,' I said finally, 'have you ever cried yourself to sleep at night because you felt inadequate and wished you were somebody else?'

She began to cry. 'How did you know?'

'Truthfully, Mary,' I answered, 'I've learned that people who *appear* to have it all together on the outside may not have it all together on the inside. I could ask almost anyone that same question at some time in their lives and get the same response.'

Often what we show on the outside is a false front designed to disguise who we really are, and we cover up the negative feelings we have about ourselves. The world would have us believe that if we appear attractive or perform well or enjoy a certain amount of status, then we will have it all together inside as well. That is not always true, however. External appearance, accomplishment and recognition don't necessarily reflect — or produce — internal peace and maturity.

In his book *The Sensation of Being Somebody*, Maurice Wagner expresses this false belief in simple equations we tend to accept. He says we mistakenly think that good appearance plus the admiration it brings equal a whole person. Or we feel that star performance plus accomplishments equal a whole person. Or we believe that a certain amount of status plus the recognition we accumulate equal a whole person. Not so. These equations are no more correct than two plus two equal six. Wagner says:

> Try as we might by our appearance, performance or social status to find self-verification for a sense of being somebody, we always come short of satisfaction. Whatever pinnacle of self-identity we achieve soon crumbles under the pressure of hostile rejection or criticism, introspection or guilt, fear or anxiety. We cannot do anything to qualify for the by-product of being loved unconditionally and voluntarily.[1]

If these equations could work for anyone, they would have worked for King Solomon. He was the king of Israel during the greatest years in its history. He had power, position, wealth, possessions and women. If a meaningful life is the result of appearance, admiration, performance, accomplishments, status or recognition, Solomon would have been the most together man who ever lived.

Not only did he possess all that a fallen humanity could hope for, but God also gave him more wisdom than any other mortal to interpret it all. What was his conclusion? 'Meaningless! Meaningless!... Utterly meaningless! Everything is meaningless' (Eccles. 1:2, NIV). Solomon sought to find purpose and meaning in life independent of God and he wrote a book about it. The book of Ecclesiastes describes the futility of humankind pursuing a meaningful life in a fallen world without God. Millions of people climb those ladders of 'success,' only to discover when they reach the top that their ladder is leaning against the wrong wall.

We also tend to buy into the negative side of the worldly success-equals-meaning formula by believing that if people have nothing, they have no hope for happiness. For example, I presented this scenario to a high school student a few years ago: 'Suppose there's a girl on your campus who has a potato body and stringy hair, who stumbles when she walks and stutters when she talks. She has a bad complexion and she struggles just to get average grades. Does she have any hope for happiness?'

He thought for a moment, then answered, 'Probably not.'

Maybe he is right in this earthly kingdom, where people live strictly on the external plane. Happiness is equated with good looks, relationships with important people, the right job and a fat bank account. Life devoid of these 'benefits' is too often equated with hopelessness.

What about life in God's kingdom? The success-equals-happiness and failure-equals-hopelessness equations don't exist. Everyone has exactly the same opportunity for a meaningful life. Why? Because wholeness and meaning in life are not the products of what you have or don't have, what you've done or haven't done. You are already a whole person and possess a life of infinite meaning and purpose because of who you are — a child of God. The only identity equation that works in God's kingdom is you plus Christ equals wholeness and meaning.

If our relationship with God is the key to wholeness, why do so many believers struggle with their identity, security, significance, sense of worth and spiritual maturity? Ignorance is probably the primary reason. The prophet Hosea said, 'My people are destroyed for lack of knowledge' (4:6). For others it is carnality, the lack of repentance and faith in God, and some are being deceived by the father of lies. This deception was brought home to me a few years ago when I was counseling a Christian girl who was the victim of satanic oppression.

I asked her, 'Who are you?'

'I'm evil,' she answered.

'You're not evil. How can a child of God be evil? Is that how you see yourself?' She nodded.

Now she may have done some evil things, but at the core of her being she wasn't evil. This was evident by the deep remorse she felt after sinning. She was basing her identity on the wrong equation. She was letting Satan's accusations influence her perception of herself instead of believing the truth.

Sadly, a great number of Christians are trapped in the same downward spiral. We fail, so we see ourselves as failures, which only leads to more failure. We sin, so we see ourselves as sinners, which only leads to more sin. We have been deceived into believing that what we do determines who we are. That false belief sends us into a tailspin of hopelessness and more defeat. On the other hand, 'The Spirit Himself bears witness with our spirit that we are children of God' (Rom. 8:16). God wants us to know who we are so we can start living accordingly. Being a child of God who is alive and free in Christ should determine what we do. Then we are working *out* our salvation (see Phil. 2:12), not for our salvation.

The Original Creation

To understand the gospel and who we are in Christ, we need to look at the creation account and the subsequent fall of humankind (see Figure 1-A). Genesis 2:7 reads: 'Then the Lord God formed man of dust from the ground, and breathed into his nostrils the breath of life; and man became a living being.' This combination of clay and divine breath is what constitutes humankind.

Theologians have debated whether the individual members of Adam's race are made up of two or three parts. Those who hold to a trichotomous view believe we are comprised of

---

ORIGINAL CREATION Genesis 1,2

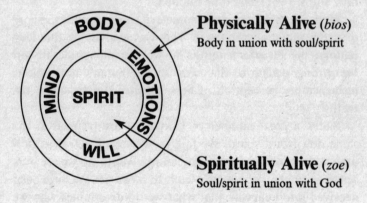

Physically Alive (*bios*)
Body in union with soul/spirit

Spiritually Alive (*zoe*)
Soul/spirit in union with God

1. Significance — Man had a divine purpose (Gen. 1:28).
2. Safety and security — All of man's needs were provided for (Gen. 1:29).
3. Belonging — Man had a sense of belonging (Gen. 2:18).

bios = The soul is in union with the body.
zoe = The soul is in union with God.

Figure 1-A

---

a body, soul (containing mind, emotions and will) and spirit. Those who hold to a dichotomous view believe we are comprised of a material and immaterial part, an outer person and an inner person. They would understand the soul and the spirit to be essentially the same.

For the sake of our discussion, we are going to describe who we are from a functional perspective. Suffice it to say, we have an outer self, a physical body that relates to this world through the five senses, and an inner self that relates to God and is created in His image (see Gen. 1:26,27). Being created in the image of God is what gives us the capacity to fully think, feel and choose. After God breathed into his nostrils the breath of life, Adam was both physically and spiritually alive.

Physically Alive

The physical life we inherited from Adam is best represented in the New Testament by the word *bios*. Bios describes the union of your physical body and your immaterial self — mind, emotions and will. To be physically alive means the soul or soul/spirit is in union with your body. To die physically means that you separate from your temporal body.

In the Bible, to die means to be separate from, and to be alive means to be in union with. Paul said to be absent from the body is to be present with the Lord (see 2 Cor. 5:8). Obviously, who you are encompasses more than your physical body, because the body is left behind when you physically die and yet you will be present with the Lord.

Although your principal identity is more than physical, in this life you cannot exist without your physical body. Your immaterial inner self needs your material outer self to live and function in this world.

For example, your physical brain is like the hardware of a computer system and your immaterial mind is like the software. A computer can't function without software, and software needs a computer to function. You need your physical brain to control your movements and responses, and you need your immaterial mind to reason and make value judgments. The brain can't function independently of how it has been programmed. The finest organic brain can't accomplish anything in a corpse that lacks a mind. Your mind can be perfectly programmed, but if your brain is damaged by Alzheimer's disease you cannot function well as a person.

As long as I live in the physical world, I must do so in a physical body. As such, I am going to take care of my body as well as I can by exercising, eating right and so on. The truth of the matter is that my body is corruptible and it is decaying. I don't look the way I looked 20 years ago, and I don't have great prospects for the next 20 years. In 2 Corinthians 5:1-4, Paul referred to the believer's body as a tent, the temporary dwelling place of the soul. Using his illustration, I must confess that my tent pegs are coming up, my poles are sagging and my seams are becoming frayed. At my age, I am just glad there is more to me than the disposable earth suit in which I walk around.

Spiritually Alive

We also inherited from Adam the capacity for spiritual life. Paul wrote: 'Though outwardly we are wasting away, yet inwardly we are being renewed day by day' (2 Cor. 4:16, NIV). He was referring to the spiritual life of the believer that doesn't age or decay as does the outer shell. To be spiritually alive — characterized in the New Testament by the word *zoe* — means that your soul or soul/spirit is in union with God. That is the condition in which Adam was created — physically alive *and* spiritually alive, in perfect union with God.

For the Christian, to be spiritually alive is to be in union with God. This spiritual life is most often conveyed in the

New Testament as being 'in Christ,' or 'in Him.' Like Adam, we were created to be in union with God. As we shall discover later in this chapter, however, Adam sinned and his union with God was severed. It is God's eternal plan to bring human creation back to Himself and restore the union He enjoyed with Adam at creation. That restored union with God, which we find 'in Christ,' is what defines who we are as children of God.

Significance

In the original creation, humankind was given a divine purpose for being here. Humanity was given dominion over all the other creatures: 'Then God said, "Let Us make man in Our image, according to Our likeness; and let them rule over the fish of the sea and over the birds of the sky and over the cattle and over all the earth, and over every creeping thing that creeps on the earth." And God created man in His own image, in the image of God He created him; male and female He created them' (Gen. 1:26,27).

Adam didn't have to search for significance. That attribute was the result of creation. Satan had to crawl on his belly like a snake in the presence of God. He was not the god of this world at that time. He usurped the authority given to Adam and his descendants after Adam sinned and lost his relationship with God.

Safety and Security

Not only did Adam have a sense of significance, but he also enjoyed a sense of safety and security. All his needs were provided. Genesis 1:29,30 records: 'Then God said, "Behold, I have given you every plant yielding seed that is on the surface of all the earth, and every tree which has fruit yielding seed; it shall be food for you; and to every beast of the earth and to every bird of the sky and to every thing that moves on the earth which has life, I have given every green plant for food."' Adam was completely cared for in the garden. All of his needs were provided. He could eat of the tree of life and live forever. He was safe and secure in the presence of God.

Belonging

Adam apparently enjoyed intimate, one-to-one communion with God, but something was missing. 'The Lord God said, "It is not good for the man to be alone; I will make him a helper suitable for him"' (Gen. 2:18). Adam and Eve not only had a sense of belonging with God, but also with each other. When God created Eve, He established human community: a meaningful, open, sharing relationship with one another. Adam and Eve were naked and unashamed. They had nothing to hide. Their bodies consisted of no dirty parts. God created them male and female and told them to be fruitful and multiply. They could openly have an intimate sexual relationship with each other in the presence of God.

The Effects of the Fall

Unfortunately, the idyllic setting in the Garden of Eden was shattered. Genesis 3 tells the sad story of Adam and Eve's lost relationship with God through sin. The effects of their fall were dramatic, immediate and far reaching, infecting every subsequent member of the human race.

Spiritual Death

What happened to Adam and Eve spiritually because of the Fall? They died. Their union with God was severed and they were separated from God. God had specifically said, 'You must not eat from the tree of the knowledge of good and evil, for when you eat of it you will surely die' (Gen. 2:17, NIV). They ate and they died.

EFFECTS OF THE FALL Genesis 3:8 – 4:9

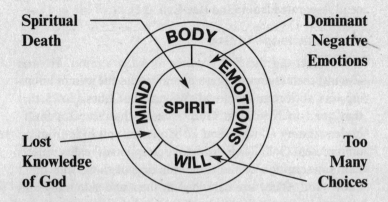

Spiritual Death — BODY — **Dominant Negative Emotions**

MIND SPIRIT EMOTIONS

Lost Knowledge of God — WILL — **Too Many Choices**

1. *Rejection* — therefore a need to belong!
2. *Guilt and shame* — therefore a need of self-worth!
3. *Weakness and helplessness* — therefore a need of strength and self-control!

Note:
All sinful behavior is a wrong attempt at meeting basic needs. The essence of sin is man living independently of God, who has said that He will meet all of our needs as we live out life in Christ..

Figure 1-B

Did they die physically? Not immediately, although physical death would be a consequence of the Fall as well. They died spiritually; they were separated from God's presence. They were physically cast out of the Garden of Eden and a cherubim waving a flaming sword was stationed at the entrance 'to guard the way to the tree of life' (Gen. 3:24). Some believe this act preserved a way back as God's plan of redemption unfolded.

Just as we inherited physical life from our first parents, so we have inherited spiritual death from them (see Rom. 5:12;

1 Cor. 15:21,22). Consequently, every human being who comes into the world is born physically alive but spiritually dead, separated from God (see Eph. 2:1).

Lost Knowledge of God

What effect did the Fall produce in Adam's mind? He and Eve lost their true perception of reality and the idea of knowing was no longer relational. We read in Genesis 3:7,8 that they tried to hide from God. Doesn't that reveal a faulty understanding of who God is? How can you hide from an omnipresent God? Their distorted perception of reality reflects Paul's description of the futile thinking of those who don't know God: 'They are darkened in their understanding and separated from the life of God because of the ignorance that is in them due to the hardening of their hearts' (Eph. 4:18, NIV).

In essence, when Adam and Eve sinned they lost a true knowledge of God. In God's original design, knowledge was relational. The Hebrew concept of knowledge implied an intimate personal relationship. For instance, 'Adam knew Eve his wife; and she conceived' (Gen. 4:1, KJV). Yet we don't generally equate a knowledge of someone with personal intimacy. When they sinned and were banished from the garden, Adam and Eve lost their relationship with God and the knowledge of God, which was intrinsic to that relationship.

In our unregenerate state, we may have known something *about* God, but we didn't *know* God because we had no relationship with Him. 'But a natural man does not accept the things of the Spirit of God; for they are foolishness to him, and he cannot understand them, because they are spiritually appraised' (1 Cor. 2:14).

The necessity of being in relationship to God to know God comes into sharp focus in John's announcement: 'And the Word [*logos* in the Greek] became flesh' (John 1:14). That was an incredibly significant statement in a world heavily influenced by ancient Greek philosophy. To the Greek philosopher, logos represented the highest form of philosophical knowledge. To say that the Word became flesh meant that the logos was incarnated, that ultimate knowledge became personal and relational. Jesus embodied the truth because He is the truth. You couldn't separate His words from who He is. The Hebrew *dabar*, translated as 'word,' also conveyed the ultimate wisdom of God.

The Gospel of John brings these two cultures and dominant concepts together in Christ. God was announcing to the world through John that the true knowledge of God, which can only be discovered in an intimate relationship with God, is now available to the world through God who came in the flesh — Jesus Christ. In Christ we are able to know God personally because we have received the 'mind of Christ' (1 Cor. 2:16) in our inner selves at salvation.

This truth has profound implications for Christian education. Knowledge to the western world has become nothing more than the collection of data. That kind of knowledge makes us arrogant, but love edifies (see 1 Cor. 8:1). Paul says, 'But the goal of our instruction is love from a pure heart and a good conscience and a sincere faith' (1 Tim. 1:5). The truth (Christ and His Word) should set us free and enable us to conform to the image of God. 'By this all men will know that you are My disciples, if you have love for one another' (John 13:35).

Dominant Negative Emotions

Adam and Eve were not only darkened in their understanding, but they also became fearful and anxious. The first emotion expressed by fallen humankind was fear (see Gen. 3:10). Fear of anything other than God is mutually exclusive to faith in God. Why is the fear of God the beginning of wisdom (see Prov. 9:10) and how does it expel all other fears?

As I was writing the book *Freedom From Fear* with my colleague Rich Miller, I became aware that we are living in an age of anxiety. People around the world are paralyzed by fear of anything and everything but God. Chuck Colson said, 'For the church in the West to come alive, it needs to resolve its identity crisis, to stand on truth, to renew its vision... and more than anything else, it needs to recover the fear of the Lord.'[2]

Another emotional by-product of sin is shame and guilt. Before Adam and Eve disobeyed God they were naked and unashamed (see Gen. 2:25). God created them as sexual beings. Their sex organs and sexual activity were holy. When they sinned, however, they were ashamed to be naked and they had to cover up (see 3:7). Many people mask the inner self for fear that others may find out what is really going on inside. When dominated by guilt and shame, self-disclosure is not likely to happen.

Humankind also became depressed and angry after the Fall. Cain brought his offering to God and, for some reason, God was displeased with it. 'So Cain was very angry, and his face was downcast. Then the Lord said to Cain, "Why are you angry? Why is your face downcast? If you do what is right, will you not be accepted? But if you do not do what is right, sin is crouching at your door; it desires to have you, but you must master it"' (Gen. 4:5-7, NIV).

Why was Cain angry and depressed? Because he didn't do what was right. In other words, God is saying, 'You don't feel your way into good behavior; you behave your way into good feelings.' Jesus said, 'If you know these things, you are blessed if you do them' (John 13:17).

While researching and writing the book *Finding Hope Again*, I discovered we are also experiencing a blues epidemic in this age of anxiety. Depression is so prevalent it is called the 'common cold' of mental illness. Visits to the doctor that resulted in a diagnosis of depression almost doubled from 1985 to 1995 in the United States, and overall there was a ten-fold increase in the twentieth century.[3]

Too Many Choices

Adam and Eve's sin also affected their will to choose. Do you realize that in the Garden of Eden they could make only one wrong choice? Everything they wanted to do was okay except eating from the tree of the knowledge of good and evil (see Gen. 2:16,17). They had the possibility of making myriad good choices and only one bad choice — *only one*!

Eventually, however, they made that one bad choice. As a result, you and I are confronted every day with myriad good *and* bad choices. Apart from the Holy Spirit in your life, the greatest power you possess is the power to choose. You can choose to pray or not pray, read your Bible or not read your Bible, go to church or not go to church. You can choose to walk according to the flesh or according to the Spirit.

Attributes Become Needs

Another long-term effect of sin is that humankind's attributes before the Fall became glaring needs after the Fall. This sad transition occurs in three areas. Each of these three needs is continuous in our lives.

1. Acceptance was replaced by rejection; therefore we have a need to belong. Even before the Fall, Adam had a need to belong. His need to belong to God was filled in the intimacy of his fellowship with God in the garden. Of all the things that were good in the garden, the only thing that was 'not good' was that Adam was alone (see Gen. 2:18). God filled that need by creating Eve.

Ever since Adam and Eve's sin alienated them from God and introduced strife into human relationships, we have experienced a deep need to belong. Even when people come to

Christ and fill their need to belong to God, they still need to belong to the community of God's people.

If your church doesn't provide opportunities for legitimate Christian fellowship for its members, they will seek it someplace else. Those who study church-growth trends have discovered that a church can give people Christ, but if it doesn't also give them friends, after a few months the church will lose them. The spiritual union of Christian fellowship — called *koinonia* in the New Testament — is not just a nice thing the church ought to provide; it is a necessary thing the church *must* provide.

You will never understand the power of peer pressure in our culture until you understand the legitimate need to belong and the fear of rejection we all share.

2. Innocence was replaced by guilt and shame; therefore the need for a legitimate sense of worth has to be restored. Those who work with people recognize that a suffering humankind struggles with a poor sense of worth. An identity crisis and a negative self-image have been human problems since the Fall. The secular advice of stroking one another's ego and picking ourselves up by our own bootstraps is not a sufficient answer. Our sense of worth is not a question of giftedness, talent, intelligence or beauty. Your sense of personal worth comes from knowing who you are as a child of God and your growth in character. We will talk more about the dimensions of our identity in Christ and how it contributes to our sense of worth in the chapters ahead.

3. Dominion was replaced by weakness and helplessness; therefore we have a need for strength and self-control. People attempt to meet this need by learning to discipline themselves or by seeking to control and manipulate others. Nobody is more insecure or sick than controllers. They wrongly believe they can establish themselves by trying to control and manipulate other people or circumstances in life. In other words, they are trying to play God. The fruit of the Spirit is not spouse control or staff control or environmental control; it is self-control (see Gal. 5:23).

On the other hand, extreme efforts at self-discipline without the grace of God often lead to legalism or perfectionism and result in self-destruction. The world would have us think we are the masters of our fates and the captains of our souls, but we really aren't. The human soul was not designed to function as a master. We cannot serve God and wealth, but we will serve one or the other (see Matt. 6:24), being deceived into thinking we are serving ourselves.

Every temptation is an attempt by the devil to get us to live our lives independently of God. Satan tempts us just as he did Jesus by appealing to our most basic and legitimate needs. The question is: Are these needs going to be met by the world, the flesh and the devil, or are they going to be met by God who promises to meet all our needs 'according to His riches in glory in Christ Jesus' (Phil. 4:19)? The most critical needs are the being needs and they are the ones most wonderfully met in Christ.

Who I Am in Christ

I Am Accepted

John 1:12	I am God's child.
John 15:15	I am Christ's friend.
Romans 5:1	I have been justified.
1 Corinthians 6:17	I am united with the Lord, and I am one spirit with Him.
1 Corinthians 6:20	I have been bought with a price. I belong to God.
1 Corinthians 12:27	I am a member of Christ's Body.
Ephesians 1:1	I am a saint.
Ephesians 1:5	I have been adopted as God's child.

Ephesians 2:18	I have direct access to God through the Holy Spirit.
Colossians 1:14	I have been redeemed and forgiven of all my sins.
Colossians 2:10	I am complete in Christ.

I Am Secure

Romans 8:1,2	I am free from condemnation.
Romans 8:28	I am assured that all things work together for good.
Romans 8:31-34	I am free from any condemning charges against me.
Romans 8:35-39	I cannot be separated from the love of God.
2 Corinthians 1:21,22	I have been established, anointed and sealed by God.
Philippians 1:6	I am confident that the good work God has begun in me will be perfected.
Philippians 3:20	I am a citizen of heaven.
Colossians 3:3	I am hidden with Christ in God.
2 Timothy 1:7	I have not been given a spirit of fear, but of power, love and a sound mind.
Hebrews 4:16	I can find grace and mercy in time of need.
1 John 5:18	I am born of God and the evil one cannot touch me.

I Am Significant

Matthew 5:13,14	I am the salt and light of the earth.
John 15:1,5	I am a branch of the true vine, a channel of His life.

John 15:16	I have been chosen and appointed to bear fruit.
Acts 1:8	I am a personal witness of Christ.
1 Corinthians 3:16	I am God's temple.
2 Corinthians 5:17-21	I am a minister of reconciliation for God.
2 Corinthians 6:1	I am God's co-worker (see 1 Corinthians 3:9).
Ephesians 2:6	I am seated with Christ in the heavenly realm.
Ephesians 2:10	I am God's workmanship.
Ephesians 3:12	I may approach God with freedom and confidence.
Philippians 4:13	I can do all things through Christ who strengthens me.

Notes

1. Maurice Wagner, *The Sensation of Being Somebody* (Grand Rapids: Zondervan Publishing House, 1975), p. 163.

2. Neil T. Anderson and Rich Miller, *Freedom From Fear* (Eugene, Oreg.: Harvest House, 1999), p. 259 (UK edition: Monarch Books).

3. Neil T. Anderson, *Finding Hope Again* (Ventura, Calif.: Regal Books, 1999), p. 32.

2
The Whole Gospel

Imagine for a moment a typical college man. Let's call him
Bill. Bill is into the college social scene. He sees himself as a
skin-wrapped package of salivary glands, taste buds and sex
drives. So how does Bill occupy his time with this self-per-
ception? By eating and by chasing girls. He eats anything and
everything in sight regardless of its nutritional value. He
chases just about anything in a skirt, but he has a special
gleam in his eye for luscious-looking Susie, the cheerleader.

Bill was chasing sweet little Susie around the campus one
day when the track coach noticed him. 'Hey, this kid can
really run!' When the coach finally caught up with Bill he
said, 'Why don't you come out for the track team?'

'Naw,' Bill answered, watching for Susie out of the corner
of his eye. 'I'm too busy.'

But the coach wasn't about to take 'naw' for an answer.
He finally convinced Bill at least to give track a try.

So Bill started working out with the track team and discovered that he really *could* run. He changed his eating and
sleeping habits and his skills improved further. He started
winning some races and posting some excellent times for his
event.

Finally Bill was invited to the big race at the state
tournament. He arrived at the track early to stretch and warm
up. Then, only a few minutes before his event, guess who
showed up: sweet little Susie, looking more beautiful and
desirable than ever. She pranced up to Bill in a scanty outfit
that accentuated her finer physical features. In her hands was
a sumptuous slice of apple pie with several scoops of ice
cream piled on the top of it.

'I've missed you, Bill,' she sang sweetly. 'If you come with me now, you can have all this and me too.'

'No way, Susie,' Bill responded.

'Why not?' Susie pouted.

'Because I'm a runner.'

What is different about Bill? What happened to his drives and glands? He is still the same guy who could pack away three burgers, two bags of fries and a quart of Pepsi without batting an eye. He is still the same guy who was just itching to get close to beautiful Susie. His understanding of himself has changed, though. He no longer sees himself primarily as a bundle of physical urges, but as a disciplined runner. He came to the tournament to run a race. That was his purpose, and Susie's suggestion was at cross-purposes with why he was there and how he perceived himself.[1]

Let's take the illustration one step further. Let's say the runner is Eric Liddell, who was the subject of the movie *Chariots of Fire*. He was committed to Christ, but he was also very fast and he represented his native Scotland in the Olympics.

When the race schedule was posted for his event, Liddell discovered his race was to be held on Sunday. Eric Liddell was committed to God and he couldn't compromise what he believed. So he withdrew from a race he might have won. Why didn't Eric Liddell run? Because he was first and foremost a child of God and he believed that competing on Sunday would compromise who he was. His belief about himself and his purpose in life determined what he did.

Many Christians are not living free and productive lives because they don't understand who they are and why they are here. Who they are is rooted in their identity and position in Christ. If they don't see themselves the way God sees them, to that degree they suffer from a false identity and poor sense of worth. They don't fully understand the gospel and the dramatic change that occurred in them the moment they trusted in Christ.

The Example of Christ

The redemptive plan of God began to unfold when Christ, the last Adam, appeared. The first thing we notice about the life of Christ was His complete dependence on God the Father. He said, 'I can do nothing on My own initiative' (John 5:30); 'I live because of the Father' (6:57); 'I proceeded forth and have come from God, for I have not even come on My own initiative, but He sent Me' (8:42); 'The words I say to you are not just my own. Rather, it is the Father, living in me, who is doing his work' (14:10, NIV).

The ultimate test came after a 40-day fast. The Holy Spirit led Jesus into the wilderness and Satan tempted Him. 'If you are the Son of God, command that these stones become bread' (Matt. 4:3). Satan wanted Jesus to use His divine attributes independently of the Father to save Himself. Jesus replied: 'Man shall not live on bread alone, but on every word that proceeds out of the mouth of God' (4:4).

Near the end of His earthly ministry, Jesus prayed, 'Now they know that everything you have given me comes from you' (John 17:7, NIV). What Jesus modeled was a life totally dependent on God the Father.

Jesus Came to Give Us Life

Like the first Adam, Jesus was born both physically and spiritually alive. This was made evident by the fact that Jesus was conceived by the Spirit of God, and born of a virgin. Unlike the first Adam, Jesus was tempted in every way, but He never sinned. He never lost His spiritual life because of any sin He committed. He kept His spiritual life all the way to the cross.

There He bled and died, taking the sins of the world upon Himself. He committed His spirit into the Father's hands as His physical life ended (see Luke 23:46). What Adam and Eve lost in the Fall was spiritual life, and Jesus came to give us life. Jesus said, 'I came that they might have life, and might have it abundantly' (John 10:10).

John declared, 'In Him was life, and the life was the light of men' (John 1:4). Notice that light does not produce life. Life produces light. Jesus said, 'I am the bread of life' (6:48) and 'I am the resurrection and the life; he who believes in Me shall live even if he dies' (11:25). In other words, those who believe in Jesus will continue to live spiritually even when they die physically. Jesus said, 'I am the way, and the truth, and the life' (14:6). The ultimate value is not our physical life, which is temporal, but our spiritual life, which is eternal.

The Whole Gospel

Many Christians are living under half a gospel. They have heard that Jesus is the Messiah who came to die for their sins, and if they pray to receive Christ, they will go to heaven when they die and their sins will be forgiven. Two things are wrong with that statement. First, it is only half the gospel. If you came across a dead man and you had the power to save him, what would you do? Give him life? If that is all you did, then he would only die again. To save the dead person, you would have to do two things. First, you would have to cure the disease that caused him to die.

The Bible says, 'The wages of sin is death' (Rom. 6:23). So Jesus went to the cross and died for our sins. Is curing the disease that caused us to die the whole gospel? No! Finish the verse: 'but the free gift of God is eternal life in Christ Jesus our Lord' (6:23). Thank God for Good Friday, but what Christians celebrate every spring is the Resurrection on

Easter Sunday. For some unknown reason, we have left the Resurrection out of the gospel presentation. Consequently, we end up with forgiven sinners instead of redeemed saints.

A second problem with the previous gospel presentation is this: it gives people the impression that eternal life is something they get when they die. That is not true. 'And the witness is this, that God has given us eternal life, and this life is in His Son. He who has the Son has the life; he who does not have the Son of God does not have the life' (1 John 5:11,12). If we don't have spiritual (eternal) life before we die physically, we can anticipate only hell.

What a Difference Christ's Difference Makes in Us!

The difference between the first and last Adam spells the difference between life and death for us. Perhaps that life-giving difference is best presented in 1 Corinthians 15:22: 'For as in Adam all die, so also in Christ all shall be made alive.' Being spiritually alive is most often portrayed in the New Testament with the prepositional phrases 'in Christ' and 'in Him.'

Everything we are going to talk about in the succeeding chapters is based on the fact that believers are alive in Christ. Being spiritually alive in Christ is the overwhelming theme of the New Testament. For example, in the six chapters of the book of Ephesians alone we find 40 references to being 'in Christ' and having Christ in you. For every biblical passage that teaches that Christ is in you, 10 teach that you are 'in Christ.' It is also the primary basis for Paul's theology. 'For this reason I have sent to you Timothy, who is my beloved and faithful child in the Lord, and he will remind you of *my ways which are in Christ*, just as I teach everywhere in every church' (1 Cor. 4:17, emphasis added).

New Life Requires New Birth

We weren't born in Christ. We were born dead in our trespasses and sins (see Eph. 2:1). What is God's plan for transforming us from being in Adam to being in Christ? Jesus said, 'Truly, truly, I say to you, unless one is born again, he cannot see the kingdom of God' (John 3:3). Physical birth gains only physical life for us. Spiritual life, the eternal life Christ promises to those who come to Him, is gained only through spiritual birth (see 3:36).

What does it mean to be spiritually alive in Christ? The moment you were born again your soul came into union with God in the same way Adam was in union with God before the Fall. You became spiritually alive and your name was written in the Lamb's book of life (see Rev. 21:27). Eternal life is not something you get when you die.

Dear believer, you are spiritually alive in Christ right now. You will never be more spiritually alive than you are right now. The only thing that will change when you die physically is that you will exchange your mortal body for a new resurrected one. Your spiritual life in Christ, which began when you personally trusted Him, will merely continue on. Salvation is not a future addition; it is a present transformation. That transformation occurs at spiritual birth, not physical death.

New Life Brings New Identity

Being a Christian is not just a matter of getting something; it is a matter of being someone. A Christian is not simply a person who is forgiven and goes to heaven. A Christian, in terms of his or her deepest identity, is a saint, a spiritually born child of God, a divine masterpiece, a child of light, a citizen of heaven. Being born again transformed you into someone who didn't exist before. What you receive as a Christian isn't the point; it is who you are. It is not what you do as a

Christian that determines who you are; it is who you are that determines what you do (see 2 Cor. 5:17; Eph. 2:10; 1 Pet. 2:9,10; 1 John 3:1,2).

Understanding your identity in Christ is essential for living the Christian life. People cannot consistently behave in ways that are inconsistent with the way they perceive themselves. You don't change yourself by your perception. You change your perception of yourself by believing the truth. If you perceive yourself wrongly, you will live wrongly because what you are believing is not true. If you think you are a no-good bum, you will probably live like a no-good bum. If, however, you see yourself as a child of God who is spiritually alive in Christ, you will begin to live accordingly. Next to a knowledge of God, a knowledge of who you are is by far the most important truth you can possess.

The major strategy of Satan is to distort the character of God and the truth of who we are. He can't change God and he can't do anything to change our identity and position in Christ. If, however, he can get us to believe a lie, we will live as though our identity in Christ isn't true.

New Life Results in a New Identity

Have you noticed that one of the most frequently used words of identity for Christians in the New Testament is 'saint'? A saint is literally a holy person. Yet Paul and the other writers of the Epistles used the word generously to describe common, ordinary, everyday Christians like you and me. For example, Paul's salutation in 1 Corinthians 1:2 reads: 'To the church of God which is at Corinth, to those who have been sanctified in Christ Jesus, saints by calling, with all who in every place call upon the name of our Lord Jesus Christ, their Lord and ours.'

Notice that Paul didn't say we are saints by hard work. He clearly states we are saints by calling. The tendency of the church is to believe that saints are people who have earned their lofty title by living a magnificent life or by achieving a certain level of maturity. In the Bible, believers are described as 'saints,' which means holy ones (e.g., Rom. 1:7; 1 Cor. 1:2; 2 Cor. 1:1; Phil. 1:1).

Being a saint does not necessarily reflect any present measure of growth in character, but it does identify those who are rightly related to God. In the *King James Version* of the Bible, believers are called 'saints,' 'holy ones' or 'righteous ones' more than 240 times. In contrast, unbelievers are called 'sinners' more than 330 times. Clearly, the term 'saint' is used in Scripture to refer to the believer, and 'sinner' is used in reference to the unbeliever.

Although the New Testament provides plenty of evidence that the believer sins, it never clearly identifies the believer as a sinner. Paul's reference to himself in which he declares, 'I am foremost [of sinners]' is often referred to as contrary (1 Tim. 1:15). Despite the use of the present tense by the apostle, several things make it much preferable to consider his description of himself as 'the foremost [of sinners]' as a reference to his preconversion opposition to the gospel. Taking this as a truthful statement, he indeed was the chief of all sinners.

Nobody opposed the work of God more zealously than he did, in spite of the fact that he could boast, 'as to zeal, a persecutor of the church; as to the righteousness which is in the Law, found blameless' (Phil. 3:6). For several reasons, I believe this refers to what Paul was before he came to Christ.

First, the reference to himself as a sinner is in support of the first half of the verse in 1 Timothy: 'Christ Jesus came into the world to save sinners' (1 Tim. 1:15). The reference to 'the ungodly and sinners' a few verses earlier (v. 9), along with the other New Testament uses of the term 'sinners' for those who are outside salvation, shows that the sinners whom

Christ came to save were outside of salvation rather than believers who can still choose to sin.

Second, Paul's reference to himself as a sinner is immediately followed by the statement, 'And yet... I found [past tense] mercy'(v. 16), clearly pointing to the past occasion of his conversion. Paul continued to be amazed at the mercy of God toward him who was the 'worst' sinner. A similar present evaluation of himself based upon the past is perceived when the apostle said, 'I am [present] the least of the apostles, who am not fit to be called an apostle, because I persecuted the church of God' (1 Cor. 15:9). Because of his past action, Paul considered himself unworthy of what by God's grace and mercy he presently was, an apostle who was in no respect 'inferior to the most eminent apostles' (2 Cor. 12:11).

Third, although declaring that he is the worst sinner, the apostle at the same time declared that Christ had strengthened him for the ministry, having considered him 'faithful,' or trustworthy, for the ministry to which he was called (see 1 Tim. 1:12). The term 'sinner,' therefore, did not describe him as a believer, but rather was used in remembrance of what he was before Christ transformed him.

The only other places in Scripture that could be referring to Christians as sinners are two references found in James. The first, 'Cleanse your hands, you sinners' (4:8) is one of 10 verbal commands urging anyone who reads this general epistle to make a decisive break with the old life. This is best understood as calling the reader to repentance and therefore salvation.

The second use of 'sinner,' found in James 5:19,20, appears to have a similar reference to unbelievers. The 'sinner' is to be turned 'from the error of his way' and thus be saved from 'death.' Because this is most likely spiritual death, it suggests that the person was not a believer. In both of these uses of 'sinner,' James is using the term as it was used among the Jews for those who disregarded the law of God and flouted standards of morality.

The fact that these 'sinners' are among those addressed by James does not necessarily mean they are believers, for Scripture teaches that unbelievers can be among the saints (see 1 John 2:19), as there surely are today in our churches. Referring to them as 'sinners' fits the description of those who have not come to repentance and faith in God, as the rest of Scripture clearly identifies believers as saints who still have the capacity to sin.[2]

The status of saint is parallel to the concept of being God's called or elect ones. Believers are those who are 'beloved of God... called as saints' (Rom. 1:7; see 1 Cor. 1:2). They are 'chosen [or elected] of God, holy, and beloved' (Col. 3:12). They are 'chosen... through sanctification by the Spirit' (2 Thess. 2:13; see 1 Pet. 1:1,2). God chose them and separated them from the world to be His people. As a result, believers are 'holy brethren' (Heb. 3:1).

By the election and calling of God, believers are set apart unto God and now belong to the sphere of His holiness. We begin our walk with God as immature babes in Christ, but we are indeed children of God. We are saints who sin, but we have all the resources in Christ we need not to sin. Paul's words to the Ephesians are an interesting combination of these two concepts of holiness. Addressing them as 'saints,' or holy ones, in 1:1, he goes on in verse 4 to say that God 'chose us in Him [Christ]... that we should be holy and blameless before Him.' By God's choosing, they were already holy in Christ, but the purpose was that they would mature in character as they conformed to the image of God.

As believers, we are not trying to become saints; we are saints who are becoming like Christ. In no way does this deny the continuous struggle with sin, but it does give the believer some hope for the future. Many Christians are dominated by the flesh and deceived by the devil. However, telling Christians they are sinners and then disciplining them if they don't act like saints seems counterproductive at best and inconsistent with the Bible at worst.

What Is True of Christ Is True of You

Because you are a saint in Christ by God's calling, you share in Christ's inheritance. 'The Spirit Himself bears witness with our spirit that we are children of God, and if children, heirs also, heirs of God and fellow heirs with Christ' (Rom. 8:16,17). Every believer is identified with Christ:

1. In His death	Romans 6:3,6; Galatians 2:20; Colossians 3:1-3
2. In His burial	Romans 6:4
3. In His resurrection	Romans 6:5,8,11
4. In His ascension	Ephesians 2:6
5. In His life	Romans 6:10,11
6. In His power	Ephesians 1:19,20
7. In His inheritance	Romans 8:16,17; Ephesians 1:11,12

The following list itemizes in first-person language who you really are in Christ. These are some of the scriptural traits that reflect who you became at spiritual birth. You can't earn them or buy them any more than a person born in the United States can earn or buy the rights and freedoms enjoyed as an American citizen. They are guaranteed to the person by the Constitution simply because he or she was born in the United States. Similarly, these traits are guaranteed to you by the Word of God simply because you were born into God's holy nation by faith in Christ.

Who Am I?

I am the salt of the earth (Matt. 5:13).

I am the light of the world (Matt. 5:14).

I am a child of God (John 1:12).

I am part of the true vine, a channel of Christ's life (John 15:1,5).

I am Christ's friend (John 15:15).

I am chosen and appointed by Christ to bear His fruit (John 15:16).

I am a slave of righteousness (Rom. 6:18).

I am enslaved to God (Rom. 6:22).

I am a son of God; God is spiritually my Father (Rom. 8:14,15; Gal. 3:26; 4:6).

I am a joint heir with Christ, sharing His inheritance with Him (Rom. 8:17).

I am a temple — a dwelling place — of God. His Spirit and His life dwells in me (1 Cor. 3:16; 6:19).

I am united to the Lord and am one spirit with Him (1 Cor. 6:17).

I am a member of Christ's Body (1 Cor. 12:27; Eph. 5:30).

I am a new creation (2 Cor. 5:17).

I am reconciled to God and am a minister of reconciliation (2 Cor. 5:18,19).

I am a son of God and one in Christ (Gal. 3:26,28).

I am an heir of God since I am a son of God (Gal. 4:6,7).

I am a saint (1 Cor. 1:2; Eph. 1:1; Phil. 1:1; Col. 1:2).

I am God's workmanship — His handiwork — born anew in Christ to do His work (Eph. 2:10).

I am a fellow citizen with the rest of God's family (Eph. 2:19).

I am a prisoner of Christ (Eph. 3:1; 4:1).

I am righteous and holy (Eph. 4:24).

I am a citizen of heaven, seated in heaven right now (Eph. 2:6; Phil. 3:20).

I am hidden with Christ in God (Col. 3:3).

I am an expression of the life of Christ because He is my life (Col. 3:4).

I am chosen of God, holy and dearly loved (Col. 3:12; 1 Thess. 1:4).

I am a son of light and not of darkness (1 Thess. 5:5).

I am a holy partaker of a heavenly calling (Heb. 3:1).

I am a partaker of Christ; I share in His life (Heb. 3:14).

I am one of God's living stones, being built up in Christ as a spiritual house (1 Pet. 2:5).

I am a member of a chosen race, a royal priesthood, a holy nation, a people for God's own possession (1 Pet. 2:9,10).

I am an alien and stranger to this world in which I temporarily live (1 Pet. 2:11).

I am an enemy of the devil (1 Pet. 5:8).

I am a child of God and I will resemble Christ when He returns (1 John 3:1,2).

I am born of God, and the evil one — the devil — cannot touch me (1 John 5:18).

I am not the great 'I am' (Exod. 3:14; John 8:24,28,58), but by the grace of God, I am what I am (1 Cor. 15:10).[3]

Because you are alive in Christ, every one of those characteristics is completely true of you, and you can do nothing to make them more true. You can, however, make these traits more meaningful and productive in your life by simply choosing to believe what God has said about you. You will not be prideful if you do, but you may be defeated if you don't.

One of the greatest ways to help yourself grow into maturity in Christ is to remind yourself continually who you are in Him. In my conferences we do this by reading the 'Who Am I?' list aloud together. I suggest you go back and read it aloud to yourself right now. Read the list once or twice a day for a week or two. Read it when you think Satan is trying to deceive you into believing you are a worthless failure.

The more you reaffirm who you are in Christ, the more your behavior will begin to reflect your true identity. Commenting on Romans chapter 6, John Stott states that the 'necessity of remembering who we are' is the way 'Paul brings his high theology down to the level of practical everyday experience,' and he continues his summary:

> So, in practice we should constantly be reminding ourselves who we are. We need to learn to talk to ourselves, and ask ourselves questions: 'Don't you know? Don't you know the meaning of your conversion and baptism? Don't you know that you have been united to Christ in His death and resurrection? Don't you know that you have been enslaved to God and have committed yourself to His obedience? Don't you know these things? Don't you know who you are?' We must go on pressing ourselves with such questions, until we reply to ourselves: 'Yes, I do know who I am, a new person in Christ, and by the grace of God I shall live accordingly.'[4]

One man drove several hundred miles to attend our Living Free in Christ conference. On his way home he decided to use the 'Who Am I?' statements as a personal prayer list. As he drove, he prayed through the list of traits one by one, asking God to burn them into his consciousness. It took him nearly five hours to drive home, and he was praying about 'Who Am I?' traits all the way. When asked about the effect this experience had on his life, he simply replied with a smile, 'Life changing.'

One of my students, who sat through this material in a seminary class, was struggling with his identity in Christ. After the class he sent the following note to me:

> Dear Dr. Anderson:
> In looking back over the material presented in class this semester, I realize that I have been freed and enlightened in many ways. I believe the most significant mater-

ial for me had to do with the fact that in Christ I am significant, accepted and secure. As I meditated on this
material I found that I was able to overcome many problems I have struggled with for years — fear of failure, feelings of worthlessness and a general sense of
inadequacy.

I began prayerfully studying the 'Who Am I?' statements given in class. I found myself going back to that
list many times during the semester, especially when I felt
attacked in the area of fear or inadequacy. I have also
been able to share this material with a class at church,
and many of my students have experienced new freedom in their lives as well. I can't speak enthusiastically
enough about helping people understand who they really
are in Christ. In my future ministry I intend to make this a
dominant part of my teaching and counseling.

The Bright Hope of Being a Child of God

As children of the sinful first Adam, we were obstinate and
unpleasant, helpless and hopeless, having nothing in ourselves to commend us to God. God's love, however, overruled
our unloveliness. Through Christ, God provided a way for us
into His family. As God's adopted child, you have been given
a new identity and a new name. You are no longer a spiritual
orphan; you are a son or daughter of God. As a child in
God's family you have become a partaker of His 'divine
nature' (2 Pet. 1:4).

If you are beginning to think you are someone special as
a Christian, you are thinking right — you *are* special! Your
specialness is not the result of anything you have done, of
course. It is all God's doing. We are what we are by the grace
of God. All you did was respond by faith to God's invitation
to be His child. As a child of God, in union with Him

because you are in Christ, you have every right to enjoy your special relationship with your heavenly Father.

How important is it to know who you are in Christ? Countless numbers of Christians struggle with their day-to-day behavior because they labor under a false perception of who they are. They consider themselves sinners who hope to make it into heaven by God's grace, but they can't seem to live above their sinful tendencies.

Look again at the hope-filled words of 1 John 3:1-3: 'See how great a love the Father has bestowed upon us, that we should be called children of God; and such we are.... Beloved, now we are children of God, and it has not appeared as yet what we shall be. We know that, when He appears, we shall be like Him, because we shall see Him just as He is. And everyone who has this hope fixed on Him purifies himself, just as He is pure.'

What is the believer's hope? That you are a child of God *now*, who is being conformed to the image of God. The person who has this hope 'purifies himself' and begins to live according to who he or she really is. You must believe you are a child of God to live like a child of God. 'God willed to make known what is the riches of the glory of this mystery among the Gentiles, which is Christ in you, the hope of glory' (Col. 1:27).

Notes

1. David C. Needham, *Birthright! Christian, Do You Know Who You Are?* (Portland, Oreg.: Multnomah Press, 1981), adapted from an illustration on page 73.

2. Confrontation with the righteousness and holiness of God frequently brought deep acknowledgment of one's own sinful condition. Paul's recognition of himself before the Lord as a 'sinful man' is not uncommon among the saints (Luke 5:8; see Gen. 18:27; Job 42:6; Isa. 6:5; Dan. 9:4). Believers are sinful, but Scripture does not seem to define their identity as sinners.

3. For deeper exploration of the scriptural truths of the 'Who Am I?' list, read *Living Free in Christ*, which contains 36 readings based on the list that will

transform your thoughts about God and yourself and that will help you live victoriously in Christ. *Living Free in Christ* is available in the UK as part of the omnibus volume *Living Free* (Monarch Books).

4. John Stott, *Romans: God's Good News for the World* (Downers Grove, Ill.: InterVarsity Press, 1994), p. 187.

3
See Yourself for Who You Really Are

Claire attended a church college ministry I was involved in several years ago. On a physical, material level, Claire had absolutely nothing going for her. She had a dumpy figure and a poor complexion. Her father was a drunken bum who had deserted his family. Her mother worked two menial jobs just to make ends meet. Her older brother, a drug addict, was always in and out of the house.

When I first met Claire, I was sure she was the ultimate wallflower. I didn't think there was any way she could compete for acceptance in a college-aged society that is attracted to physical beauty and material success. To my pleasant surprise, though, everybody in the group liked Claire and loved to be around her. She had lots of friends, and eventually she married the nicest guy in the college department.

What was her secret? Claire simply accepted herself for who God said she was in Christ, and she confidently committed herself to God's great goal for her life: to love people and grow in Christ. She wasn't a threat to anyone. Instead, she was so positive and caring toward others that everyone loved her.

Derek, a man in his early 30s, was enrolled in our missions program at Talbot School of Theology several years ago. I barely knew Derek until he attended a conference where I spoke about the critical importance of understanding our spiritual identity in Christ. The next week he came to see me and tell me his story.

Derek grew up with a father who demanded perfection in everything his son did. Derek was an intelligent, talented young man, but no matter how hard he tried or how well he succeeded, he seemed unable to please his father. The man continually pushed his son for better performance.

Striving to fulfill his father's expectations, Derek earned an appointment to the United States Naval Academy and qualified for flight school. He achieved what most young men only dream about: becoming a member of the elite corps of Navy fliers.

'After I completed my obligation to the Navy,' Derek told me, 'I decided that I wanted to please God with my life. But I saw God as a perfectionistic heavenly shadow of my earthly father, and I figured the only way I could fulfill His expectations for me was to become a missionary. I'll be honest with you. I enrolled in the missions program for the same reason I went to Annapolis: to please a demanding Father.

'Then I attended your conference last Saturday. I had never heard that I am unconditionally loved and accepted by my heavenly Father and I never understood who I already am in Christ. I've always worked so hard to please Him by what I do, just as I struggled to please my natural father. I didn't realize that I already please Him by who I am in Christ. Now I know that I don't have to be a missionary to please God, so I'm changing my major to practical theology.'

Derek studied for a practical theology degree for about a year. Then he had the opportunity to serve on a short-term missions team in Spain. When Derek returned from his trip he burst into my office and excitedly told me about his ministry experience in Spain. 'I'm changing my major again,' he concluded.

'To missions, right?' I responded with a smile.

'Right,' Derek beamed. 'But I'm not going into missions because I need God's approval. I know God already loves and accepts me as His child. Now I'm planning to be a missionary because I love Him and want to serve Him.'

I told Derek, 'That is the fundamental difference between being driven and being called.'

Theology Before Practicality

The experiences of Claire and Derek illustrate the importance of establishing our Christian lives on what we believe instead of how we behave. We need a firm grip on the truth of God's Word before we will experience much success at practical Christianity. We need to understand who we are as a result of who God is and what He has done. A fruitful Christian life is the result of living by faith according to what God said is true.

The problem is that we try to base our spiritual growth and maturity on practical sections of the Scriptures and spend too little time internalizing the doctrinal sections. For example, Paul's letters tend to fall into two major parts. The first part is generally called the doctrinal section, such as Romans 1 – 8, Ephesians 1 – 3, Colossians 1 – 2 and so on. These sections reveal what we need to *know* about God, ourselves, sin and salvation. The second half of the letters is the practical section: Romans 12 – 15, Ephesians 4 – 6, Colossians 3 – 4 and so on. These passages describe what we need to do to live our faith in daily experience.

In our zeal to correct the problems in our lives, we skip the doctrinal first half and jump to the practical second half of God's Word. We want a quick fix, a rule or instruction we can apply like a Band-Aid to make things better. We don't have time to wade through the deep theological concepts of Scripture; we want a practical solution and we want it now.

Perhaps you have already discovered that a Band-Aid approach to daily living doesn't work. Why not? Because you need an adequate foundation of truth to live a practical life of faith. How can you hope to 'stand firm against the schemes of the devil' (Eph. 6:11) if you have not internalized that you are already victoriously 'raised... up with Him, and seated... with Him in the heavenly places, in Christ Jesus' (2:6)?

How can you rejoice in hope and persevere in tribulation (see Rom. 12:12) without the confidence of knowing you have been justified by faith and 'have peace with God through our Lord Jesus Christ' (5:1)? When your basic belief system about God and yourself is shaky, your day-to-day behavior system will be shaky. When your belief system is intact and your relationship with God is based on truth, however, you will have very little trouble working out the practical aspects of daily Christianity.

Positional and Progressive Sanctification

Most Christians are aware that salvation for the believer is past, present and future tense. By that, I mean we have been saved (past tense; see Eph. 2:4,5,8), we are being saved (present tense; see 1 Cor. 1:18; 2 Cor. 2:15) and someday we shall fully be saved from the wrath that is to come (future tense; see Rom. 5:9,10; 13:11). We have not yet experienced the totality of salvation, but I believe we can have the assurance of it.

Paul says, 'You were sealed in Him with the Holy Spirit of promise, who is given as a pledge of our inheritance, with a view to the redemption of God's own possession, to the praise of His glory' (Eph. 1:13,14). John says, 'These things I have written to you who believe in the name of the Son of God, in order that you may know that you have eternal life' (1 John 5:13).

In reference to the believer, sanctification is also past, present and future tense. We have been sanctified (past tense, see 1 Cor. 6:19; 2 Pet. 1:3,4), we are being sanctified (present tense, see Rom. 6:22; 2 Cor. 7:1) and we shall someday be fully sanctified (future tense, see 1 Thess. 3:12,13; 5:23,24). The doctrine of sanctification begins at our new birth and ends in our glorification. Past-tense sanctification is usually referred to as positional sanctification, and refers to the position or the status the believer has in Christ. Present-tense sanctification is referred to as progressive or experiential sanctification.

The positional truth of who we are in Christ is real truth and it is the only basis for the progressive sanctification that follows. Just as the past reality of salvation is the basis for the present-tense working out of our salvation, so is our position in Christ the basis for our growth in Christ. In other words, we are not trying to become children of God; we are already children of God who are becoming like Christ.

It is my firm belief that if we fully appropriated the first half of Paul's Epistles, which establish us in Christ, we would naturally (or supernaturally) live the second half. For a comprehensive study of sanctification see *God's Power at Work in You*,[1] coauthored with Dr. Robert Saucy.

Get Right with God First

A few years ago a pastor asked me to counsel a couple from his church — the music director and his wife. I have never seen a family so blown apart in my life. They came into the room screaming at each other. Their relationship was characterized by infidelity and abuse. They were ready to leave my office in two different directions. I prayed silently to the Lord, *If there's any way of saving this marriage, You're the only one who knows about it.*

After listening to their bitter complaints against each other for several minutes, I interrupted them. 'I think you need to forget about your marriage. There's no way we can save it — not now, not in this condition. But may I implore you individually to get right with God by restoring your personal relationship with Him?' I had their attention.

I turned to the wife. 'Is there a way you can get away for a while all by yourself?'

She thought for a moment, then nodded. 'My sister has a cabin in the hills. I think she'll let me use it.'

'Good. Here are some tapes I want you to listen to. Go away for a few days and saturate yourself with these messages. Find out who you are in Christ and commit yourself to aligning your torn-up internal world with Him.'

Surprisingly, she agreed. I asked the husband to make the same commitment and handed him an identical set of tapes. He also agreed. As they left my office I had little hope that I would ever see them together again.

Two years later I was sitting in a restaurant after church when that same music director walked in with his three children. *Oh, no,* I thought, *they've split up for good.* I kept out of his sight because I felt sorry for him and didn't want to face him. In a few minutes his wife walked into the restaurant and sat down in the same booth. They looked as happy and contented as any Christian family I have ever seen. I was really puzzled.

Suddenly the couple looked my way, recognized me and got out of their booth to come see me. 'Hi, Neil, it's good to see you,' they greeted me cheerfully.

'Yes, it's good to see you two.' I really wanted to say, 'It's good to see you two *together,*' but thought better of it. 'How are you doing?' I wouldn't have been surprised if they had told me they were divorced and they had met in the restaurant for the children's sake.

'We're doing great, Neil,' the wife answered. 'I did what you told me to do. I went up into the hills alone for two weeks, listened to your tapes and got my life right with God.'

'I did the same,' the husband added. 'And we were able to work out the problems in our marriage.' We rejoiced together about what God had done for them first as individuals and then as a family.

This couple discovered that getting right with each other

began with getting right with God. Getting right with God always begins with settling once and for all the fact that God is your loving Father and you are His accepted child. That is the foundational truth from which you live.

You are a child of God, you are created in His image, you have been justified and positionally declared righteous by Him because of Christ's finished work and your faith in Him. As long as you believe that and walk accordingly, your daily experience of practical Christianity will result in growth. You will struggle, though, if you question the finished work of Christ, and try to become somebody you already are.

We don't serve God to gain His acceptance; we are accepted, so we serve God. We don't follow Him to be loved; we are loved, so we follow Him. It is not what we do that determines who we are; it is who we are that determines what we do. 'Beloved, *now* we are children of God' (1 John 3:2, emphasis added). That is why you are called to live by faith (see Rom. 1:16,17).

To live the victorious Christian life you have to believe what is already true about you. Will you have opposition to believing this truth? Of course! The father of lies (see John 8:44) has deceived the whole world (see Rev. 12:9), and he accuses the brethren day and night (see 12:10). If that isn't enough, others will put you down. We have to keep reminding ourselves of these positional truths.

The Fallout from God's Grace

The following list supplements the 'Who Am I?' list in chapter 2. These statements further describe your identity in Christ. Read this list aloud to yourself repeatedly until it becomes a part of you. Pray through the list occasionally, asking God to cement these truths in your heart:

Since I Am in Christ

Since I am in Christ, by the grace of God...

I have been justified — completely forgiven and made righteous (Rom. 5:1).

I died with Christ and died to the power of sin's rule over my life (Rom. 6:1-6).

I am free forever from condemnation (Rom. 8:1).

I have been placed into Christ by God's doing (1 Cor. 1:30).

I have received the Spirit of God into my life that I might know the things freely given to me by God (1 Cor. 2:12).

I have been given the mind of Christ (1 Cor. 2:16).

I have been bought with a price; I am not my own; I belong to God (1 Cor. 6:19,20).

I have been established, anointed and sealed by God in Christ, and I have been given the Holy Spirit as a pledge guaranteeing our inheritance to come (2 Cor. 1:21; Eph. 1:13,14).

Since I have died, I no longer live for myself, but for Christ (2 Cor. 5:14,15).

I have been made righteous (2 Cor. 5:21).

I have been crucified with Christ and it is no longer I who live, but Christ lives in me. The life I am now living is Christ's life (Gal. 2:20).

I have been blessed with every spiritual blessing (Eph. 1:3).

I was chosen in Christ before the foundation of the world to be holy and am without blame before Him (Eph. 1:4).

I was predestined — determined by God — to be adopted as God's son (Eph. 1:5).

I have been redeemed and forgiven, and I am a recipient of His lavish grace (Eph. 1:17).

I have been made alive together with Christ (Eph. 2:5).

I have been raised up and seated with Christ in heaven (Eph. 2:6).

I have direct access to God through the Spirit (Eph. 2:18).

I may approach God with boldness, freedom and confidence (Eph. 3:12).

I have been rescued from the domain of Satan's rule and transferred to the kingdom of Christ (Col. 1:13).

I have been redeemed and forgiven of all my sins. The debt against me has been canceled (Col. 1:14).

Christ Himself is in me (Col. 1:27).

I am firmly rooted in Christ and am now being built in Him (Col. 2:7).

I have been made complete in Christ (Col. 2:10).

I have been spiritually circumcised (Col. 2:11).

I have been buried, raised and made alive with Christ (Col. 2:12,13).

I died with Christ and I have been raised up with Christ. My life is now hidden with Christ in God. Christ is now my life (Col. 3:1-4).

I have been given a spirit of power, love and self-discipline (2 Tim. 1:7).

I have been saved and set apart according to God's doing (2 Tim. 1:9; Titus 3:5).

Because I am sanctified and am one with the Sanctifier, He is not ashamed to call me brother (Heb. 2:11).

I have the right to come boldly before the throne of God to find mercy and grace in time of need (Heb. 4:16).

I have been given exceedingly great and precious promises by God by which I am a partaker of God's divine nature (2 Pet. 1:4).

Recently, a pastor who was attending one of my conferences on resolving spiritual conflicts pulled me aside after a session. His comments to me reaffirmed my conviction that understanding our spiritual inheritance is the key to resolving our daily conflicts.

'A lady in our church dropped by for counseling this week,' he began. 'She has been struggling in her relationship with her alcoholic husband. She was at her wit's end, feeling terribly defeated. She came to tell me she was calling it quits on their marriage.

'I pulled out the list of statements you shared with us declaring who we are in Christ. I said, "Here, read this aloud." She read about halfway through the list and began to cry. She said, "I never realized all this was true of me. I feel that maybe there is hope for me after all."'

Isn't that incredible? The truth about who you are in Christ makes such a big difference in your success at handling the challenges and conflicts of life. It is imperative to your growth and maturity that you believe God's truth about who you are.

Relationship Versus Harmony

Considering all this emphasis on God's complete acceptance of us in Christ, you may be wondering, *What happens to this ideal relationship with God when we sin? Does our failure interfere with God's acceptance of us?* Let me respond by using a very simple illustration.

When I was born physically, I had a father. His name was Marvin Anderson. As his son, I not only have Marvin Anderson's last name, but I also have Marvin Anderson's blood coursing though my veins. Marvin Anderson and Neil Anderson are blood related.

Could I possibly do anything that would change my blood relationship to my father? What if I ran away from home and changed my name? I would still be Marvin Anderson's son, wouldn't I? What if he kicked me out of the house? What if he disowned me? Would I still be his son? Of course! We are related by blood and nothing can change that.

Could I do anything that would affect the harmony of our relationship as father and son? Yes, indeed — and by the time I was five years old I had discovered almost every way! My relationship with my father was never in jeopardy, but the harmony of our relationship was interrupted countless times by my behavior.

What determined whether I lived in harmony with my father? Trust and obedience. The relationship area was settled for life when I was born into Dad's family as his son. The harmony problem was addressed repeatedly as a result of my behavior and misbehavior. I discovered very early in life that if I obeyed Dad I lived in harmony with him. If I didn't obey him we were out of harmony. Whether we were in harmony or not, however, he was always my father.

In the spiritual realm, when I was born again I became a member of God's family. God is my Father and I enjoy an eternal relationship with Him through the precious blood of Christ (see 1 Pet. 1:18,19). As a child of God, can I do anything that will change my relationship with Him? Now I realize that I may step on some theological toes here. The question of eternal security is still a topic of debate among Christians. For the sake of this discussion, I am less concerned about that debate than I am about making a distinction between two separate areas. Our relationship with God is based on the blood of the Lord Jesus Christ. We are saved by how we believe, not by how we behave.

A lot of Scripture supports the assurance of salvation. Paul asks in Romans 8:35: 'Who shall separate us from the love of Christ?' He then answers that no created thing 'shall be able to separate us from the love of God, which is in Christ Jesus our Lord' (8:39). Jesus declared: 'My sheep hear My voice,… and I give eternal life to them, and they shall never perish; and no one shall snatch them out of My hand' (John 10:27,28). I am a born-again child of God, in spiritual union with Him by

His grace, which I received through faith. My relationship with God was settled when I was born into His family.

Can I do anything that will interfere with the *harmony* of my relationship with God? Absolutely! Harmony with God is based on the same concerns as harmony with my earthly father: trust and obedience. When I trust and obey God I live in harmony with Him. When I don't perfectly respond to God, the harmony of our relationship is disturbed and my life will reflect it. I love my heavenly Father and I want to live in harmony with Him, so I strive to live by faith according to what He says is true. Even when I fail to take Him at His Word or choose to walk by the flesh, my relationship with Him is not at stake, because we are related by the blood of Jesus Christ.

Believing the Truth About Others

A pastor asked me, 'How can I get out of my church?'

'Why do you want out?' I asked. 'What's wrong with your church?'

'I've got a bunch of losers in my church.'

'Losers? I wonder if they are really losers or if they just see themselves as losers because that's how you see them.'

He reluctantly agreed that it was probably the latter. He was right, because there are no losers in the kingdom of God — none whatsoever. How can children of God be losers when they have already gained eternal life? As important as it is for you to believe in your true identity as a child of God, it is equally important that you perceive other Christians for who they are in Christ and treat them accordingly. I believe that the greatest determinant for how we treat people is how we perceive them. If we view people as losers we will begin to treat them that way. If, however, we believe our brothers and sisters in Christ are redeemed saints, we will treat them as saints and they will be greatly helped in behaving as saints.

Studies have shown that, in the average home, for every positive statement, a child receives 10 negative statements. The school environment is only slightly better; students hear seven negative statements from their teachers for every one positive statement. No wonder so many children are growing up thinking they are losers. Every day, parents and teachers are conveying what they believe to their children and students.

These studies go on to point out that it takes four positive statements to negate the effect of one negative statement. You probably verify that finding every time you wear a new suit or dress. Some of your friends may say, 'Oh, what a good looking outfit.' It only takes one comment such as 'It's really not you' to send you scurrying back to the store for a refund. We affect others significantly by what we say about them, and what we say is determined by what we believe about them.

The New Testament clearly states that we are saints who sin. Children of God who say they don't sin are called liars (see 1 John 1:8). We are not to judge one another; instead, we are called to accept other believers as children of God, and to build up each other.

If we could memorize just one verse from the New Testament, put it into practice and never violate it, I believe we would resolve half the problems in our homes and churches. The verse is Ephesians 4:29: 'Let no unwholesome word proceed from your mouth, but only such a word as is good for edification according to the need of the moment, that it may give grace to those who hear.'

Isn't it amazing that you and I have the power to give grace to others through the proper use of our words? If we said nothing to put others down, and only built up others as Ephesians 4:29 commands, we would be part of God's construction crew in the church instead of members of Satan's wrecking crew.

Relating to God

When I was in the eighth grade, we had a program called Religious Day Instruction. Every Tuesday afternoon the afternoon classes were shortened so we could go to the church of our choice for the last hour. It wasn't forced religion; students could choose to go to study hall, but I went to the church of my mother's choice. One nice fall day, I decided to skip Religious Day Instruction. I played in the park, and came back in time to catch the bus for my ride home to the farm. I thought I had gotten away with it, but I did not!

The next day the principal called me in and hauled me over the coals. Then he said, 'I have arranged for you to be home Thursday and Friday.' I was shocked. Suspended from school for two days for skipping Religious Day Instruction? I was not looking forward to seeing my parents, and the ride home was miserable. I thought about playing sick for two days, or hiding in the woods when I should have been in school. I couldn't do it, and I knew I had to face my authority figures. I went to my mother because I knew there would be some mercy there.

'Mom,' I said, 'I got suspended from school for two days for skipping Religious Day Instruction.'

At first she was shocked, then she smiled and said, 'Oh, Neil, I forgot to tell you. We called the school to see if you could stay home Thursday and Friday to help us pick corn.'

Now if I had known that, would I have dreaded seeing my parents? Would the school-bus ride home have been miserable? Of course not, but I didn't know that staying home Thursday and Friday was already justified. That is how many Christians live their lives. They live their lives as though they are walking on glass. They can't make any mistakes because if they do, the hammer of God will fall on them.

Dear Christian reader, the hammer fell. It fell on Christ. He died 'once for all' our sins (Rom. 6:10). We are not sinners in the hands of an angry God. We are saints in the hands of a loving God who has called us to 'draw near with a sincere heart in full assurance of faith, having our hearts sprinkled clean from an evil conscience and our bodies washed with pure water' (Heb. 10:22). 'For through Him [Christ] we both have our access in one Spirit to the Father' (Eph. 2:18); 'in whom we have boldness and confident access through faith in Him' (Eph. 3:12).

Some Christian leaders believe we should emphasize the sinful side of our human nature as a motivation to live righteously. I respectfully disagree. How can we motivate by guilt when, 'There is therefore now no condemnation for those who are in Christ Jesus' (Rom. 8:1)? How can we motivate by fear when, 'God has not given us a spirit of timidity, but of power and love and discipline' (2 Tim. 1:7)? I believe we ought to tell believers the truth about who they are in Christ and motivate them to live accordingly. To illustrate this truth, let me share the following testimony sent to me by a missionary who read the first edition of this book:

> Though I have been a Christian for many years, I never understood God's forgiveness and my spiritual inheritance. I have been struggling for years with a particular sin. I was in Bible college when I began this horrible practice. I never thought this living hell would ever end. I would have killed myself had I not thought that was a sin. I felt God had turned His back on me and I was doomed to hell because I couldn't overcome this sin. I hated myself. I felt like such a failure.
>
> The Lord led me to purchase your book *Victory over the Darkness*. I feel like a new Christian, like I've just been born again. My eyes are now open to God's love, and I realize that I am a saint who has chosen to sin. I can finally say I am free, free of Satan's bondage and aware of the lies he has been feeding me.

I would confess to God and beg His forgiveness when I sinned, but the next time I fell deeper into Satan's grasp because I couldn't accept God's forgiveness and I couldn't forgive myself. I always thought the answer lay in drawing closer to God, but I went to Him in confusion, believing I was a sinner who couldn't be loved. No more! Through the Scriptures and the way you presented them to me, I am no longer a defeated Christian. I now know I am alive in Christ and dead to sin and a slave of righteousness. I now live by faith according to what God said is true. Sin has no power over me, Satan has lost his grip on me.

Note

1. Neil T. Anderson and Robert Saucy, *God's Power at Work in You* (London: Monarch Books 2001).

4
Something Old, Something New

Attend any Bible-believing church and ask the congregation, 'How many believe that you are a sinner?' They will all raise their hands. Then ask, 'How many believe you are a saint?' Few if any would raise their hands. Why is that? Some have never been taught differently. Others think it would be prideful to identity themselves as saints. Many believe the label 'sinner' best fits their present condition. They sin so they must be sinners. Even if you told them they are both saint and sinner, they will believe the latter and probably not the former because of their experiences.

Being a saint who is alive and free in Christ does not mean spiritual maturity or sinlessness, but it does provide the basis for hope and future growth. Despite God's provision for us in Christ, we are still far less than perfect. We are saints who sin. Our position in Christ is settled, but our daily performance is often marked by personal failure and disobedience that disappoints us and disrupts the harmony of our relationship with God. We groan with the apostle Paul: 'For the good that I wish, I do not do; but I practise the very evil that I do not wish. Wretched man that I am! Who will set me free from the body of this death?' (Rom. 7:19,24).

In our attempts to understand the failure that often disturbs our sense of sainthood, we struggle with such biblical terms as flesh, nature and old man (self). What do these terms really mean? Are they distinct in themselves or interchangeable elements of the same problem? Defining these terms becomes even more difficult when the editorial teams of some modern Bibles translate 'flesh' (*sarx*) as old nature or sin nature.

Admittedly, this is a difficult theological area. Bible scholars have wrestled with these questions for centuries and I don't in any way pretend to have the final answers. In this chapter, however, I want to explore some of these terms that often confuse Christians who are attempting to understand the sinful side of their sainthood. I believe a clearer biblical grasp of these terms will further assist you in understanding who you are and pave the way for greater spiritual maturity.

The Nature of the Problem

The Bible says we were dead in our 'trespasses and sins' (Eph. 2:1) and 'were by *nature* children of wrath' (2:3, emphasis added). In other words, we were born physically alive but spiritually dead. We had neither the presence of God in our lives nor the knowledge of His ways. Consequently, we all learned to live our lives independently of God. This learned independence is one of the chief characteristics of the flesh.

'For the flesh sets its desire against the Spirit, and the Spirit against the flesh; for these are in opposition to one another' (Gal. 5:17). They are in opposition because the Holy Spirit, like Jesus, will not operate independently of our heavenly Father, but the flesh does. The flesh may be defined as existence apart from God — a life dominated by sin or a drive opposed to God. The flesh is self-reliant rather than God-dependent; it is self-centered rather than Christ-centered.

Such is the state of fallen humankind: sinful by nature and spiritually dead (i.e., separated from God). In addition, the heart, which is the center of our being, 'is more deceitful than all else and is desperately sick' (Jer. 17:9). Paul says, 'for all have sinned and fall short of the glory of God' (Rom.

3:23). Fallen humankind live their lives 'in the flesh,' and 'those who are in the flesh cannot please God' (Rom. 8:8). Humankind were depraved. Every aspect of their beings was corrupted and they could do nothing to save themselves.

Positionally, several things changed at salvation. First, God transferred us from the domain of darkness 'to the kingdom of His beloved Son' (Col. 1:13).

Second, sin's dominion through the flesh has been broken. As a believer, you are no longer in the flesh, you are in Christ. Paul explains, 'However, you are not in the flesh but in the Spirit, if indeed the Spirit of God dwells in you. But if anyone does not have the Spirit of Christ, he does not belong to Him' (Rom. 8:9).

Paul also equates the idea of being 'in the flesh' with being 'in Adam.' 'For as *in Adam* all die, so also *in Christ* all shall be made alive' (1 Cor. 15:22, emphasis added). Christians are no longer in the flesh, but because the characteristics of the flesh remain in believers, they have a choice. They can walk (or live) according to the flesh (see Gal. 5:19-21) or they can walk (or live) according to the Spirit (see 5:22,23). This positional change can be shown as follows:

In Adam		In Christ
Old man (self)	by ancestry	New man (self)
Sin nature Ephesians 2:1-3	by nature 2 Peter 1:4	Partaker of divine nature
In the flesh Romans 8:8	by birth Romans 8:9	In the Spirit
Live according to the flesh	by choice	Live according to the Spirit or the flesh Galatians 5:16-18

We Have Been Grafted In

Concerning our nature, Paul says, 'you were formerly darkness, but now you are light in the Lord' (Eph. 5:8). Are we both light and darkness? Paul also said, 'Therefore if any man is in Christ, he is a new creature; the old things passed away; behold, new things have come' (2 Cor. 5:17).

Are we partly new creature and partly old creature? Does the Christian have two natures? Perhaps an illustration will help answer that question. In Arizona, city parks and boulevards are decorated with ornamental orange trees that are a much hardier stock than the trees that produce the sweet oranges we eat. Because they can survive colder temperatures, they are used for root stock.

The ornamental orange is allowed to grow to a certain height; then it is cut off, and a new life (such as a navel orange) is grafted into it. Everything that grows above the graft takes on the new nature of the sweet orange. Everything below the graft retains the physical characteristics of the ornamental orange. Only one tree remains when it is fully grown. The *physical* growth of the tree is still dependent upon the roots that go deep into the soil for water and nutrition. What grows above the graft takes on the nature of what was grafted into it.

People don't look at a grove of navel oranges and say, 'That grove is nothing more than a bunch of root stock!' They would call them navel orange trees because they would identify the trees by their fruit. That is how we should be known.

Jesus said, 'So then, you will know them by their fruits' (Matt. 7:20). Paul says, 'Therefore from now on we recognize no man according to the flesh' (2 Cor. 5:16). In other words, we are not supposed to recognize Christians for who they were in Adam, but for who they now are in Christ. That is why the Bible doesn't identify believers as sinners but instead identifies them as saints.

The natural person is like an ornamental orange tree, who may look good but cannot bear any fruit that isn't bitter. The fruit will only drop to the ground and bring forth more natural stock that will only appear to look good for a season.

Let me present another observation from the tree illustration. How would you define the nature of the tree? Would it have two natures? It depends upon whether you are talking about the whole tree, which does have two natures (root stock and navel), or if you are just talking about the part of the tree that grows above the graft (the new creation), which has just one nature (navel). This is something of a semantic problem. When Paul talks about the new 'I,' is he talking about who he was before Christ in combination with who he now is in Christ, or is he referring only to the new creation in Christ?

Spiritual growth in the Christian life requires a relationship with God who is the fountain of spiritual life, a relationship that brings a new seed or root of life. As in nature, unless there is some seed or root of life within an organism, no growth can take place. So also unless there is a root of life within the believer (i.e., some core of spiritual life), growth is impossible. There is nothing to grow. That is why Paul's theology is all based on our position in Christ.

'As you therefore have received Christ Jesus the Lord, so walk *in Him*, having been firmly rooted and now being built up *in Him*' (Col. 2:6,7, emphasis added). To build up believers (progressive sanctification), they must first be firmly rooted in Christ (positional sanctification). To grow and bear fruit, Christians, their marriages and their ministries must all be organically centered in Christ.

A New Heart and a New Spirit

According to Scripture, the center of the person is the heart. It is the 'wellspring of life' (Prov. 4:23, NIV). In our natural state, 'The heart is deceitful above all things and beyond cure' (Jer. 17:9, NIV). It is deceitful because it has been conditioned from the time of birth by the deceitfulness of a fallen world, rather than by the truth of God's Word.

One of the greatest prophecies concerning our salvation is found in Ezekiel 36:26 (NIV): 'I will give you a new heart and put a new spirit in you; I will remove from you your heart of stone and give you a heart of flesh.'

The new covenant by which every Christian lives says, 'I will put my laws in their hearts' (Heb. 10:16, NIV). In other words, 'All the ornamental oranges that will choose to put their trust in God and believe His Word shall be navel oranges.' The moment you were grafted into the vine you were sanctified or set apart as a child of God. 'You are already clean' (John 15:3), and you shall continue to be sanctified as He prunes you so that you may grow and bear fruit.

The same thought is captured in Paul's testimony: 'I have been crucified with Christ and I no longer live, but Christ lives in me. The life I live in the body, I live by faith in the Son of God, who loved me and gave himself for me'(Gal. 2:20, NIV). Paul says I died, but I live, obviously a new and different person (see also Col. 3:1-3). In other words, my old ornamental tree has been cut off; I no longer live as an ornamental orange, I now live as a new navel orange.

A New Man

Parallel to the concept of being a new creation in Christ is the teaching that the believer has put on the 'new self' (Col. 3:10), or more literally the new man. The new man at times refers both to the new individual (i.e., 'self') in Christ as well as the new humankind, the new creation united in Christ, with Christ as its head. F. F. Bruce says, 'the new man who is created is the new personality that each believer becomes when he is reborn as a member of the new creation whose source of life is Christ.'[1]

What does it mean to be a new man? Does it mean that every aspect of the believer is new in reality? We still look the same physically, and we still have many of the same thoughts, feelings and experiences.

Picture, for instance, the ornamental orange tree that has just had a tiny new stem grafted into it. Because so much appears to be the same, it is sometimes taught that our 'new-ness' refers only to our position in Christ. The newness is only what we have seen in relation to our position of right-eousness and holiness in justification and positional sanctifi-cation. There is no real change in us until we are finally transformed in glorification. That, however, would be like teaching justification without regeneration (we are forgiven, but there is no new life). If we are still ornamental orange trees, how can we be expected to bear navel oranges? We have to believe that our new identity is in the life of Christ and commit ourselves to grow accordingly.

If you are a new creation in Christ, have you ever won-dered why you still think and feel at times the same way you did before? Because everything you learned before you knew Christ is still programmed into your memory. There is no mental delete button. That is why Paul says, 'Do not conform any longer to the pattern of this world, but be transformed by the renewing of your mind' (Rom. 12:2, NIV).

Let me illustrate. When I was in the Navy, we called the captain of our ship 'the Old Man.' My first Old Man was tough and crusty, and nobody liked him. He drank with the chiefs, belittled his junior officers and made life miserable for the rest of us. He was a lousy Old Man. If I planned to survive on board that ship, however, I had to do it under his authority relating to him as my Old Man. Then one day he got transferred to another ship. I no longer had any relationship with him and I was no longer under his authority.

Then we got a new skipper who was very much different from the Old Man who trained me. So how do you think I related to the new skipper? At first I responded to him just as I had been conditioned to respond to the first Old Man. As I got to know the new skipper, though, I realized he wasn't a crusty old tyrant like the Old Man who was once my authority. He wasn't out to harass his crew. He was a good guy, really concerned about us, but I had been programmed for two years to react a certain way when I saw a captain's braids. I didn't need to react that way any longer; but it took several months to recondition myself to the new skipper.

When you were dead in your trespasses and sins, you also served under a cruel self-serving skipper. The admiral of that fleet is Satan, the prince of darkness, the god and ruler of this world. By God's grace, you have been 'delivered... from the domain of darkness, and transferred... to the kingdom of His beloved Son' (Col. 1:13). You now have a new skipper; your new self is infused with the divine nature of Jesus Christ, your new admiral. As a child of God, you are no longer under the authority of Satan and dominated by sin and death. The old man is dead.

New Things Have Come

Despite the fact that all believers at times still live according to the old self, like Paul, they are new persons — new in relationship to God and new in themselves. The change that takes place in us when we come to Christ involves two dimensions.

First, we have a new master. As mortals we have no choice

but to live under a spiritual power — either our heavenly Father or the god of this world. At salvation, the believer in Christ experiences a change in the power that dominates life.

Second, there is an actual change in the nature of believers so that the propensities of their lives or the deepest desires of their hearts are now oriented toward God rather than toward self and sin.

This becomes evident when believers choose to sin. They are being convicted. What they are doing is no longer consistent with who they really are in Christ. I have counseled hundreds of Christians who are questioning their salvation because of their struggle with sin. The fact that it even bothers them is the best argument for their salvation. It is the nature of a natural person to sin. On the other hand, I have talked to people who profess to be Christians, but seem to have little or no remorse for sin. I would have to question their salvation. If we are children of God, we are not going to live comfortably with sin.

Why do you need the nature of Christ within you? So you can *be* like Christ, not just *act* like Him. God has not given us the power to imitate Him. He has made us partakers of His nature so that we can actually *be* like Him. You don't become a Christian by acting like one. You are not on a performance basis with God. He doesn't say, 'Here are My standards, now you measure up.' He knows you can't solve the problem of an old sinful self by simply improving your behavior. He must change your nature, give you an entirely new self — the life of Christ in you — which is the grace you need to measure up to His standards.

That was the point of Christ's message in the Sermon on the Mount: 'Unless your righteousness surpasses that of the scribes and Pharisees, you shall not enter the kingdom of heaven' (Matt. 5:20). The scribes and Pharisees were the religious perfectionists of their day. They had external behavior down to a science, but their hearts were like the insides of a tomb: reeking of death. Jesus is interested only in creating new persons from the inside out by infusing in them a brand new nature and creating in them a new self. Only after He changes who you are and makes you a partaker of His divine nature will you be able to change your behavior.

A New Master

Because we are identified with Christ in His death and resurrection, we have become new and are part of the new humanity. In this change, we have a new power of dominion in our lives. This is clearly expressed in Romans 6:5-7 (NIV): 'If we have been united with him... in his death, we will certainly also be united with him in his resurrection. For we know that our old self was crucified with him so that the body of sin might be done away with, that we should no longer be slaves to sin — because anyone who has died has been freed from sin.' 'Old self' in this passage literally means old man. The old man in relation to the believer has been crucified in Christ and he has put on the new man (see Col. 3:10).

Paul says, 'Even so consider yourselves to be dead to sin, but alive to God in Christ Jesus' (Rom. 6:11). We don't consider it so to make it so. We are to continuously believe we are alive in Christ and dead to sin because it is so. Believing anything doesn't make it true. God said it is true; therefore we believe it. Death is the ending of a relationship, not an existence. Sin is still present, appealing and powerful; but when you are tempted to sin, you can say, 'I don't have to do that. By the grace of God I can live a righteous life.'

To illustrate, look at Romans 8:1,2: 'There is therefore now no condemnation for those who are in Christ Jesus. For the law of the Spirit of life in Christ Jesus has set you free from the law of sin and of death.' Is the law of sin and of death still operative? Yes, that is why Paul calls it a law. You can't do away with a law, but you can overcome it by a greater law, which is the 'law... of life in Christ Jesus.'

For instance, as mortals we can't fly in our own strength, but we can fly in an airplane because an airplane has a power greater than the law of gravity. If you don't think the law of gravity is still in effect, then flip the switch at 30,000 feet. You will crash and burn. If we walk by faith according to what God says is true in the power of the Holy Spirit, we will 'not carry out the desire of the flesh' (Gal. 5:16). If we believe a lie and walk according to the flesh, we will crash and burn.

Saved and Sanctified by Faith

Paul says in Romans 6:6, 'our old self was crucified' (past tense). We try and try to put the old man to death and we can't do it. Why not? Because he is already dead. Because many Christians are not living the abundant life, they incorrectly reason, 'What experience has to occur for this to be true?' The only thing that had to happen for that to be true happened nearly two thousand years ago, and the only way you can enter into that experience is by faith.

A dear pastor who heard of my ministry asked for an appointment with me. He said, 'I have struggled for 22 years in ministry and I finally think I know what the answer is. In my devotions I read the following passage in Colossians 3:3 (NIV), "For you died, and your life is now hidden with Christ in God." That's it, isn't it?'

I assured him it was, then he asked, 'How do I do that?'

I suggested he read the passage just a little bit slower. This dear man for 22 years had been desperately trying to become somebody he already was, and so do many other believers. We cannot do for ourselves what Christ has already accomplished for us.

Too many Christians are trying to show that the Bible is true by the way they live. It will never work for them. We accept what God says is true and live accordingly by faith, and this abundant life works out in our experience. If we try to make it true by the way we live, we will never get there. Paul points out the futility of that thinking in Galatians 3:2 (NIV): 'I would like to learn just one thing from you: Did you receive the Spirit by observing the law, or by believing what you heard? Are you so foolish? After beginning with the Spirit, are you now trying to attain your goal by human effort?'

We are saved by faith and we walk or live by faith. We have been sanctified by faith and we are being sanctified by faith and by faith alone. We are neither saved nor sanctified by how we behave, but by how we believe.

God's work of atonement changes sinners to saints. The radical change, regeneration, is effected at the moment of salvation. The ongoing change in the believer's daily walk continues throughout life. The progressive work of sanctification, however, is only fully effective when the radical, inner transformation by regeneration is realized and appropriated by faith.

As a new Christian you were like a lump of coal: unattractive, somewhat fragile and messy to work with. After time and pressure, however, coal becomes hardened and beautiful. Although the original lump of coal is not a diamond, it consists of the right substance to become a diamond. Right now, you are a diamond in the rough, but given enough time and pressure, you will be like a diamond, revealing the glory of God.

Anthony Hoekema comments, 'You are new creatures now! Not totally new, to be sure, but genuinely new. And we who are believers should see ourselves in this way: no longer as depraved and helpless slaves of sin, but as those who have been created anew in Christ Jesus.'[2]

Balancing the Indicative and the Imperative

The greatest tension in the New Testament is between the indicative (what God has already done and what is already true about us), and the imperative (what remains to be done as we respond to God by faith and obedience in the power of the Holy Spirit). You have to know and believe positional truth to successfully progress in your sanctification or you are going to try doing for yourself what God has already done for you.

The balance between the indicative and the imperative is about equal in Scripture, but I have not observed that in our churches. Most preaching I have heard focuses on the imperatives. People could go to a good evangelical church for years and never hear the message that they are children of God who are alive and free in Christ. We need to worship God for all He has done, and rest in the finished work of Christ. We need to hear again and again the wonderful identity and position we already have in Christ; then we will be better prepared to receive the instructions and assume our responsibility for living the Christian life.

In Summary

I was asked if I taught the eradication of the sinful nature at the new birth. One cannot give a simple yes or no answer to that question. If you are asking, 'Do you believe that the old man is dead?' the answer is yes. I am no longer in Adam, I am spiritually alive in Christ. If you are asking, 'Do you believe that the Christian can still sin and walk or live according to the flesh?' the answer is yes. New believers are dominated by the flesh and deceived by the devil. It takes time to renew the mind and overcome the patterns of the flesh.

If you asked me, 'Do you believe that you have a new nature?' I would answer yes, because God has given me a new heart and I am now spiritually alive. My 'new self' is oriented toward God. I have become a partaker of the divine nature (see 2 Pet. 1:4), and 'I joyfully concur with the law of God in the inner man' (Rom. 7:22). If you asked me, 'Are you a sinner or a saint?' I would joyfully respond, 'I believe I am a saint by the grace of God and I intend to live my life as His child in the way He intended me to live by faith in the power of the Holy Spirit.'

Don't forget that our entire being was morally corrupt before we came to Christ. Our minds were programmed to live independently of God and the desires of our flesh are in opposition to the Spirit of God. The flesh, our old nature, has to be crucified by the believer (see Gal. 5:24). I do not believe in instant maturity. It will take us the rest of our lives to renew our minds, and conform to the image of God. The seed that was sown in us by God is only a beginning. Being a child of God and being free in Christ is positional truth and the birthright of every believer. Because of a lack of repentance and ignorance of the truth, many believers are not living like liberated children of God. How tragic! Perhaps the following illustration I used in *God's Power at Work in You* will explain part of the reason why.

> Slavery in the United States was abolished by the 13th Amendment on December 18th, 1865. How many slaves were there on December 19th? In reality, none, but many still lived like slaves. Many did, because they never learned the truth, others knew and even believed that they were free but chose to live as they had been taught.
>
> Several plantation owners were devastated by this proclamation of emancipation. 'We're ruined! Slavery has been abolished. We've lost the battle to keep our slaves.' But their chief spokesman slyly responded, 'Not necessarily, as long as these people think they're still slaves, the proclamation of emancipation will have no practical effect. We don't have a legal right

over them anymore, but many of them don't know it. Keep your slaves from learning the truth, and your control over them will not even be challenged.'

'But, what if the news spreads?'

'Don't panic. We have another barrel in our gun. We may not be able to keep them from hearing the news, but we can still keep them from understanding it. They don't call me the father of lies for nothing. We still have the potential to deceive the whole world. Just tell them that they misunderstood the 13th Amendment. Tell them that they are going to be free, not that they are free already. The truth they heard is just positional truth, not actual truth. Someday they may receive the benefits, but not now.'

'But, they'll expect me to say that. They won't believe me.'

'Then pick out a few persuasive ones who are convinced that they're still slaves and let them do the talking for you. Remember, most of these free people were born as slaves and have lived like slaves. All we have to do is to deceive them so that they still think like slaves. As long as they continue to do what slaves do, it will not be hard to convince them that they must still be slaves. They will maintain their slave identity because of the things they do. The moment they try to profess that they are no longer slaves, just whisper in their ear, "How can you even think you are no longer a slave when you are still doing things that slaves do?" After all, we have the capacity to accuse the brethren day and night.'

Years later, many have still not heard the wonderful news that they have been freed, so naturally they continue to live the way they have always lived. Some have heard the good news, but evaluated it by what they are presently doing and feeling. They reason, 'I'm still living in bondage, doing the same things I have always done. My experience tells me that I must not be free. I'm feeling the same way I was before the proclamation, so it must not be true. After all, your feelings always tell the truth.' So they continue to live according to how they feel, not wanting to be hypocrites!

One former slave hears the good news, and receives it with great joy. He checks out the validity of the proclamation, and finds out that the highest of all authorities has originated the decree. Not only that, but it personally cost the authority a tremendous price which He willingly paid, so that he could be free. His life is transformed. He correctly reasons that it would be hypocritical to believe his feelings, and not believe the truth. Determined to live by what he knows to be true, his experiences began to change rather dramatically. He realizes that his old master has no authority over him and does not need to be obeyed. He gladly serves the one who set him free.[3]

Notes

1. E. K. Simpson and F. F. Bruce, *Commentary on the Epistles to the Ephesians and the Colossians* (Grand Rapids: Eerdmans, 1957), p. 273.

2. Anthony A. Hoekema, *Created in God's Image* (Grand Rapids: Eerdmans/ Paternoster, 1986), p. 110.

3. Neil T. Anderson and Robert Saucy, *God's Power at Work in You* (London: Monarch Books, 2001), pp. 25-27.

5
Becoming the Spiritual Person God Wants You to Be

Before the turn of the twentieth century, an asylum in the suburbs of Boston housed severely retarded and disturbed individuals. One of the patients was a girl who was simply called Little Annie. She was totally unresponsive to others in the asylum. The staff tried everything possible to help her, yet without success. Finally she was confined to a cell in the basement of the asylum and given up as hopeless.

A Christian woman worked at the asylum, and she believed that every one of God's creatures needed love, concern and care. So she decided to spend her lunch hours in front of Little Annie's cell, reading to her and praying that God would free her from her prison of silence. Day after day the Christian woman came to Little Annie's door and read, but the little girl did not respond. Months went by. The woman tried to talk with Little Annie, but it was like talking to an empty cell. She brought little tokens of food for the girl, but they were never received.

Then one day a brownie was missing from the plate the caring woman retrieved from Little Annie's cell. Encouraged, she continued to read to her and pray for her. Eventually, the little girl began to answer the woman through the bars of her cell. Soon the woman convinced the doctors that Little Annie needed a second chance at treatment. They brought her up from the basement and continued to work with her. Within two years Little Annie was told she could leave the asylum and enjoy a normal life.

She chose not to leave, though. She was so grateful for the

love and attention she was given by the dedicated Christian woman that she decided to stay and love others as she had been loved. So Little Annie stayed on at the institution to work with other patients who were suffering as she had suffered.

Nearly half a century later, the Queen of England held a special ceremony to honor one of the most inspiring women in the United States, Helen Keller. When asked to what she would attribute her success at overcoming the dual handicap of blindness and deafness, Helen Keller replied, 'If it hadn't been for Anne Sullivan, I wouldn't be here today.'

Anne Sullivan, who tenaciously loved and believed in an incorrigible blind and deaf girl named Helen Keller, was Little Annie. Because one selfless Christian woman in the dungeon of an insane asylum believed that a hopeless little girl needed God's love, the world received the marvelous gift of Helen Keller.

What does it take to be that kind of Christian? What is needed to move us beyond our inconsequential selfish, fleshly pursuits to deeds of loving service to God and others? What was the essence of Christian maturity that motivated Anne Sullivan's benefactress to such a significant ministry?

First, it requires a firm understanding of who you are in Christ. You can't become like Jesus unless you are His divine offspring. You have to be grafted into the vine because apart from Christ you can do nothing (see John 15:5).

Second, you must crucify daily the old sin-trained flesh and walk in accordance with who you are in Christ and 'be transformed by the renewing of your mind' (Rom. 12:2).

Third, it requires the grace of God. 'For sin shall not be master over you, for you are not under law, but under grace' (Rom. 6:14). We cannot live righteous lives by human effort based on external standards. Under the covenant of grace, we live by faith according to what God says is true in the power of the Holy Spirit.

To live under grace we need to learn how to walk or live by the Spirit (see Gal. 5:16-18). How do we walk by the Spirit? If I answered that question by offering three steps and a formula, I would be putting you back under the law again. The Holy Spirit is a *He* to whom we relate as our divine guide, not an *it* that can be boxed and quantified. We are talking about walking with God, which is a Father-and-son relationship.

The apostle John said of the Spirit: 'The wind blows where it wishes and you hear the sound of it, but do not know where it comes from and where it is going; so is everyone who is born of the Spirit' (John 3:8). Being filled and led by the Spirit may take you places you never planned; but the will of God will never lead you where the grace of God cannot keep you. I think we need to 'pull in the oars and put up the sail.' Let's explore some of the guidelines in Scripture for walking by the Spirit.

Three Persons and the Spirit

In 1 Corinthians 2:14 – 3:3, Paul distinguishes between three kinds of people in relation to life in the Spirit: natural persons, spiritual persons and fleshly persons. The simple diagrams in this chapter will help you understand the differences pertaining to spiritual life that exist among these three kinds of individuals.

Ephesians 2:1-3 contains a concise description of the natural person Paul identified in 1 Corinthians 2:14 (see Figure 5-A). This person is spiritually dead, separated from God. Living completely independent from God, the natural person sins as a matter of course.

The natural man has a soul, in that he can think, feel and choose. As the arrows on the diagram show, however, his mind, and subsequently his emotions and his will, are directed by his flesh, which acts completely apart from the

THE NATURAL PERSON
Life 'in the Flesh'
1 Corinthians 2:14

FLESH (Rom. 8:8)
Though flesh can mean the body, it is the learned independence which gives sin its opportunity. The natural man, who tries to find purpose and meaning in life independently of God, is going to struggle with inferiority, insecurity, inadequacy, guilt, worry and doubts.

BODY
Tension or migraine headaches, nervous stomach, hives, skin rashes, allergies, asthma, some arthritis, spastic colon, heart palpitations, respiratory ailments, etc.

EMOTIONS
Bitterness, anxiety, depression, etc.

MIND
Obsessive thoughts, fantasy, etc.

WILL
(Gal. 5:16–18)
Walk after the flesh.

SPIRIT
Man's spirit is dead to God (Eph. 2:1–3); thus, the natural man is unable to fulfill the purpose for which he was created. Lacking life from God, sin is inevitable.

immorality	jealousy
impurity	disputes
sensuality	dissensions
idolatry	factions
sorcery	envying
enmities	drunkenness
strife	carousing
outbursts of anger	

Figure 5-A

God who created him. The natural man may think he is free to choose his behavior. Because he lives *in* the flesh, however, he invariably walks *according* to the flesh and his choices reflect the 'deeds of the flesh' listed in Galatians 5:19-21.

Living in a stressful age and having no spiritual base for coping with life or making positive choices, the natural person may fall victim to one or more of the physical ailments listed on the diagram. Medical doctors tell us that more than 50 percent of the population is physically sick for psychosomatic reasons. Possessing peace of mind and the calm assurance of God's presence in our lives positively affects our physical health. 'He who raised Christ Jesus from the dead will also give life to your mortal bodies through His Spirit who indwells you' (Rom. 8:11).

The natural person's actions, reactions, habits, memories and responses are all governed by the flesh. 'Whatever is not from faith is sin' (Rom. 14:23). The natural person cannot help but struggle with feelings of inferiority, insecurity, inadequacy, guilt, worry and doubt.

The spiritual man also has a body, soul and spirit. Yet, as illustrated in Figure 5-B, this individual has been remarkably transformed from the natural person he was before spiritual birth. At conversion, his spirit became united with God's Spirit. The spiritual life that resulted from this union is characterized by forgiveness of sin, acceptance in God's family and a positive sense of worth.

The soul of the spiritual man also reflects a change generated by spiritual birth. He now receives his impetus from the Spirit, not from the flesh. His mind has been renewed and transformed. His emotions are characterized by peace and joy instead of turmoil. He is also free to choose not to walk according to the flesh, but to walk according to the Spirit. As the spiritual man exercises his choice to live in the Spirit, his life exhibits the fruit of the Spirit (see Gal. 5:22,23).

THE SPIRITUAL PERSON
Life 'in the Spirit'
1 Corinthians 2:15

FLESH (Rom. 8:8)
The crucifying of the flesh is the believer's responsibility on a day-by-day basis as he considers himself dead to sin.

BODY
Temple of God (1 Cor. 6:19,20)
Present as a living and holy sacrifice (Rom. 12:1)

MIND
Transformed (Rom. 12:2)
Single-minded (Phil. 4:6–8)
Girded for action (1 Pet. 1:13)

EMOTIONS
Peace (Col. 3:15)
Joy (Phil. 4:4)

WILL
(Gal. 5:16–18)
Walk after the Spirit.

love
joy
peace
patience
kindness
goodness
faithfulness
gentleness
self-control

SPIRIT (Rom. 8:9)
Salvation (John 3:3; 1 John 3:9)
Forgiveness (Acts 2:38; Heb. 8:12)
Assurance (Rom. 8:16)
Security (Eph. 1:13,14)
Acceptance (1 John 3:1)
Worth (Eph. 2:10)

Figure 5-B

The body of the spiritual person has also been transformed. It is now the dwelling place for the Holy Spirit and is being offered as a living sacrifice of worship and service to God. The flesh, conditioned to live independently from God under the old self, is still present in the spiritual man, but he responsibly crucifies the flesh and its desires daily as he considers himself alive in Christ and dead to sin.

'That all looks and sounds great,' you may say. 'But I'm a Christian and I still have some problems. I know I'm spiritually alive, but sometimes my mind dwells on the wrong kinds of thoughts. Sometimes I give in to behavior from the wrong list: the deeds of the flesh instead of the fruit of the Spirit. Sometimes I entertain the desires of the flesh instead of crucifying them.'

The description of the spiritual person is the ideal. It is the model of maturity toward which we are all growing. God has made every provision for us to experience personally the description of the spiritual person in His Word (see 2 Pet. 1:3). However, most of us live somewhere on the slope between this mountaintop of spiritual maturity and the depths of fleshly behavior described in Figure 5-C. As you walk according to the Spirit, be assured that your growth, maturity and sanctification toward the ideal model are in process.

Notice that the spirit of the fleshly person is identical to that of the spiritual person. The fleshly person is a Christian, spiritually alive in Christ and declared righteous by God; but that is where the similarity ends. Instead of being directed by the Spirit, this believing man chooses to follow the impulses of his flesh. As a result, his mind is occupied by carnal thoughts and his emotions are plagued by negative feelings. Though he is free to choose to walk after the Spirit and produce the fruit of the Spirit, he continues to involve himself in sinful activity by willfully walking after the flesh.

THE FLESHLY PERSON
Life 'According to the Flesh'
1 Corinthians 3:3

FLESH (Rom. 8:8)
The ingrained habit patterns still appeal to the mind to live independently of God.

BODY
Tension or migraine headaches, nervous stomach, hives, skin rashes, allergies, asthma, some arthritis, spastic colon, heart palpitations, respiratory ailments, etc.

MIND
Double-minded

BODY

FLESH

MIND

EMOTIONS

SPIRIT

WILL

EMOTIONS
Unstable

SPIRIT
(Rom. 8:9)
Alive but quenched
(1 Thess. 5:19)

WILL (Gal. 5:16–18)
Walk after the flesh (often).

Walk after the Spirit (seldom).

immorality	outbursts of	love
impurity	anger	joy
sensuality	disputes	peace
idolatry	dissensions	patience
sorcery	factions	kindness
enmities	envying	goodness
strife	drunkenness	faithfulness
jealousy	carousing	gentleness
		self-control

Figure 5-C

The fleshly man's physical body is a temple of God, but it is being defiled. He often exhibits the same troubling physical symptoms experienced by the natural person because he is not operating in the manner God created him to operate. He is not presenting his body to God as a living sacrifice, but indulging his physical appetites at the whim of his sin-trained flesh. Because he is yielding to the flesh instead of crucifying it, the fleshly man is also subject to feelings of inferiority, insecurity, inadequacy, guilt, worry and doubt.

Several years ago, I conducted a little personal research to discover how many Christians are still the victims of their flesh. I presented the same following question to 50 consecutive Christians who talked to me about problems in their lives: 'How many of the following characteristics describe your life: inferiority, insecurity, inadequacy, guilt, worry and doubt?' Every one of the 50 answered, 'All six.' Here were 50 born-again children of God who were so bogged down by the flesh that they struggled with the same problems of self-doubt that inundate unbelievers who live only in the flesh.

If I asked you the same question, how would you answer? From my counseling experiences, I imagine that many of you would admit that some or all of these six traits describe you. It is evident to me that a staggering number of believers don't know how to live their lives by faith in the power of the Holy Spirit.

Are you struggling with feelings of inferiority? To whom or to what are you inferior? You are a child of God seated with Christ in the heavenlies (see Eph. 2:6). Do you feel insecure? Your God will never leave you nor forsake you (see Heb. 13:5). Inadequate? You can do all things through Christ who strengthens you (see Phil. 4:13). Guilty? There is no condemnation for those who are in Christ (see Rom. 8:1). Worried? You can have the peace of God and learn to cast your anxiety upon Christ (see John 14:27; Phil. 4:6; 1 Pet.

5:7). Doubt? God provides wisdom for the asking (see Jas. 1:5).

Why is there often such great disparity between these two kinds of Christians: spiritual and fleshly? Why are so many believers living so far below their potential in Christ? Why are so few of us enjoying the abundant, productive life we have already inherited? We should be able to say every year, 'I am more loving, peaceful, joyful, patient, kind and gentle than I was last year.' If we can't honestly say that, then we are not growing.

'His divine power has granted to us everything pertaining to life and godliness, through the true knowledge of Him who called us by His own glory and excellence' (2 Pet. 1:3). Yet, countless numbers of Christians have been born-again for years — even decades — and have yet to experience significant measures of victory over sin. Ignorance, lack of repentance and faith in God, and unresolved conflicts keep people from growing.

The world and the flesh are not the only enemies of our sanctification. We have a living, personal enemy — Satan — who attempts to accuse, tempt and to deceive God's children. Paul wrote about Satan: 'We are not ignorant of his schemes' (2 Cor. 2:11). Perhaps Paul and the Corinthians weren't ignorant, but a lot of present-day Christians surely are. We live as though the kingdom of darkness doesn't exist. Our naivety in this area is exacting a crippling toll that keeps many Christians from experiencing their freedom in Christ.

Parameters of the Spirit-Filled Walk

When we first became Christians, we were similar to one-third-horsepower lawn mower engines. We could accomplish something but not very much because we were not very mature. Our goal as Christians is to become DC9 Caterpillar engines — real powerhouses for the Lord. Without gas, though, neither a lawn mower nor a bulldozer can accomplish anything. Neither can we accomplish anything apart from Christ (see John 15:5). No matter how mature you are, you can never be productive unless you are walking by faith in the power of the Holy Spirit.

When it comes to walking according to the flesh and walking in the Spirit, our wills are like toggle switches. The wills of new Christians seem to be spring-loaded toward fleshly behavior. New believers are going to live according to what they know, and they don't know very much about the Spirit-filled life. The wills of mature Christians are spring-loaded toward the Spirit. They make occasional poor choices, but they are daily learning to crucify the flesh and walk by faith in the power of the Holy Spirit.

Walking by the Spirit is relationship, not regimentation. To illustrate, think about your marriage. You may have started your marriage by relying on rules for effective communication, meeting each other's sexual needs and so on. If after several years you can't even talk to each other or make love without following an outline or list of steps, however, your marriage relationship is still in infancy. In a mature marriage, communication flows naturally from two who love each other.

Another example is prayer. Perhaps you learned to pray using the simple acrostic ACTS: adoration, confession, thanksgiving, supplication. If, however, you have been a Christian for a few years and your prayer life is no deeper than an acrostic, you have never learned to pray by the Spirit (see Eph. 6:18). Prayer is a two-way communication with God that requires listening as well as petitioning.

Paul defines what it means to walk by the Spirit in Galatians 5:16-18: 'Walk by the Spirit, and you will not carry out the desire of the flesh. For the flesh sets its desire against the Spirit, and the Spirit against the flesh; for these are in opposition to one another, so that you may not do the things that you please. But if you are led by the Spirit, you are not under the Law.' Actually, this passage mainly tells us what walking by the Spirit is not, but that is helpful because it gives us two parameters within which we can freely live.

What the Spirit-Filled Walk Is Not

First, Paul said that walking according to the Spirit is not license. License is a disregard for rules and regulations constituting an abuse of privilege. Some Christians wrongly assert that walking by the Spirit and living under grace means, 'I can do whatever I want to do.' Walking by the Spirit means, 'You may not do the things that you please.' Living by the Spirit doesn't mean you are free to do whatever you want to do. That would be license. It means you are free to live a responsible, moral life — something you were incapable of doing when you were a bond servant of sin.

I was invited to speak to a religion class at a Catholic high school on the topic of Protestant Christianity. At the end of my talk, an athletic-looking, streetwise student raised his hand and asked, 'Do you have a lot of don'ts in your religion?'

I answered, 'I don't think I have any that God doesn't, but I think what you are really asking me is, "Do I have any freedom?"' He nodded.

'Sure, I'm free to do whatever I want to do,' I answered.

His face mirrored his disbelief. 'Get serious,' he said.

I responded, 'I am free to make the decision to rob a bank. But I'm mature enough to realize that I would be in bondage to that act for the rest of my life. I would always have to look over my shoulder wondering if I would someday be caught. I would have to cover up my crime, possibly go into hiding and eventually pay for what I did. I'm also free to tell a lie. But if I told a lie, I would have to remember who I told the lie to and what I told them.'

What some people think is freedom is nothing more than license that leads to bondage. Freedom doesn't just lie in the exercise of choice; it ultimately lies in the consequences of those choices. The Spirit of truth will always lead us to freedom, but the desires of the flesh will lead us to sin and bondage. The commandments of God are not restrictive; they are protective. Our real freedom is in the ability to choose to live responsibly within the context of the protective guidelines God has established for our lives.

Second, walking by the Spirit is also not legalism. 'If you are led by the Spirit, you are not under the Law' (Gal. 5:18). If you want to relate to God purely on the basis of moral law, then you need to listen to Paul's words in Galatians 3:10: 'For as many as are of the works of the Law are under a curse.' You will be a driven person or a guilt-ridden dropout. 'Is the Law then contrary to the promises of God? May it never be! For if a law had been given which was able to impart life, then righteousness would indeed have been based on law' (Gal. 3:21). The law is powerless to give life.

Telling people that what they are doing is wrong does not give them the power to stop doing it. Christians have been notorious at trying to legislate spirituality with don'ts: Christians don't drink, don't smoke, don't dance, don't attend movies, don't play cards, don't wear makeup and so on. Others may claim not to be legalistic, but all they have done is gone from negative legalism (don't do this and don't do that) to positive legalism (do this and do that). We are 'servants of a new covenant, not of the letter, but of the Spirit; for the letter kills, but the Spirit gives life' (2 Cor. 3:6).

The law also has the capacity to stimulate the desire to do what it intended to prohibit (see Rom. 7:5,8)! Let me illustrate. What happens when you tell a child, 'You can go here, but you can't go there.' The moment you say that, where does the child want to go? There! He probably didn't even want to go there until you told him he couldn't go. A Christian school published a list of movies the students could not see. Guess which ones they all wanted to see? Why is the forbidden fruit the most desirable? Apparently it was in the Garden of Eden as well.

Christianity is a relationship, not a ritual or a religious code of ethics. We could not keep the commandments by human effort living under the law. The law was a 'tutor to lead us to Christ, that we may be justified by faith' (Gal. 3:24). In Christ we can actually live by faith according to the righteous laws of God in the power of the Holy Spirit.

Suppose you were walking along a very narrow mountain road. On the right side is a cliff too steep to climb down and too far to jump. On the other side of the road is a roaring forest fire. Ahead of you is a church and a roaring lion is behind you. Which way do you run? Off to your right is an option. Just sail off that cliff. Can you imagine the initial thrill? There are serious consequences to that decision, though, like the sudden stop at the end. That is the nature of temptation. If it didn't initially look good, you wouldn't be tempted. Giving in to temptation always has serious consequences. When people advocate free sex, they are advocating license that has deadly consequences to meaningful relationships and even life.

On the left is another option, but you will be burned by legalism as well. The accuser will give you no peace when you try to live under the law. The only path of freedom is straight ahead, but no church building or group of people will provide an adequate sanctuary. A devil is roaring around like a hungry lion seeking someone to devour (see 1 Pet. 5:8), and your only sanctuary is in Christ. No physical place can provide a spiritual sanctuary for you on planet Earth.

What the Spirit-Filled Walk Is

If the Spirit-filled walk is neither license nor legalism, then what is it? It is liberty. 'Now the Lord is the Spirit; and where the Spirit of the Lord is, there is liberty' (2 Cor. 3:17).

Our freedom in Christ is one of the most precious commodities we have received from our spiritual union with God. Because the Spirit of the Lord is in you, you are free to become the person God created you to be. You are no longer compelled to walk according to the flesh as you were before conversion. You are not even compelled to walk according to the Spirit, but you are inwardly bent in that direction. You have the choice to walk according to the Spirit or to walk according to the flesh.

Walking according to the Spirit implies two things. First, it is not *sitting* in the Spirit. Walking by the Spirit is not sitting around in some holy piety expecting God to do it all. Second, it is not *running* in the Spirit. The Spirit-filled life is not an endless round of exhausting activities in which we are trying to do it all by ourselves. Thinking we will become more spiritual if we try harder is a typical error of many believers. If Satan can't tempt us to be immoral, he will simply try to make us busy.

How much fruit can we bear if we try to do it all by ourselves? None! Apart from Christ we can do nothing (see John 15:5). How much gets accomplished in the kingdom of God if we expect God to do it all by Himself? Not much! God has committed Himself in this age to work through the Church (see Eph. 3:10). We have the privilege to water and plant, and God causes the increase (see 1 Cor. 3:6-9). If we don't water and plant, nothing grows.

A pastor was working in his garden one day when one of his deacons paid a visit. 'My, the Lord sure gave you a beautiful garden,' the deacon said. To which the pastor responded, 'You should have seen it when God had it by Himself.'

This truth is illustrated by Jesus in Matthew 11:28-30: 'Come to Me, all who are weary and heavy-laden, and I will give you rest. Take My yoke upon you, and learn from Me, for I am gentle and humble in heart; and you shall find rest for your souls. For My yoke is easy, and My load is light.'

In His youth, Jesus was a carpenter. In those days, carpenters didn't frame houses; they fashioned wooden doors and yokes. Jesus metaphorically used those products to describe the spiritual life. For instance, Jesus is the door to spiritual life (see John 10:9), and a yoke is a wooden beam that fits over the shoulders of two oxen. How well does the yoke work if only one person is in it? You would be better off not having it on you. It only works if two are yoked together and pulling in the same direction.

A young ox is trained by putting it in a yoke with an old seasoned ox who 'learned obedience from the things which He suffered' (Heb. 5:8). The typical nature of the young ox is to think the pace is too slow and to run ahead, but all it would get is a sore neck. 'Though youths grow weary and tired, and vigorous young men stumble badly, yet those who wait for the Lord will gain new strength; they will mount up with wings like eagles, they will run and not get tired, they will walk and not become weary' (Isa. 40:30,31). Some young oxen will be tempted to drop out, but life goes on and the debts pile up. Others will be tempted to stray off to the left or the right. Then one day the young ox thinks, *This old ox knows what he is talking about and how to walk; I think I will learn from Him.*

I once owned a rather dumb dog named Buster. I bought a choke chain and sent Buster off to dog obedience school with my son. It didn't work. So one day I thought I would take Buster for a walk. I said 'walk' not 'run.' So I put the choke chain on Buster and off we went. I was the master and I knew where I wanted to go on this 'walk.' Buster just about choked himself to death trying to run ahead, but I was determined to be the master and walk at my pace. Then he would stop and sniff a flower or some gross thing, but I kept on walking.

'Did that dumb dog ever learn to walk by its master?' you ask. No, it never did, and I have met a lot of Christians who haven't either. Some try to run ahead of God and burn out. Others fall into temptation and stray off to the left or the right. Some just drop out even though their Master is saying, 'Come to Me, all who are weary and heavy-laden, and I will give you rest' (Matt. 11:28). We can find rest for our souls if we learn to live by faith in the power of the Holy Spirit.

Being Led by the Spirit

We are also being 'led by the Spirit' (Rom. 8:14). The Lord used another metaphor to describe our relationship with Him. He is the Shepherd and we are the sheep of His pasture. Sheep need to be shepherded. I know because as a farm boy in Minnesota, I had the privilege to be a shepherd of sheep. In the spring after the snow melted, we would herd the sheep along the roadside for them to eat the fresh green grass. We had to keep them moving or they would eat until they bloated and died. We chased them from the back, just as an Australian sheep dog barks at the heels of the sheep.

While studying in Israel, I watched a shepherd tend his flock on a hillside outside Bethlehem. The shepherd sat on a rock while the sheep grazed. Then he stood up, said a few words to the sheep and walked away. The sheep looked up and followed him. Unlike my experience of chasing the sheep from the back, the shepherds of Israel lead from the front even to this day. Suddenly, the words of Jesus in John 10:27 took on new meaning to me: 'My sheep hear My voice, and I know them, and they follow Me.' Paul said, 'For all who are being led by the Spirit of God, these are sons of God' (Rom. 8:14).

The Proof Is in the Fruit

How can you know if you are walking according to the flesh or according to the Spirit? Take a look at your life. 'Now the deeds of the flesh are evident, which are: immorality, impurity, sensuality, idolatry, sorcery, enmities, strife, jealousy, outbursts of anger, disputes, dissensions, factions, envying,... and things like these' (Gal. 5:19-21). These deeds are spiritually dead acts which do not reflect the life of Christ. So if people have outbursts of anger, are they living according to the Spirit? Can they blame someone else for their outburst of anger? No, that is a deed of their flesh. Jesus said, 'That which proceeds out of the man, that is what defiles the man' (Mark. 7:20).

We must learn to have enough self-awareness to know when we are living according to the flesh and to assume responsibility for our own attitudes and actions. We need to walk in the light and learn to confess our sins, which means to consciously agree with God. When a deed of the flesh becomes evident, mentally acknowledge that to God and ask Him to fill you with His Holy Spirit. The more you practise that simple little discipline, the more you will live according to the Spirit.

'The fruit of the Spirit is love, joy, peace, patience, kindness, goodness, faithfulness, gentleness, self-control' (Gal. 5:22,23). Notice it said fruit, not fruits of the Spirit. Fruit comes from something that is living. It is the result of abiding in Christ and the ultimate expression is love, which is the character of God. 'We have come to know and have believed the love which God has for us. God is love, and the one who abides in love abides in God, and God abides in him' (1 John 4:16).

6
The Power of
Believing the Truth

Nearly 60 years ago outside Nashville, Tennessee, a little girl was born with major health problems that left her crippled. She had a large, wonderful Christian family. While her brothers and sisters enjoyed running and playing outside, she was confined to braces.

Her parents took her into Nashville periodically for physiotherapy, but the little girl's hope was dim. 'Will I ever be able to run and play like the other children?' she asked her parents.

'Honey, you only have to believe,' they responded. 'You have to trust in God because with God all things are possible.'

She took her parents' counsel to heart and began to believe that God could make her walk without braces. Unbeknown to her parents and doctors, she practised walking without her braces with the aid of her brothers and sisters. On her 12th birthday, she surprised her elders by removing her braces and walking around the doctor's office unassisted. Her doctors couldn't believe her progress. She never wore the braces again.

Her next goal was to play basketball. She continued to exercise her faith and courage — as well as her underdeveloped legs — and tried out for the school basketball team. The coach selected her older sister for the team, but the courageous girl was told she wasn't good enough to play. Her father, a wise, loving man, told the coach, 'My daughters come in pairs. If you want one, you have to take the other also.' Reluctantly, the coach added the girl to the team. She was given an outdated uniform and allowed to work out with the other players.

One day she approached the coach. 'If you will give me an extra 10 minutes of coaching each day, I'll give you a world-class athlete.' He laughed, then realized she was serious. He halfheartedly agreed to give her some additional time playing two on two with her best friend and a couple of boys. Before long her determination started to pay off. She showed tremendous athletic skill and courage, and soon she was one of the team's best players.

Her team went to the state basketball championships. One of the referees at the tournament noticed her exceptional ability and asked if she had ever run track. Of course she hadn't! The referee, who also happened to be the coach of the internationally famous Tiger Belles track club, encouraged her to try running. So after the basketball season she tried out for track. She began running and winning races. She also earned a berth in the state track championships.

At the age of 16, she was one of the best young runners in the country. She went to the Olympics in Australia and won a bronze medal for anchoring the 400-meter relay team. Not satisfied with her accomplishment, she worked diligently for four more years and returned to the Olympics in Rome in 1960. There, Wilma Rudolph won the 100-meter dash, the 200-meter dash and anchored the winning 400-meter relay team — all in world-record times. She capped the year by receiving the prestigious Sullivan Award as the most outstanding amateur athlete in the United States. Wilma Rudolph's faith and hard work had paid off.

When you hear inspiring stories of faith such as Wilma Rudolph's, do you sometimes wonder, *Is faith really the critical element that allows some people to rise above seemingly incredible odds and achieve things others cannot? Can faith also do great things for me?*

The Essence of Faith

Faith in God is indispensable to the Christian life. The author of Hebrews capsulized it by writing: 'Without faith it is impossible to please Him, for he who comes to God must believe that He is, and that He is a rewarder of those who seek Him' (11:6). Believing who God is, what He says and what He does is the key to the kingdom of God.

Consider how important the concept of faith is. You are saved by faith (see Eph. 2:8,9), and you 'walk by faith, not by sight' (2 Cor. 5:7). In other words, faith is the basis for our salvation and the means by which we live. If we are going to continue living free in Christ, we need to keep in mind three simple faith concepts.

1. Faith Depends on Its Object

The truth is, everyone lives by faith. The only difference between Christian faith and non-Christian faith is the object of our faith. The critical issue is *what* you believe or *who* you believe in. Telling people to live by faith is invalid if they have no understanding of the object of their faith. You can't have faith in faith. Faith has no validity without an object.

The truth is, we live every moment of every day by faith. However, some of our faith objects are valid but others aren't. For instance, suppose you are driving a car and see a green light. You would probably drive through the intersection without giving your action a second thought, and you would do it by faith. First, you believed the light was red in the other direction even though you couldn't see it. Second, you believed the drivers coming from the other direction saw the red light and would stop. That is a lot of faith, but if you didn't believe that, you wouldn't go through too many intersections or you would proceed very cautiously. We trust people or things that have proven to be reliable over a long time period.

What happens when the object of your faith proves unreliable? You give up on it — maybe not immediately, but how many failures would you tolerate before saying never again? Once faith is lost, it is very difficult to regain. Your ability to believe isn't the problem; it is the object of your faith that has proven to be untrustworthy.

If you have had a few auto accidents as a result of careless drivers, your ability to trust other drivers may be seriously shaken, and rightfully so. That is why our relationships are so fragile. One act of unfaithfulness can all but destroy a marriage. You can forgive your spouse and commit yourself to make the marriage work, but it will take months and even years to gain back the trust that was lost. You would be foolish to trust someone or something that has proven to be unreliable.

The most accepted faith object by the world's population is the fixed order of the universe, primarily the solar system. You set your watch, plan your calendar and schedule your day believing that the earth will continue to revolve on its axis and rotate around the sun at its current speed. If the earth's orbit shifted just a few degrees and the sun appeared two hours late, the whole world would be thrown into chaos. So far the laws governing the physical universe have been among the most trustworthy faith objects we have.

The ultimate faith object, of course, is not the sun, but the Son, because 'Jesus Christ is the same yesterday and today, yes and forever' (Heb. 13:8). The fact that God is immutable is what makes Him eminently trustworthy (see Num. 23:19; Mal. 3:6). God cannot change, nor can His Word. 'The grass withers, the flower fades, but the word of our God stands forever' (Isa. 40:8). This eternal consistency is why God is faithful and why we can put our trust in Him.

2. How Much Faith You Have Is Dependent Upon How Well You Know the Object of Your Faith

When people struggle with their faith in God, it is not because their faith object has failed or is insufficient. It is because they don't have a true knowledge of God and His ways. They expect Him to respond in a certain way or answer prayer a certain way — their way,. not His — and when He doesn't comply they say, 'Forget you, God.' The problem is not with God. He is the perfect faith object. Faith in God fails only when people have a faulty understanding of Him.

If you want your faith in God to increase, you must increase your knowledge of God. If you have little knowledge about God and His Word, you will have little faith. If you have great knowledge of God and His Word, you can potentially have great faith. Faith cannot be pumped up by coaxing yourself, *If only I can believe! If only I can believe!* You can believe because belief is a choice we all have to make.

Any attempt to push yourself beyond what you know to be true about God and His ways is to move from faith to presumption. You choose to believe God according to what you know to be true from His Word. The only way to increase your faith is to increase your knowledge of God, who is the believer's only legitimate faith object. That is why Paul wrote that 'faith comes from hearing, and hearing by the word of Christ' (Rom. 10:17).

The only limit to your faith is your knowledge and understanding of God, which grows every time you read your Bible, memorize a Scripture verse, participate in a Bible study or meditate on His Word. Can you see the practical, tangible potential for your faith to grow as you endeavor to know God through His Word? It is bound only by the infinite nature of God! I doubt whether there is a Christian alive who has lived up to his or her faith potential based on what he or she already knows to be true.

It is important to know that God is under no obligation to humankind. We can't maneuver or manipulate God through prayer. He is under obligation to Himself and to remain faithful to His covenant promises and His Word. We have a covenant relationship with God that we can count on being true. If God declares something to be true, you simply believe Him and live according to what is true. If God didn't say it, no amount of faith in the world will make it so. Believing doesn't make God's Word true. His Word is true; therefore we believe it.

Let me illustrate how our faith grows. When my son, Karl, was a toddler, I would stand him up on the table and encourage him to jump from the table into my arms. He would waver in unbelief for a moment and then fall into my arms. Then I would stand back a little bit farther, which made the step of faith a little bit bigger. Then one day I took him outside and put him on the limb of a tree and encouraged him to jump. This was a greater leap of faith, but he did it. As he continues to climb the tree of life, however, can I always be the ultimate object of his faith? There was a time when Karl thought I could answer any question and defeat any foe.

We have an obligation as parents to do more than lead our children to a saving knowledge of our Lord Jesus Christ. We need to help them understand their spiritual identity and heritage. The ultimate object of their faith changes when they become children of God. I can't go everywhere my children go, but God can and He does.

3. Faith Is an Action Word

When I was encouraging Karl to take a step of faith, did he believe I would catch him? Yes. How did I know he believed? Because he jumped. Suppose he wouldn't jump. Suppose I asked Karl, 'Do you believe I will catch you, Karl?' and he answered, 'Yes,' but never jumped.

Does Karl really believe I will catch him if he doesn't jump? According to James, that is just wishful thinking. He says, 'Faith, if it has no works, is dead, being by itself. But someone may well say, "You have faith, and I have works; show me your faith without the works, and I will show you my faith by my works"' (Jas. 2:17,18). In other words, really believing will affect one's walk and one's talk. If we believe God and His Word, we will live accordingly. Everything we do is essentially a product of what we have chosen to believe.

Distortions of Faith

Faith without action is one distortion, but the New Age and Positive Confession movements offer two other distortions of what it means to biblically believe. The New Age belief says, 'If you believe hard enough, it will become true.' Christianity says, 'It is true; therefore we believe it.' Believing something doesn't make it true and not believing something doesn't make it false. Not believing in hell doesn't lower the temperature down there one degree.

The Positive Confession movement has another interpretation of faith that is partially true. Consider the words of Jesus in Matthew 17:20: 'Because of the littleness of your faith; for truly I say to you, if you have faith as a mustard seed, you shall say to this mountain, "move from here to there," and it shall move; and nothing shall be impossible to you.'

The Positive Confession movement correctly points out that the mountain doesn't move until you tell it to. In other words, even the smallest faith doesn't work until it is acted upon, which is the emphasis of the passage in Matthew 17. But the Positive Confession teaching becomes distorted when one thinks the mountain has to move simply because one says it. Taking the Positive Confession idea too far borders on New Age thinking, which says we can create reality with our minds. To do that, we would have to be gods, and that is exactly what the New Agers are teaching.

There is only one Creator and only one who can speak anything into existence. 'With God all things are possible' (Matt. 19:26) and we can do all things through Christ who strengthens us, but we have never been given the privilege to determine for ourselves what we want to believe. The New Agers want us to believe we are God, and the 'name and claim it' proponents want us to act as though we are God. God wants His children to believe Him and live accordingly.

Those distortions often arise when the church is not living up to its potential. Consequently, many people think the church is an infirmary where sick people go. We limp along in unbelief, hoping the rapture will come soon and take us out of this miserable defeat. The church is not an infirmary; it is a military outpost under orders to storm the gates of hell. Every believer is on active duty, called to take part in fulfilling the Great Commission (see Matt. 28:19,20).

Thankfully, the church has an infirmary that ministers to the weak and the wounded, but the infirmary exists only for the purpose of the military outpost. Our real calling is to be change agents in the world, taking a stand, living by faith and fulfilling our purpose for being here.

I think it was J. C. Penney who said, 'Whether you think you can or whether you think you cannot, either way you are right.' The world understands the problem of unbelief. It stresses the power of positive thinking, which is illustrated in the following poem:

If You Believe You Can, You Can

> If you think you are beaten — you are.
> If you think you dare not — you don't.
> If you want to win but think you can't,
> It is almost a cinch you won't.
> If you think you'll lose — you've lost.
> For out of the world we find
> That success begins with a fellow's will;
> It's all in the state of mind.
> Life's battles don't always go
> To the stronger or the faster man;
> But sooner or later the man that wins
> Is the one who thinks he can.[1]

Consider what the world has accomplished just by believing in itself. How much more could we accomplish if we really believed in God? The Christian community has been somewhat reluctant to buy into the power of positive thinking, and for good reason. We are not called to just think positive thoughts; we are called to think the truth. Without God as the object of our faith, thinking is merely a function of the mind that cannot exceed its input and attributes. Attempting to push the mind beyond its limitations will result only in moving from the world of reality to fantasy.

The Christian, however, has far greater potential for success in life through the power of believing the truth. Belief incorporates the mind, but is not limited by it. Faith actually transcends the limitations of the mind and incorporates the real but unseen world. The believer's faith is as valid as its object, which is the living (Christ) and written (Bible) Word of God. If you have the infinite God of the universe as the object of your Christian faith, you can go wherever God leads you.

Someone has said that success comes in 'cans' and failure in 'cannots.' Believing you can live a victorious Christian life takes no more effort than believing you cannot. So why not believe that you can walk by faith in the power of the Holy Spirit, that you can resist the temptations of the world, the flesh and the devil, and that you can grow as a Christian. It is your choice. The following 'Twenty Cans of Success,' taken from God's Word, will expand your knowledge of our faith object: the almighty God. Building your faith by internalizing these truths will lift you from the miry clay of the cannots to sit with Christ in the heavenlies.

Twenty Cans of Success

1. *Why should I say I can't when the Bible says I can do all things through Christ who gives me strength (Philippians 4:13)?*

2. *Why should I worry about my needs when I know that God will take care of all my needs according to His riches in glory in Christ Jesus (Philippians 4:19)?*

3. *Why should I fear when the Bible says God has not given me a spirit of fear, but of power, love and a sound mind (2 Timothy 1:7)?*

4. *Why should I lack faith to live for Christ when God has given me a measure of faith (Romans 12:3)?*

5. *Why should I be weak when the Bible says that the Lord is the strength of my life and that I will display strength and take action because I know God (Psalm 27:1; Daniel 11:32)?*

6. *Why should I allow Satan control over my life when He that is in me is greater than he that is in the world (1 John 4:4)?*

7. *Why should I accept defeat when the Bible says that God always leads me in victory (2 Corinthians 2:14)?*

8. *Why should I lack wisdom when I know that Christ became wisdom to me from God and God gives wisdom to me gen-*

erously when I ask Him for it (1 Corinthians 1:30; James 1:5)?

9. *Why should I be depressed when I have hope and can recall to mind God's loving-kindness, compassion and faithfulness (Lamentations 3:21-23)?*

10. *Why should I worry and be upset when I can cast all my anxieties on Christ who cares for me (1 Peter 5:7)?*

11. *Why should I ever be in bondage knowing that there is freedom where the Spirit of the Lord is (2 Corinthians 3:17)?*

12. *Why should I feel condemned when the Bible says there is no condemnation for those who are in Christ Jesus (Romans 8:1)?*

13. *Why should I feel alone when Jesus said He is with me always and He will never leave me nor forsake me (Matthew 28:20; Hebrews 13:5)?*

14. *Why should I feel as if I'm cursed or have bad luck when the Bible says that Christ rescued me from the curse of the law that I might receive His Spirit by faith (Galatians 3:13,14)?*

15. *Why should I be unhappy when I, like Paul, can learn to be content whatever the circumstances (Philippians 4:11)?*

16. *Why should I feel worthless when Christ became sin for me so that I might become the righteousness of God (2 Corinthians 5:21)?*

17. *Why should I feel helpless in the presence of others when I know that if God is for me, who can be against me (Romans 8:31)?*

18. *Why should I be confused when God is the author of peace and He gives me knowledge through His spirit who lives in me (1 Corinthians 2:12; 14:33)?*

19. *Why should I feel like a failure when I am more than a conqueror through Christ who loved me (Romans 8:37)?*

20. *Why should I let the pressures of life bother me when I can take courage knowing that Jesus has overcome the world and its problems (John 16:33)?*

What Happens When I Stumble in My Walk of Faith?

Have you ever thought God is ready to give up on you because, instead of walking confidently in faith, you sometimes stumble and fall? Do you ever fear that there is a limit to God's tolerance for your failure and that you are walking dangerously near that outer barrier or have already crossed it? Many Christians are defeated by that kind of thinking. They believe God is upset with them, that He is ready to dump them or that He has already given up on them because their daily performance is less than perfect.

It is true that the walk of faith can sometimes be interrupted by moments of personal unbelief, rebellion or even satanic deception. During those moments, we think God has surely lost His patience with us and is ready to give up on us. We will probably give up if we think God has. We stop walking by faith in God, slump dejectedly by the side of the road and wonder, *What's the use?* We feel defeated, our purpose for being here is suspended and Satan is elated.

God Loves You Just the Way You Are

The primary truth you need to know about God for your faith to remain strong is that His love and acceptance are unconditional. When your walk of faith is strong, God loves you. When your walk of faith is weak, God loves you. When you are strong one moment and weak the next, God still loves you. God's love for you is the great eternal constant in the midst of all the inconsistencies of your daily walk.

When Mandy came to see me, she appeared to have her life all together. She was a Christian who was very active in her church. She had led her alcoholic father to Christ on her father's deathbed. She was an attractive lady who had a nice husband and two wonderful children, but she had attempted suicide at least three times.

'How can God love me?' Mandy sobbed. 'I'm such a failure, such a mess.'

'Mandy, God loves you, not because you are lovable, but because it is His nature to love you. God simply loves you — period, because God is love.'

'But when I do bad I don't feel like God loves me,' she argued.

'Don't trust those feelings. He loves all His children all the time, whether we do good or bad. That's the heart of God. When the 99 sheep were safe in the fold, the heart of the shepherd was with the one that was lost. When the prodigal son squandered his life and inheritance, the heart of his father was with him, and he lovingly welcomed his son home. Those parables reveal that God's heart is full of love for us even when we are lost.'

'But I've tried to take my own life, Neil. How can God overlook that?'

'Just suppose, Mandy, that your son grew despondent and tried to take his own life. Would you love him any less? Would you kick him out of the family? Would you turn your back on him?'

'Of course not. If anything I'd feel sorry for him and try to love him more.'

'Are you telling me that a perfect God isn't as good a parent to you as you, an imperfect person, are to your children?'

Mandy got the point. She began to realize that God, as a loving parent, loves and forgives His children.

God Loves You No Matter What You Do

God wants us to do good, of course. The apostle John wrote: 'I write this to you so that you will not sin.' John continues by reminding us that God has already made provision for our failures so that His love continues constant in spite of what we do: 'But if anybody does sin, we have one who speaks to the Father in our defense — Jesus Christ, the Righteous One. He is the atoning sacrifice for our sins, and not only for ours but also for the sins of the whole world' (1 John 2:1,2, NIV).

One reason we doubt God's love is that we have an adversary who uses every little offense to accuse us of being good-for-nothings. Your advocate, Jesus Christ, however, is more powerful than your adversary. He has canceled the debt of your past, present and future sins. No matter what you do or how you fail, God will still love you because the love of God is not dependent upon its object; it is dependent upon His character. Because He loves you, He will discipline you in order that you 'may share His holiness' (Heb. 12:10).

When our children were small, a young couple who baby-sat them gave them each a hamster. They named their hamsters after the couple. Karl's was Johnny and Heidi's was Patty.

One night I came home from work and my wife, Joanne, met me at the door. 'You'd better go talk to Karl,' she said solemnly.

'What's the matter?'

'I think Karl threw Johnny this afternoon.'

I went to Karl and asked him point blank, 'Did you throw Johnny this afternoon?'

'No,' he answered firmly.

'Yes he did, yes he did,' Heidi accused, as only a big sister can. They argued back and forth, but Karl would not admit to throwing his hamster.

Unfortunately for poor Karl, there was an eyewitness that afternoon. When I asked Heidi's friend if Karl had thrown the hamster, she said yes.

Again I confronted Karl, this time with one of those over-sized plastic whiffle bats that make a lot of noise on a child's behind without inflicting any damage. 'Karl, throwing Johnny is not that big a deal. But you need to be honest with me. Did you throw Johnny?'

'No.' *Whack!*

'Karl, tell me the truth. Did you throw Johnny?'

'No.' *Whack!*

No matter how much I threatened, Karl wouldn't confess. I was frustrated and finally I gave up.

A couple of days later Joanne met me at the door again. 'You'd better go talk to Karl.'

'What's wrong this time?'

'Johnny died.'

I found Karl in the backyard mourning over his little hamster, which was stretched out on a small piece of cloth. We talked about death and dying, then buried Johnny and went to the pet store to buy a new hamster. While I was there, I also got sucked into buying a tweety bird!

I thought the incident had ended, but the next day Joanne met me at the door again.

'Now what's the problem?' I sighed.

'Karl dug up Johnny.'

I again found Karl in the backyard mourning over the stiff, dirt-encrusted hamster lying on a piece of cloth.

'Karl, I think the problem is that we didn't give Johnny a Christian funeral.'

So I made a little cross out of two sticks, and Karl and I talked about death and dying some more. Then we buried Johnny again and placed the cross on top of the little grave. 'Karl, I think you need to pray now,' I said.

'No, Dad. You pray.'

'Karl, Johnny was your hamster. I think you need to pray.'

Finally, he agreed. This was his prayer: 'Dear Jesus, help me not to throw my new hamster.'

What I couldn't coax out of him with a plastic bat, God worked out in his heart.

Why did Karl lie to me? He thought if he admitted to throwing his pet, I wouldn't love him. He was willing to lie so he could hold on to my love and respect, which he feared he would lose if he admitted his misbehavior.

I reached down and wrapped my arms around my little son. 'Karl, I want you to know something. No matter what you do in life, I'm always going to love you. You can be honest with me and tell me the truth. I may not approve of everything you do, but I'm always going to love you.'

What I expressed to Karl that day is a small reflection of the love God has for you. He says to you, 'I want you to know something. No matter what you do in life, I'm always going to love you. You can be honest with Me and tell Me the truth. I may not approve of everything you do, but I'm always going to love you.'

Note

1. Author and source unknown.

7
You Can't Live Beyond What You Believe

Walking by faith is a little bit like playing golf. When my son, Karl, was about 10 years old, I introduced him to the game of golf. I gave him a little starter set of clubs and took him to the course with me. Karl would tee up his ball and whale away at it with his mightiest swing. Usually he sprayed the ball all over the place. Because he could only hit it 60 or 70 yards at best, his direction could be off by 15 degrees or so and his ball would still be in the fairway.

As he grew up and got a bigger set of clubs, Karl was able to drive the ball off the tee 150 yards and farther. If, however, his drive was still 15 degrees off target, his ball no longer stayed in the fairway; it usually went into the rough. Accuracy is even more important for golfers who can blast a golf ball 250 yards off the tee. The same 15-degree deviation that allowed little Karl's short drives to remain in the fairway will send a longer drive soaring out of bounds.

Your Christian walk is the direct result of what you believe. If your faith is off, your walk will be off. If your walk is off, you need to take a good look at what you believe. Suppose you began your Christian walk just 15 degrees off in your teenage years. You are still in the fairway of life, but if you continue to live the same way for many years, life may start to get pretty rough and eventually you may find yourself out of bounds. That is the classic midlife crisis. You thought you understood well what constituted success, fulfillment and satisfaction, but now you are discovering that what you had believed about life wasn't quite true. The longer you persist in a faulty belief system, the less fulfilling and productive your daily walk of faith will be.

Walking by faith simply means that you function in daily life on the basis of what you believe. In fact, you are already walking by faith; you can't *not* walk by faith. People may not always live what they profess, but they will always live what they believe. If your behavior is off, you need to correct what you believe because your misbehavior is the result of your disbelief. The writer of Hebrews said, 'Remember those who led you, who spoke the word of God to you; and considering the result of their conduct, imitate their faith' (13:7).

To better understand what you presently believe, take a few minutes to complete the following Faith Appraisal. Simply evaluate yourself in each of the eight categories by circling a number from one to five that best represents you, five being high. Then complete each of the eight statements as concisely and truthfully as possible.

Faith Appraisal

	Low				High
1. How successful am I?	1	2	3	4	5
I would be more successful if…					
2. How significant am I?	1	2	3	4	5
I would be more significant if…					
3. How fulfilled am I?	1	2	3	4	5
I would be more fulfilled if…					
4. How satisfied am I?	1	2	3	4	5
I would be more satisfied if…					
5. How happy am I?	1	2	3	4	5
I would be happier if…					
6. How much fun am I having?	1	2	3	4	5
I would have more fun if…					

7. How secure am I?   1   2   3   4   5
      I would be more secure if...
8. How peaceful am I?   1   2   3   4   5
      I would have more peace if...

Whatever you believe are the answers to 'I would be more successful if... ,' 'I would be more significant if... ,' etc. constitute your present belief system. You are right now walking by faith according to what you believe. Assuming your basic physiological needs (food, shelter, safety and so on) are met, you are motivated to live a successful, significant, fulfilled, satisfied, happy, fun, secure and peaceful life. That is perfectly fine because God hasn't called you to be an insecure, insignificant, unfulfilled failure. Chances are you may not have the same definitions for these eight qualities of life that God does, and therefore your walk by faith may not be achieving what you want.

Feelings Are God's Red Flag of Warning

From birth, you have been developing in your mind a means for experiencing these eight values and reaching other goals in life. Consciously or subconsciously, you continue to formulate and adjust your plans for achieving these goals.

Sometimes, however, your well-intended plans and noble-sounding goals are not completely in harmony with God's plans and goals for you. *How can I know if what I believe is right?* you may be wondering. *Must I wait until I am 45 years old or until I experience some kind of midlife crisis to discover that what I believed in these eight areas was wrong?*

I don't think so. I believe God has designed you in such a way that you can know on a moment-by-moment basis if your belief system is properly aligned with God's truth. God has established a feedback system designed to grab your attention so you can examine the validity of your goals and beliefs. When an experience or relationship leaves you feeling angry, anxious or depressed, those emotional signposts are there to alert you that you may be cherishing a faulty goal based on a wrong belief.

Anger Signals a Blocked Goal

When your activity in a relationship or a project results in feelings of anger, it is usually because someone or something has blocked your goal, something or somebody is preventing you from accomplishing what you wanted. How do you feel in a traffic jam when it is preventing you from getting to an important meeting on time?

Suppose a wife and mother says, 'My goal in life is to have a loving, harmonious, happy Christian family.' Who can block that goal? Every person in her family can block that goal — not only *can*, they *will*! A homemaker clinging to the belief that her sense of worth is dependent on her family will crash and burn every time her husband or children fail to live up to her image of family harmony. She could become a very angry and controlling woman or a defeated victim of life's circumstances. Either option could drive family members even farther away from her and each other.

What if a pastor's goal is to reach his community for Christ? Good goal? It is a wonderful desire, but if his sense of worth and success as a pastor is dependent on that happening, he will experience tremendous emotional turmoil. Every person in the community can block his goal. Furthermore, two old board members may even try to block his goal. Pastors who believe their success is dependent on others will end up fighting with their boards, controlling members, praying their opposition out of the church or quitting.

'Whatever is not from faith is sin' (Rom. 14:23); therefore, an outburst of anger should prompt us to reexamine what we believe and the mental goals we have formulated to accomplish those beliefs.

My daughter, Heidi, helped me with this process one Sunday morning while I was trying to hustle my family out the door for church. I had been waiting in the car for several minutes before I stomped back into the house and shouted angrily, 'We should have left for church 15 minutes ago!'

All was silent for a moment, then Heidi's soft voice floated around the corner from her bedroom: 'What's the matter, Dad; am I blocking your goal?' That is the question you need to hear right before you preach!

Anxiety Signals an Uncertain Goal

When you feel anxious in a task or a relationship, your anxiety may be signaling that achieving your goal may be uncertain. You are hoping something will happen, but you have no guarantee it will. You can control some of the factors but not all of them.

For example, a teenager may believe her happiness at school depends on her parents' allowing her to attend a school dance. Not knowing how they will respond, she is anxious. If they say no, she will be angry because her goal was blocked. If she knows all along that there was no possible chance of their saying yes, she will be depressed because her goal will not be achieved.

Depression Signals an Impossible Goal

When you base your future success on something that can never happen, you have an impossible, hopeless goal. Your depression is a signal that your goal, no matter how spiritual or noble, may never be reached. We can be depressed for biochemical reasons, but if there is no physical cause, then depression is often rooted in a sense of hopelessness or helplessness.

I was speaking at a church conference on depression when a woman who was attending invited my wife and me to her home for dinner with her family. The woman had been a Christian for 20 years, but her husband was not a Christian. After I arrived, I quickly realized that the real reason this woman had invited me to dinner was to win her husband to Christ.

I discovered later that the woman had been severely depressed for many years. Her psychiatrist insisted that her depression was endogenous and she staunchly agreed. I believe, however, her depression stemmed from an impossible goal. For 20 years she had based her success as a Christian on winning her husband and children to Christ. She had prayed for them, witnessed to them and invited guest preachers home for dinner. She had said everything she could say and done everything she could do, but to no avail. As the futility of her efforts loomed larger, her faith faltered, her hope dimmed and her depression grew.

We had a nice dinner and I had an enjoyable conversation with her husband. He was a decent man who adequately provided for the physical needs of his family. He simply didn't see any need for God in his life. I shared my testimony and tried to be a positive example of a Christian. The last time I saw the woman, she was holding on to slim threads of hope. Her depression affected her positive attitude in the home, and her witness to her husband only weakened, further obliterating her goal.

You should, of course, desire that your loved ones come to Christ, and pray and work to that end. When you base your sense of worth as a Christian friend, parent or child on the salvation of your loved ones, however, realize that this goal may be beyond your ability or right to control. Witnessing is sharing our faith in the power of the Holy Spirit and leaving the results to God. We can't save anyone. Depression often signals that you are desperately clinging to a goal you have little or no chance of achieving, which is not a healthy goal.

Sometimes depression reveals a faulty concept of God. David wrote: 'How long, O LORD? Will you forget me forever? How long will you hide your face from me?...How long will my enemy triumph over me?' (Ps. 13:1,2, NIV). Had God really forgotten David? Was He actually hiding from David? Of course not. David had a wrong concept of God, feeling that He had abandoned him to the enemy. David's wrong concept led him to an impossible goal: victory over his enemies without God's help. No wonder he felt depressed!

The remarkable thing about David is that he didn't stay in the dumps. He evaluated his situation and realized, 'Hey, I'm a child of God. I'm going to focus on what I know about Him, not on my negative feelings.' From the pit of his depression he wrote: 'I trust in your unfailing love; my heart rejoices in your salvation' (v. 5). Then he decided to make a positive expression of his will: 'I will sing to the Lord, for he has been good to me' (v. 6). He willfully moved away from his wrong concept and its accompanying depression and returned to the source of his hope.

With God all things are possible. He is the God of all hope. Turn to God when you are feeling down, as David did. 'Why are you in despair, O my soul? And why are you disturbed within me? Hope in God, for I shall again praise Him, the help of my countenance, and my God' (Ps. 43:5).

Wrong Responses to Those Who Frustrate Goals

If our goals can be blocked or uncertain, how do we respond to someone or something that threatens our success? We may attempt to control or manipulate people or circumstances who stand between us and the achievement of our goals.

For example, a pastor's goal is to have the finest youth ministry in the community. However, one of his board members attempts to block his goal by insisting that a music ministry is more important. Every attempt by the pastor to hire a youth pastor is vetoed by the influential board member who wants to hire a music director first. The pastor's sense of worth and success in ministry is on the line. So he shifts into a power mode to push the stumbling block out of the way. He lobbies his cause with other board members. He solicits support from denominational leaders. He preaches about the importance of youth ministry to gain congregational support. He looks for a way to change the opposition's mind, or remove him from the board, because he believes his success in ministry is dependent on reaching his goal of having a great youth ministry.

Suppose a mother believes that her sense of worth depends on how well her children turn out. Her goal is to raise perfect little Christians who will become doctors and lawyers. As her children reach their teen years and begin to express their independence, however, their behavior doesn't always match her ideal. She is heading for a collision course because her children want their freedom and she wants to control them. She must control their behavior because she believes her success as a mother depends on it. If they don't attend the functions she wants them to attend, they can't go anywhere. If they don't listen to the music she expects them to listen to, they lose their radio and TV privileges. Somehow she never heard that parenting is an 18-year process of letting go, and the fruit of the spirit is self-control, not child control.

It is not hard to understand why people try to control others. They believe their sense of worth is dependent on other people and circumstances. This is a false belief, as evidenced by the fact that the most insecure people you will ever meet are manipulators and controllers.

People who cannot control those who frustrate their goals will probably respond by getting bitter, angry or resentful. Or they may simply resort to a martyr complex, which I perceived in the woman whose husband wouldn't come to Christ. She had been unsuccessful at getting him into the Kingdom and her faith and hope had shriveled to depression. So she resigned herself to bear her cross of a hopeless goal and hang on until the rapture. Unless she adjusts her goals, she will live the rest of her life in bitter defeat.

How Can I Turn Bad Goals into Good Goals?

Let me ask you a faith-stretching question: If God wants something done, can it be done? In other words, if God has a goal for your life, can it be blocked, or is its fulfillment uncertain or impossible?

I am personally convinced that no goal God has for my life is impossible or uncertain, nor can it be blocked. I can't imagine God saying, 'I've called you into existence, I've made you My child and I have something for you to do. I know you won't be able to do it, but give it your best shot.' That's ludicrous! It's like saying to your child, 'I want you to mow the lawn. Unfortunately, the lawn is full of rocks, the mower doesn't work and there's no gas. But give it your best shot.' When an authority figure issues a command that cannot be obeyed, the authority of the leader is undermined in the minds of those who are in submission.

God had a staggering goal for a young maid named Mary. An angel told her she would bear a Son while still a virgin, and her Son would be the Savior of the world. When she inquired about this seemingly impossible feat, the angel simply said, "'Nothing will be impossible with God'" (Luke 1:37).

You wouldn't give your children tasks they couldn't possibly complete, and God doesn't assign to you goals you can't achieve. His goals for you are possible, certain and achievable. We need to understand His goals for our lives and then say with Mary: 'Behold, the bondslave of the Lord; be it done to me according to your word' (v. 38).

Goals Versus Desires

To live successful lives, we need to distinguish a godly goal from a godly desire. This liberating distinction can spell the difference between success and failure, inner peace and inner pain for the Christian.

A godly goal is any specific orientation that reflects God's purpose for your life and is not dependent on people or circumstances beyond your ability or right to control. Who do you have the ability and right to control? Virtually no one but yourself. The only person who can block a godly goal or render it uncertain or impossible is you. If you adopt the attitude of cooperation with God's goals as Mary did, your goal can be reached.

A godly desire is any specific result that depends on the cooperation of other people, the success of events or favorable circumstances you have no right or ability to control. You cannot base your success or sense of worth on your desires, no matter how godly they may be, because you cannot control their fulfillment. Some of your desires will be blocked, remain uncertain and eventually prove to be impossible. Let's face it, life doesn't always go our way and many of our desires will not be met.

We will struggle with anger, anxiety and depression when we elevate a desire to a goal in our own minds. By comparison, when a desire isn't met, you will only face disappointment. Life is full of disappointments and we all must learn to live with them. However, dealing with the disappointments of unmet desires is a lot easier than dealing with the anger, anxiety and depression of goals that are based on wrong beliefs.

Does God make a distinction between a goal and a desire?

Yes, I think He does. "'For I have no pleasure in the death of anyone who dies," declares the LORD GOD. "Therefore, repent and live"' (Ezek. 18:32). It is God's desire that we all repent and live, but not all will.

John wrote, 'My little children, I am writing these things to you that you may not sin' (1 John 2:1). Certainly the integrity, sovereignty and success of God is not dependent upon whether or not we sin. God has no blocked goals. It is God's *desire* that everyone repent, although not everyone will.

Then does God have any genuine goals — specific results that cannot be blocked? Praise the Lord, *yes*! For example, Jesus Christ will return and take us home to heaven to be with Him forever — it will happen. Satan will be cast into the abyss for eternity — count on it. Rewards will be distributed to the saints for their faithfulness — look forward to it. These are not desires that can be thwarted by the fickle nature of a fallen humanity. What God has determined to do, He will do.

When you begin to align your goals with God's goals and your desires with God's desires, you will rid your life of a lot of anger, anxiety and depression. The homemaker who wants a happy, harmonious family is expressing a godly desire, but she cannot guarantee that it will happen. Her goal is to become the wife and mother God wants her to be. The only one who can block that goal for her life is herself.

She may object, 'But what if my husband has a midlife crisis or my kids rebel?' Those kinds of problems are not blocking her goal to be the wife and mother God called her to be. Such trials will surely test her faith. If anything, difficulties in the family should further encourage her commitment. If her husband should ever need a godly wife and her children a godly mother, it is in times of trouble. Family difficulties refine her goal of being the woman God wants her to be.

The pastor whose success and sense of worth are based on

his goal to win his community for Christ, have the best youth ministry in town or increase giving to missions by 50 percent, is headed for a fall. These are worthwhile desires, but no pastor should deem himself a success or failure based on whether or not they are achieved. His goal is to be the pastor God called him to be. No member of his church or community can block that goal.

The Goal Is to Become the Person God Called You to Be

It should be obvious by now that God's basic goal for your life is character development: becoming the person God wants you to be. Sanctification is God's goal for your life (see 1 Thess. 4:3). Nobody and nothing on planet Earth can keep you from being the person God called you to be. Certainly, a lot of distractions, diversions, disappointments, trials, temptations and traumas come along to disrupt the process. Every day you will struggle against the world, the flesh and the devil, each of which are opposed to your success at being God's person.

Paul teaches that the tribulations we face are actually a means of achieving our supreme goal of maturity: 'We also exult in our tribulations, knowing that tribulation brings about perseverance; and perseverance, proven character; and proven character, hope; and hope does not disappoint, because the love of God has been poured out within our hearts through the Holy Spirit who was given to us' (Rom. 5:3-5).

James offers similar counsel: 'Consider it all joy, my brethren, when you encounter various trials, knowing that the testing of your faith produces endurance. And let endurance have its perfect result, that you may be perfect and complete, lacking in nothing' (Jas. 1:2-4).

The word 'exultation' means heightened joy. To be under

tribulation means to be under pressure, and perseverance means to remain under pressure. Persevering through tribulations results in proven character, which is God's goal for us.

Suppose a Christian wife asked for help because her husband had just left her. What kind of hope could you give her? Would you say, 'Don't worry, honey, we'll win him back'? That is a legitimate desire, but is a wrong goal that could lead to manipulation and control. Attempts to manipulate him to come back may be the same kind of controlling behavior that caused him to leave in the first place.

It would be better to say, 'I will help you work through this crisis (perseverance) to become the person God wants you to be (proven character). If you haven't committed yourself to be the wife and mother God has called you to be, would you now? You can't change him, but you can change yourself, which is the best way to win him back anyway. Even if he doesn't come back, you can come through this crisis with proven character, which is where your hope lies.'

She may rightly ask, 'What if the problem was 90 percent his?' She doesn't have any control over that. By committing to change herself, she is responsibly dealing with what she can control. Her transformation may be just the motivation her husband needs to change himself and restore the relationship.

Trials and tribulations reveal wrong goals, but they can actually be the catalyst for achieving God's goal for our lives, which is our sanctification — the process of conforming to His image. During these times of pressure, our emotions raise their warning flags, signaling blocked, uncertain or impossible goals based on our desires instead of God's goal of proven character.

Someone may say, 'My marriage is hopeless,' and then try to solve the problem by changing partners. If you think your first marriage is hopeless, be aware that second marriages are failing at a far higher rate. Others think their jobs or churches are hopeless. So they change jobs, only to discover their new job or church is just as hopeless. They should hang in there and grow up. Now, there may be legitimate times to change jobs or churches, but if we are just running from our own immaturity, it will follow us wherever we go.

Is there an easier way to being God's person than through enduring tribulations? Believe me: I have been looking for one. I must honestly say, though, that it has been the dark, difficult times of testing in my life that have brought me to where I am today. We need occasional mountaintop experiences, but the fertile soil for growth is always down in the valleys of tribulation, not on the mountaintops.

Paul says, 'The goal of our instruction is love' (1 Tim. 1:5). Notice that if you make that your goal, then the fruit of the Spirit is love, joy (instead of depression), peace (instead of anxiety) and patience (instead of anger). The following poem from an unknown author expresses well the message of this chapter:

> 'Disappointment — His appointment,'
>   Change one letter, then I see
> That the thwarting of my purpose
>   Is God's better choice for me.
> His appointment must be blessing,
>   Tho' it may come in disguise,
> For the end from the beginning
>   Open to His wisdom lies.
>
> 'Disappointment — His appointment,'
>   No good will He withhold,
> From denials oft we gather
>   Treasures of His love untold.
> Well He knows each broken purpose

Leads to fuller, deeper trust,
And the end of all His dealings
Proves our God is wise and just.

'Disappointment — His appointment,'
Lord, I take it, then, as such,
Like clay in the hands of a potter,
Yielding wholly to Thy touch.
My life's plan is Thy molding;
Not one single choice be mine;
Let me answer, unrepining —
'Father, not my will, but Thine.'

8
God's Guidelines for
the Walk of Faith

A few years ago, I accepted an invitation to speak at a church retreat the weekend after Mother's Day. A month before the retreat, the pastor called to tell me that the conference center had been double booked, so their retreat had to be moved ahead one week. He asked if I could still be there the Friday, Saturday and Sunday of Mother's Day weekend.

I wasn't about to schedule anything that would take me away from my family on Mother's Day, but my wife, Joanne, overheard the conversation and suggested I go ahead with the retreat. I told her I didn't want to be away on her special day, but she insisted I go. So I did.

During a break in the retreat, I visited the little gift shop in the grounds and got a wonderful idea for making up to my family for being away on Mother's Day. One of the gift items in the shop was a cute little basket containing a package of muffin mix and a jar of apple jelly. I decided I would get up early on Monday morning and fix a delicious, banquet-style breakfast for Joanne, Heidi and Karl — complete with eggs, sausage and muffins.

So on Monday morning I rose with the chickens, had my devotions and started making breakfast. I was stirring the muffin mix, singing and feeling great when sleepy-eyed Karl wandered into the kitchen. He grabbed a box of cereal and an empty bowl and headed for the table.

'Hey, Karl, just a second. We're not having cereal this morning. We're going to sit around the table together and have a big breakfast with muffins.'

'I don't like muffins, Dad,' he mumbled, opening the cereal box.

'Wait, Karl,' I insisted, starting to get annoyed. 'We're going to sit around the table together and have a big breakfast with muffins.'

'But I don't like muffins, Dad,' he repeated as he got ready to fill his bowl.

I lost it. 'Karl, we're going to sit around the table together and have a big breakfast with muffins!' I barked. Karl closed the cereal box, threw it into the cupboard and stomped back to his room. The kid blocked my goal!

When I realized what I had done, I went to Karl's room and said, 'I'm sorry, son. You can have cereal.'

He said, 'I don't like cereal.'

Like me, I am sure you have suffered your share of blocked goals, which are described in the previous chapter. You had this great plan to do something wonderful for God, your church, your family or a friend. Then your plan was thrown into disarray by hectic, daily events over which you had no control. A pileup on the freeway kept you from getting to work on time. Your husband was late for the special dinner you planned. Your child decided to be the lead guitarist in a rock band instead of becoming a doctor, as you had planned. You didn't get your way at the board meeting.

When you base your sense of worth on the success of your own personal plans, your life will be one long, emotional roller-coaster ride. The only way to get off the roller coaster is to walk by faith according to the truth of God's Word.

Proper Guidelines Lead to a Proper Walk

As far as the devil is concerned, the next best thing to keeping you chained in spiritual darkness or having you live as an emotional wreck is confusing your belief system. He lost you in the eternal sense when you became a child of God. If he can muddy your mind and weaken your faith with partial truths, however, he can neutralize your effectiveness for God and stunt your growth as a Christian.

We have already determined that God wants you to be successful, fulfilled and happy. It is imperative for your spiritual maturity, though, that your beliefs about success, significance, fulfillment, satisfaction, happiness, fun, security and peace be anchored in the Scriptures.

In this chapter, I want to review each of these belief areas from the foundation of God's Word. Compare these eight descriptions with the eight statements you wrote for the Faith Appraisal in the previous chapter. These descriptions may help you make some vital adjustments that will steer you back to the middle of the fairway.

1. Success. Key Concept: Goals

A few years ago, a young woman flew to Los Angeles from the East Coast to spend a Saturday with me in counseling. She said she had deep spiritual problems. She did, and I was surprised the airplane stayed in the air with her in it. She was hearing demonic voices and was plagued with many problems.

Mattie quoted to me 3 John 2: 'Beloved, I pray that in all respects you may prosper and be in good health.'

'If God has promised prosperity, success and health to me, why is my life all screwed up?' she complained.

'There's more to that verse,' I said. 'Finish reading it.'

'Just as your soul prospers,' she continued.

I asked her pointedly, 'How is your soul doing?' Mattie then told me her sad story. She had submitted to three abortions as a result of illicit sexual affairs; she withdrew from drugs several times; and she was presently living with another man outside of marriage. I felt like telling her, 'I think the verse is working.'

Success is related to goals. If you rated yourself low in the success category, you are probably having difficulty reaching your goals in life. If you aren't reaching your goals, it is probably because you are working on the wrong goals.

A good summary of God's goal for us is found in 2 Peter 1:3-10:

> His divine power has granted to us everything pertaining to life and godliness, through the true knowledge of Him who called us by His own glory and excellence. For by these He has granted to us His precious and magnificent promises, in order that by them you might become partakers of the divine nature, having escaped the corruption that is in the world by lust. Now for this very reason also, applying all diligence, in your faith supply moral excellence, and in your moral excellence, knowledge; and in your knowledge, self-control, and in your self-control, perseverance, and in your perseverance, godliness; and in your godliness, brotherly kindness, and in your brotherly kindness, love. For if these qualities are yours and are increasing, they render you neither useless nor unfruitful in the true knowledge of our Lord Jesus Christ. For he who lacks these qualities is blind or short-sighted, having forgotten his purification from his former sins. Therefore, brethren, be all the more diligent to make certain about His calling and choosing you; for as long as you practice these things, you will never stumble.

Notice that God's goal begins with who you are on the basis of what God has already done for you. He has given you 'life and godliness'; justification has already happened and sanctification has already begun. You are already a partaker of the 'divine nature, having escaped' (past tense) sin's corruption. What a great start!

Your primary job now is to adopt God's character goals diligently — moral excellence, knowledge, self-control, perseverance, godliness, brotherly kindness and Christian love — and apply them to your life. Focusing on God's goals will lead to ultimate success: success in God's terms. Peter promises that as these qualities increase in your life through practice, you will be useful and fruitful and you will never stumble. That is a legitimate basis for a true sense of worth and success and nobody can keep you from accomplishing it!

Notice also that this list does not mention talents, intelligence or gifts that are not equally distributed to all believers. Your identity and sense of worth aren't determined by those qualities. Your sense of worth is based on your identity in Christ and your growth in character, both of which are equally accessible to every Christian. Those Christians, like Mattie, who are not committed to God's goals for character are sad stories of failure. According to Peter, they have forgotten their purification from former sins. They have forgotten who they are in Christ.

Another helpful perspective of success is seen in Joshua's experience of leading Israel into the Promised Land. God said to him:

> Be strong and very courageous; be careful to do according to all the law which Moses My servant commanded you; do not turn from it to the right or to the left, so that you may have success wherever you go. This book of the law shall not depart from your mouth, but you shall meditate on it day and night, so that you may be careful to do according to all that is written in it; for then you will make your way prosperous, and then you will have success (Josh. 1:7,8).

Was Joshua's success dependent on other people or favorable circumstances? Absolutely not. Success hinged entirely on living according to God's Word. If Joshua believed what God said and did what God told him to do, he would succeed. Sounds simple enough, but God immediately put Joshua to the test by giving him a rather unorthodox battle plan for conquering Jericho. Marching around the city for seven days and then blowing a horn weren't exactly approved military tactics in Joshua's day!

Joshua's success was conditional on obeying God regardless of how foolish His plan seemed. As Joshua 6 records, Joshua's success had nothing to do with the circumstances of the battle and everything to do with obedience. Success is accepting God's goal for our lives and by His grace becoming what He has called us to be.

2. Significance. Key Concept: Time

Significance is a time concept. What is forgotten in time is of little significance. What is remembered for eternity is of great significance. Paul wrote to the Corinthians: 'If any man's work... remains, he shall receive a reward' (1 Cor. 3:14). He instructed Timothy: 'Discipline yourself for the purpose of godliness... since it holds promise for the present life and also for the life to come' (1 Tim. 4:7,8). If you want to increase your significance, focus your energies on significant activities: those that will remain for eternity.

Stu, the pastor of a small church, attended one of my classes at Talbot School of Theology. He was in his mid-30s and married when he found out he had cancer. The doctors gave him less than two years to live.

One day Stu came to talk to me. 'Ten years ago somebody gave a prophecy about me in church,' he began. 'They said I was going to do a great work for God. I've led a few hundred people to Christ, but I haven't had a great work for God yet. Do you think God is going to heal me so the prophecy can be fulfilled?'

I registered shock by his statement and said, 'You've led a few hundred people to Christ and don't think you have accomplished a great work for God? Stu, I know some significant pastors in large churches who can't make that claim. I know some great theologians who have led very few people to Christ. If a few hundred people are believers today because of you, and they have influenced who knows how many other people for Christ, I'd call that a great work for God.' Stu is now with the Lord, having completed his significant ministry of reaching hundreds for Christ.

One of the few heroes of my life is Billy Graham. He has been verbally shot at from the right and from the left, but he has remained true to his calling to preach the gospel. One day, several years ago, I happened to see him walking through the lobby of the Century Plaza Hotel in Los Angeles. I had never met him before and I couldn't pass up the opportunity. I caught up with him and said, 'I wanted to meet you, Dr. Graham, even though I'm just a lowly pastor.'

He warmly returned my greeting and then brought me up short by saying, 'There's no such thing as a lowly pastor.'

He was right. There is no such thing as a lowly pastor or a lowly child of God. We are in the significant business of collecting treasures for eternity. What we do and say for Christ in this world, no matter how insignificant it seems, will last forever.

3. Fulfillment. Key Concept: Role Preference

Fulfillment in life can be summarized by the simple slogan, 'Bloom where you're planted.' Peter said it this way: 'As each one has received a special gift, employ it in serving one another' (1 Pet. 4:10). Fulfillment is discovering our own uniqueness in Christ and using our gifts and talents to edify others and to glorify the Lord.

God allowed me to understand this simple principle before I entered the ministry while still employed as an aerospace engineer. I knew God wanted me to be an ambassador for Him on the job, so I started a breakfast Bible study in the bowling alley next door to the office. My announcement about the Bible study had been posted in our office for only about an hour when a Jewish fellow pulled it off the wall and brought it to me. 'You can't bring Jesus in here,' he objected.

'I can't do otherwise,' I said. 'Every day I walk in here Jesus comes in with me.' He was not impressed with my response!

One of the men who found Christ through the Bible study became a flaming evangelist. He passed out tracts everywhere he went. When I left that aerospace firm to enter seminary, he took over the Bible study.

A few months later I went back to visit my friends in the Bible study. 'Do you remember the Jewish fellow?' the leader asked.

'Sure, I remember him,' I said, recalling his brash opposition to our Bible study.

'Well, he got sick and almost died. I went to the hospital and visited him every night. Finally I led him to Christ.'

I was ecstatic at the realization that I had become a spiritual grandparent. The sense of fulfillment was exhilarating. It all happened because I started a simple little Bible study where I worked so I could do what Paul said: 'Do the work of an evangelist, fulfill your ministry' (2 Tim. 4:5).

God has a unique place of ministry for each of us. It is important to your sense of fulfillment that you realize your calling in life. The key is to discover the roles you occupy in which you cannot be replaced, and then decide to be what God wants you to be in those roles. For example, of the six billion people in the world, you are the only one who occupies your unique role as husband, father, wife, mother, parent or child in your home. God has specially planted you to serve Him by serving your family in that environment.

Furthermore, you are the only one who knows your neighbors as you do. You occupy a unique role as an ambassador for Christ where you work. These are your mission fields and you are the worker God has appointed for the harvest there. Your greatest fulfillment will come from accepting and occupying God's unique place for you to the best of your ability. Sadly, many miss their calling in life by looking for fulfillment in the world. Find your fulfillment in the kingdom of God by deciding to be an ambassador for Christ in the world (see 2 Cor. 5:20).

4. Satisfaction. Key Concept: Quality

Satisfaction comes from living righteously and seeking to raise the level of quality in relationships, service and product. Jesus said, 'Blessed are those who hunger and thirst for righteousness, for they shall be satisfied' (Matt. 5:6). Do you believe that? If you do, what are you doing? You are hungering and thirsting after righteousness, and if you aren't doing that, then you really don't believe it.

What causes you to become dissatisfied with someone or something? It is usually because the quality of the relationship, service or product has diminished. I often ask people if they can remember when they became dissatisfied. Inevitably, they identify the time when the quality of a relationship, a service rendered or their work diminished.

Satisfaction is a quality concern, not a quantity concern. You will achieve greater satisfaction from doing a few things well than from doing many things in a haphazard or hasty manner. The key to personal satisfaction is not found in broadening the scope of your activities but in deepening them through a commitment to quality.

The same is true in relationships. If you are dissatisfied in your relationships, perhaps you have spread yourself too thin. Solomon wrote, 'A man of many friends comes to ruin, but there is a friend who sticks closer than a brother' (Prov. 18:24). It may be nice to know a lot of people on the surface, but you need a few really good friends who are committed to a quality relationship with you.

That is what our Lord modeled for us. He taught the multitudes and equipped 70 for ministry, but He invested most of His time in the 12 disciples. Out of those 12, He selected three — Peter, James and John — to be with Him on the Mount of Transfiguration, on the Mount of Olives and in the Garden of Gethsemane. While suffering on the cross, Jesus committed to John, perhaps His closest friend, the care of His mother. That is a quality relationship, and we all need the satisfaction that quality relationships bring.

5. Happiness. Key Concept: Wanting What You Have

The world's concept of happiness is having what we want. Madison Avenue tells us we need a flashier car, a sexier cologne or any number of items that are better, faster or easier to use than what we already have. We watch the commercials and read the ads, and we become antsy to acquire all the latest fashions, fads and fancy doodahs. We are not really happy until we get what we want.

God's concept of happiness is summed up in the simple proverb: 'Happy is the man who wants what he has.' As long as you are focusing on what you don't have, you will be unhappy. When you begin to appreciate what you already have, however, you will be happy all your life.

Paul wrote to Timothy, 'But godliness with contentment is great gain. For we brought nothing into the world, and we can take nothing out of it. But if we have food and clothing, we will be content with that' (1 Tim. 6:6-8, NIV).

Actually, you already have everything you need to make you happy forever. You have Christ. You have eternal life. You are loved by a heavenly Father who has promised to supply all your needs. No wonder the Bible repeatedly commands us to be thankful (see 1 Thess. 5:18). If you really want to be happy, learn to be content with life and thankful for what you already have in Christ.

6. Fun. Key Concept: Uninhibited Spontaneity

Fun is uninhibited spontaneity. Have you ever planned a major fun event? Chances are, the last time you really had fun was spontaneous, after you threw off your inhibitions. Worldly people know they need to get rid of their inhibitions to have fun. That is one reason they drink.

The secret to enjoying uninhibited spontaneity as a Christian is to remove unscriptural inhibitors. Chief among the inhibitors of Christian fun is our fleshly tendency to keep up appearances. We don't want to look out of place or be thought less of by others, so we stifle our spontaneity with a form of false decorum. That is people pleasing, and Paul suggested that anybody who lives to please people isn't serving Christ (see Gal. 1:10). The joyless cry, 'What will people say?' The liberated in Christ respond, 'Who cares what people say? I care what God says; I stopped playing for the grandstand a long time ago when I started playing for the coach.'

I love the uninhibited joy of King David. He was so happy about returning the Ark to Jerusalem that he leaped and danced before the Lord in celebration. He knew there was joy in the presence of God. Michal, his party-pooping wife, however, thought his behavior was unbecoming to a king, and she told him so in no uncertain terms. David said, 'Too bad for you, lady. I'm dancing before the Lord, not before you or anybody else. And I'm going to keep dancing whether you like it or not' (see 2 Sam. 6:21). As it turned out, Michal was the person God judged in the incident, not David (see v. 23). It is a lot more fun pleasing the Lord than trying to please people.

7. Security. Key Concept: Relating to the Eternal

Insecurity means depending upon temporal things that we have no right or ability to control. Do you realize that God is shaking the foundations of this world? Insecurity is a global problem. Some tough days are ahead for this fallen world. It doesn't take a genius to determine that. An exploding population and decreasing natural resources indicate we are fast heading on a collision course.

Our security can be found only in the eternal life of Christ. Jesus said no one can snatch us out of His hand (see John 10:27-29). Paul declared that nothing can separate us from the love of God in Christ (see Rom. 8:35-39) and that we are sealed in Him by the Holy Spirit (see Eph. 1:13,14). How much more secure can you get than that?

Everything we now have we shall lose some day. Jim Elliot (a missionary who was killed along with four other men by the Auca Indians in Ecuador, South America, in 1956) said, 'He is no fool who gives what he cannot keep to gain what he cannot lose.'[1]

Paul said, 'But whatever things were gain to me, those things I have counted as loss for the sake of Christ. More than that, I count all things to be loss in view of the surpassing value of knowing Christ Jesus my Lord, for whom I have suffered the loss of all things, and count them but rubbish in order that I may gain Christ' (Phil. 3:7,8).

8. Peace. Key Concept: Establishing Internal Order

Peace on earth, good will toward men; that is what everybody wants. That is a great desire but a wrong goal. Nobody can guarantee external peace because nobody can control people or circumstances. Nations sign and break peace treaties with frightening regularity. One group of peace marchers confronts another group of peace marchers and they end up beating each other over the head with their placards. Couples lament that there would be peace in their home 'if only he/she would shape up.'

The peace of God is internal, not external. Peace *with* God is something you already have (see Rom. 5:1). The peace *of* God is something you need to appropriate daily in your inner world in the midst of the storms that rage in the external world (see John 14:27).

A lot of things can disrupt your external world because you can't control all your circumstances and relationships. You *can* control the inner world of your thoughts and emotions, however, by daily allowing the peace of God to rule in your heart. Chaos may be occurring all around you, but God is bigger than any storm. I keep a little plaque on my desk that reminds me: 'Nothing will happen to me today that God and I cannot resolve.' Personal worship, prayer and interaction with God's Word enable us to experience the peace of God (see Phil. 4:6,7; Col. 3:15,16).

Often when I share these eight critical points of the Christian's belief system, I hear people say, 'Well, I suppose that's true, but I still believe...' Which will they live by: what they acknowledge as true or what they 'still believe'? Always the latter — *always*! Walking by faith is simply choosing to believe what God says is true and to live accordingly by the power of the Holy Spirit.

Note

1. Elisabeth Elliot, *Shadow of the Almighty: The Life and Testament of Jim Elliot* (San Francisco: Harper and Row Publishers, 1958), p. 15.

9
Winning the Battle
for Your Mind

Several years ago, Shelley, a Talbot student's wife, audited my class on spiritual conflicts. About halfway through the course she stopped me in the hallway one day and simply said, 'You have no idea what's going on in my life.' She was right; I had no idea! I encouraged her to keep attending and to apply the truths she had learned to her life.

At the conclusion of the course, Shelley handed me the following letter:

> Dear Neil,
>
> I just want to thank you again for how the Lord has used your class to change my life. The last two years of my life have been a constant struggle for the control of my mind. I was ignorant of my position and authority in Christ, and equally ignorant of Satan's ability to deceive me. I was constantly afraid. My mind was bombarded by hostile, angry thoughts. I felt guilty and wondered what was wrong with me. I didn't understand how much bondage I was in until I came to your class.
>
> I was always taught that demons didn't really affect Christians. But when you began to describe a person influenced by demons, I just about passed out from shock. You were describing me! For the first time in my life I can identify Satan's attack and really resist him. I'm not paralyzed by fear anymore and my mind is much less cluttered. As you can tell, I'm pretty excited about this!

> When I read the Scriptures now, I wonder why I couldn't see all this before. But as you know, I was deceived.
>
> Thanks again so much.
>
> Shelley

Shelley was a Christian long before she audited my course, but she didn't understand the battle that was going on in her mind. She was being 'destroyed for lack of knowledge' (Hos. 4:6). Shelley represents untold numbers of Christians who are ignorant of Satan's schemes (see 2 Cor. 2:11). When struggling believers resolve their personal and spiritual conflicts through repentance and faith in God, they, too, will experience their freedom in Christ that Shelley wrote about.

Faith in God is the Christian way to live and humanistic philosophical reasoning is the human way, but they are often in conflict. Having faith in God is not unreasonable, and I am not suggesting you ignore your responsibility to think. On the contrary, we are required by God to think and make conscious choices. God is a rational God and He does work through our ability to reason. The problem is that our ability to reason is limited and prone to rationalization.

The Lord said: 'For as the heavens are higher than the earth, so are My ways higher than your ways, and My thoughts than your thoughts' (Isa. 55:9). We are incapable of determining God's thoughts through human reasoning; therefore, we are dependent on divine revelation.

Plan A in Figure 9-A is living God's way by faith. Plan B is living our way by humanistic reasoning. The humanist would say, 'I don't see it God's way' or 'I don't believe in God's way, so I will do it my way.' Solomon urged us to live God's way when he wrote, 'Do not lean on your own understanding [Plan B]. In all your ways acknowledge Him [Plan A]' (Prov. 3:5,6).

The strength of Plan A is determined by your personal

GOD'S WAY VERSUS MAN'S WAY

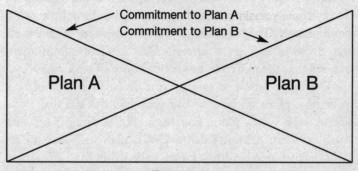

Figure 9-A

conviction that God's way is always right and by how committed you are to believe Him. The strength of Plan B is determined by the amount of time and energy you invest in entertaining thoughts that are contrary to God's Word. Plan B is saturated with defense mechanisms and strongholds raised against the knowledge of God. All new believers are dominated by Plan B because that is all they know until they get to know God and His ways.

For example, God's plan is that marriage be a monogamous, lifetime commitment. Suppose a Christian wife begins to reason, *I don't know if this marriage is going to last. Just in case it doesn't, I'd better get a job to secure my future.* Any commitment she makes to Plan B decreases her commitment to Plan A. The more she thinks about Plan B, the better are the chances she is going to need it. She is actually making plans for the marriage to fail.

I don't have a Plan B for my marriage because I made a commitment to Joanne for life. I try not to entertain thoughts contrary to my commitment to her, even though I am tempted to. Every believer will be tempted to think the slippery slope of Plan B. I received a letter from the wife of a former seminary student who was serving as a pastor. She said, 'I knew I was in trouble when I saw on his desk the book *Creative Divorce.*' He was considering Plan B and he chose it. Today some young people are marrying but have little or no commitment. They are thinking, *If the marriage doesn't work out, I can always get a divorce.* That kind of commitment assures that the marriage has little chance of surviving.

The more time and energy you invest in contemplating your own plans on how to live your life, the less likely you are to seek God's plan. You begin flip-flopping back and forth between acknowledging God's plan and leaning on your own understanding. James called this kind of person double-minded, 'unstable in all his ways' (Jas. 1:8). When you continue to vacillate between God's Plan A and your Plan B, your spiritual growth will be stunted, your maturity in Christ will be blocked, and your daily experience as a Christian will be marked by disillusionment, discouragement and defeat.

Where do Plan B thoughts originate? There are three primary sources. First, your flesh still generates humanistic thoughts and ideas. Your flesh is that part of you that was trained to live independently of God before you became a Christian. Before salvation there was no Plan A in your life; you were separated from God, ignorant of His ways and determined to succeed and survive by your own resources and natural abilities.

When you were born again, you became a new person, but nobody pressed the Clear button in your memory. You brought with you into your new faith all the old Plan B habits and thought patterns of the flesh. So, although your new self desires to live dependently on God and follow Plan A, your flesh persists in suggesting Plan B ways to live independently of God.

Second, we are continually being influenced by this fallen

world. The mass media and the worldly environment are dominated by Plan B thinking.

Third, the god of this world has opposed the Word of God since the Garden of Eden. This father of lies will tempt, accuse and deceive God's children just as he did Eve, if we let him. In addition, false prophets and teachers, mediums and spiritists will also lead many astray.

The essence of the battle for the mind is the conflict between Plan A and Plan B impulses from the world, the flesh and the devil. You may think you are the helpless victim in this battle, being slapped back and forth like a hockey puck, but you are anything but helpless. In fact, God has provided all we need to win this battle for our minds.

Strongholds of the Mind

The nature of the battle is presented in 2 Corinthians 10:3-5:

> For though we walk in the flesh, we do not war according to the flesh, for the weapons of our warfare are not of the flesh, but divinely powerful for the destruction of fortresses. We are destroying speculations and every lofty thing raised up against the knowledge of God, and we are taking every thought captive to the obedience of Christ.

The weapons in this passage are different from the defensive armor described in Ephesians 6. The image presented here is similar to an offensive, battering ram that is designed to tear down strongholds. What are these strongholds or fortresses of the mind, and how have they been raised against the knowledge of God?

Environmental Stimulation

Recall that we were all born physically alive but spiritually dead in a fallen world (see Eph. 2:1-3). We had neither the presence of God in our lives nor the knowledge of His ways, so we learned to live our lives independently of God. Infants have no vocabulary and no attitudes or beliefs about anything. Everything we learned in the early formative years of our lives was assimilated from the environment in which we were raised, in two ways.

First, we learned primarily from prevailing experiences. Attitudes and beliefs were formed from long-term exposure to the homes in which we were raised, the neighborhoods where we played, the schools we attended, the friends we had and the churches we attended or didn't attend. All these childhood experiences shaped our worldviews.

It is important to realize that two children raised in the same environment will interpret their experiences differently. Two children can also have radically different childhood experiences. One could be raised in a friendly environment where the parents protected the children from harmful influences. Another child could be raised in a hostile environment and exposed to the filth of this world. However, both need Christ equally as much.

Second, beliefs and attitudes are also formed in our minds from traumatic experiences such as the death of a parent, a divorce in the home, or mental, physical or sexual abuse. Unlike prevailing experiences that are assimilated into our minds over time, these traumatic experiences are burned into our minds because of their intensity; and they will leave lasting impressions.

Paul said, 'Do not conform any longer to the pattern of this world, but be transformed by the renewing of your mind' (Rom. 12:2, NIV). The point is we all were conformed to this world, albeit differently, and we still can be. Even as Christians we can still listen to the wrong music, watch the wrong programs, have the wrong friends and think the wrong thoughts. We will still be tempted to live our lives independently of God because we are living in a fallen world.

Temptation

Temptation always comes by way of a thought, and the key to resisting temptation is to take that initial thought captive to the obedience of Christ. I found a humorous 'Cathy' cartoon strip that illustrates how an unchecked initial thought carries her away like a runaway freight train:

Frame 1: 'I will take a drive, but won't go near the grocery store.'

Frame 2: 'I will drive by the grocery store, but will not go in.'

Frame 3: 'I will go in the grocery store, but will not walk down the aisle where the Halloween candy is on sale.'

Frame 4: 'I will look at the candy, but not pick it up.'

Frame 5: 'I will pick it up, but not buy it.'

Frame 6: 'I will buy it, but not open it.'

Frame 7: 'Open it, but not smell it.'

Frame 8: 'Smell it, but not taste it.'

Frame 9: 'Taste it, but not eat it.'

Frame 10: 'Eat, eat, eat, eat, eat!'

The Scriptures teach that God has provided a way of escape from every temptation (see 1 Cor. 10:13). As illustrated by Cathy's experience, however, the escape probably would have occurred before the first frame. Cathy lost the battle when she decided to go for a drive. If you don't take captive the initial thought, you will probably lose the battle to temptation. We all have to learn how to practise threshold thinking. We need to take the way of escape the moment our thoughts are contrary to the truth and righteousness.

For example, a man struggling with lust sees a pornographic picture. He has the opportunity to respond by thinking, *My relationship with sin has ended. I don't have to give in to this. I choose right now to take this thought captive to the obedience of Christ. I'm not going to look at it and I'm not going to think about it.* He stops looking at the picture and gets rid of the magazine or leaves the place of temptation. If he hesitates at the threshold, stares at the picture and begins to fantasize about it, he will trigger an emotional landslide, producing a physical response that will be difficult to stop. He must capture the initial tempting thought or it will probably capture him.

Consideration and Choice

If you begin to mull over a tempting thought in your mind, your emotions will be affected and the likelihood of yielding to that temptation is increased. The fact that our emotions are a product of our thought lives is the general opinion of mental health workers. We can't directly control our feelings, but we can control what we think. That is why the mind is the control center of all activities. You don't do anything without first thinking it. The physical and emotional responses to our thoughts may be so fast that we could think we have no control over the process, but we do. Every believer has a No button. 'For as he thinks within himself, so he is' (Prov. 23:7).

If what we think does not reflect truth, then what we feel does not reflect reality. Suppose on Monday you heard a rumor around the office that you were going to get laid off on Friday. You become more and more anxious each day. Then on Thursday you receive a memo from your boss asking you to go to his office at 10:00 A.M. on Friday. Your mind is entertaining all kinds of thoughts such as, *Walk in there and hand him your resignation, or Why wait until tomorrow?* Tell him off today.' Friday comes and you are a bundle of nerves. When you open the door to his office, the top brass of the company shout in unison, 'Surprise, you have just been promoted to top management!'

When you thought you would be fired, your feelings of anger did not conform to reality because what you believed wasn't true. The joy and relief you felt after the promotion did conform to reality because then you knew the truth. Many Christians don't feel saved, don't feel God loves them because of old thoughts raised against the knowledge of God. When we tear down those strongholds and take every thought captive in obedience to Christ, our emotions will begin to conform to the reality of God's love. If we choose to believe the lie, our emotions will take us further down the temptation trail.

Action, Habit and Stronghold

Once your consideration of a temptation triggers an emotional response leading to a Plan B choice, you will act upon that choice and own that behavior. You may resent your actions or claim you are not responsible for what you do. However, you *are* responsible for your actions at this stage because you will have failed to take a tempting thought captive when it first appeared at the threshold of your mind.

People who study human behavior tell us that if you continue to repeat an act for six weeks, you will form a habit. If you exercise that habit long enough, a stronghold will be established. Once a stronghold of thought and response is entrenched in your mind, your ability to choose and to act contrary to that pattern is very difficult. It is like driving an old truck down the same dirt road for so long that deep ruts are established. After a while, you won't even have to steer the truck. It will naturally stay in the ruts of the road and any attempt to steer out of them will be met with resistance.

A stronghold is a mental habit pattern. It is memory traces burned into our minds over time or by the intensity of traumatic experiences. For instance, inferiority is a stronghold. Nobody is born inferior to anyone else, but you could be struggling with an inferiority complex if you kept getting the message from the world that everyone is stronger, smarter and prettier than you.

Being the adult child of an alcoholic can be the basis for a mental stronghold. Suppose three boys were raised in a home in which the father becomes an alcoholic. When the father comes home drunk and belligerent every night, the oldest son thinks he is big enough to stand up for himself. He says to his father, 'You lay one hand on me, mister, and you're in trouble.'

The middle child doesn't believe he can stand up to his father so he accommodates and becomes the classic enabler. He greets him by saying, 'Hi, Dad. Are you feeling okay? Can I get you anything, Dad? Do you want me to call anybody?'

The youngest son is totally intimidated by his father. When Dad comes home, he scurries out of sight and hides in the closet or under the bed. He stays clear of his dad and avoids conflict.

Twenty years later their father is long gone and these three men are confronted with a hostile situation. How do you think they will respond? The oldest one will fight; the middle one will appease; and the youngest one will run away. That is the way they learned to handle hostility. Their deeply ingrained patterns of thinking and responding have formed strongholds in their minds.

Hostility is a stronghold. The man or woman who struggled with hostile thoughts and behavior learned to be pugnacious or argumentative when threatened. That is how he or she learned to cope in difficult situations. He or she will not find it easy to learn to love his or her enemy, bless those who curse him or her and turn the other cheek.

Homosexuality is a stronghold. In God's eyes there is no such thing as a homosexual. He created us male and female. However, homosexual thoughts, feelings and behavior can usually be traced to past negative experiences or tempting thoughts. Such experiences precipitate sexual feelings, fantasies and disorientations, causing some to believe a lie about their sexual identity.

Anorexia and bulimia are mental strongholds. Eating disorders have little to do with food. A 95-pound woman standing in front of a mirror believes she is fat and can't see the deception! She is the victim of negative thought patterns about herself that have been burned into her mind over time, or they could have originated during traumatic experiences such as rape or incest.

Renewing the Mind

Do we have to remain victims of these mental strongholds for the rest of our lives? Absolutely not! If we have been trained wrong, can we be retrained? If we have learned to believe a lie, can we now choose to believe the truth? If we have programmed our computers wrong, can they be reprogrammed? Absolutely, but we have to want to renew our minds. How? Our lives are transformed as we renew our minds through the hearing of God's Word, Bible studies, personal discipleship and Christ-centered counseling (see Rom. 12:2). Because some of these strongholds are thoughts raised against the knowledge of God (see 2 Cor. 10:5), learning to know God as a loving Father and yourself as His accepted child is a starting place.

More is going on in your mind than prior negative conditioning. You are not just up against the world system in which you were raised and the resultant flesh patterns you have chosen to adopt. You are also up against the devil who is scheming to fill your mind with thoughts that are opposed to God's plan for you.

In addition to previous thoughts that formed mental strongholds, we have the present-day responsibility to manage our thoughts according to 2 Corinthians 10:5: 'We are taking every thought [noema] captive to the obedience of Christ.' Why do these thoughts need to be taken captive? Because they are contrary to God's ways and they may be the enemy's thoughts.

Notice how Paul uses the word 'thoughts' (noema) in 2 Corinthians in relation to Satan's activity. In 3:14 and 4:4, Paul reveals that Satan is behind the spiritual hardness and blindness of unbelievers: 'But their minds [*noema*] were hardened.... The god of this world has blinded the minds [noema] of the unbelieving.'

Paul also states that Satan is deceiving and dividing believers: 'I am afraid, lest as the serpent deceived Eve by his craftiness, your minds [noema] should be led astray from the simplicity and purity of devotion to Christ' (2 Cor. 11:3). We are not ignorant of his [Satan's] schemes [noema]' (2 Cor. 2:11).

Satan's strategy is to introduce his thoughts and ideas into your mind and deceive you into believing they are yours. It happened to King David. Satan 'moved David to number Israel' (1 Chron. 21:1), an act God had forbidden, and David acted on Satan's idea. Did Satan manifest himself to David and audibly say, 'I want you to number Israel'? I doubt it. David was a godly man and he wouldn't have obeyed Satan. What if Satan slipped the idea into David's mind in first-person singular? What if the thought came to David as, 'I need to know how large my army is; I think I'll count the troops'? These were David's thoughts; at least he thought they were, but that isn't what Scripture says.

If Satan can place a thought in your mind — and he can — it isn't much more of a trick for him to make you think it is your idea. If you knew it was Satan, you would reject the thought, wouldn't you? When he disguises his suggestions as your thoughts and ideas, however, you are more likely to accept them. That is his primary deception.

I doubt that Judas initially realized it was Satan's idea to betray Jesus, but Scripture clearly reveals it was. 'And during supper, the devil having already put into the heart of Judas Iscariot, the son of Simon, to betray Him' (John 13:2). Judas probably thought he was prompting Jesus to deliver Israel from the Romans. The fact that Judas was a thief was what made him vulnerable to Satan.

Ananias and Sapphira might have thought it was their idea to withhold some of their offering while getting the strokes and attention from others who believed they had given everything. If they knew it was Satan's idea, they probably wouldn't have done it, but Scripture clearly reveals the source of their thoughts. 'Peter said, "Ananias, why has Satan filled your heart to lie to the Holy Spirit, and to keep back some of the price of the land?"' (Acts 5:3).

One of our Talbot students brought Tina to me for counseling. Tina was experiencing tremendous emotional difficulty as the result of an incredible background. As a child and teenager, she had witnessed sacrificial and ritual abuse and had repeatedly been violated sexually by her father, her brother and her brother's friend. She watched as her little pet puppy dog was sacrificed as a burnt offering in satanic worship.

Her hope for escaping her background was to enter the field of psychology. She finished her master's degree and tried to enroll in a doctoral program, but her personal life was in shambles.

I shared with Tina that Jesus Christ could set her free if she would open her life to Him. 'Would you like to make that decision for Christ?' I asked.

She shook her head. 'I'll do it later.'

Having heard Tina's story, I was suspicious of what was going on in her mind. 'Tina, are you hearing opposing thoughts to what I have been saying? They could be threatening you or me.'

'Yes,' Tina answered, her face blanched with shock and amazement.

'You're being told a lie, Tina, and Satan is the father of lies.' I shared with her further from God's Word, and within 10 minutes she gave her heart to Christ.

If Satan can get you to believe a lie, you can lose some element of control in your life. Suppose I was devious and persuaded you to believe a lie. Would believing that lie have some effect on your life? Suppose I started a rumor that your spouse was unfaithful; and you heard it. Would believing that lie affect how you felt about your husband and how you related to him? Therefore, if you fail to take every thought captive to the obedience of Christ, you may be allowing Satan to influence your life in a negative direction.

Expose the Lie and You Win the Battle

Satan is a defeated foe; therefore, his power is limited, but he still has the ability to deceive 'the whole world' (Rev. 12:9). Jesus said: 'The devil... does not stand in the truth, because there is no truth in him. Whenever he speaks a lie, he speaks from his own nature; for he is a liar, and the father of lies' (John 8:44). Satan has no authority or power over you except what you yield to him when you are deceived into believing his lies.

How much deception is actually going on in Christians today I can only speculate. In my ministry I encounter false beliefs in nearly every counseling session. Many Christians are hearing voices in their minds, but they are afraid to tell anyone for fear others will think they are going crazy.

Most Christians I counsel are plagued by difficulties in their thoughts that negatively affect their personal lives and devotion to God. These mental distractions usually reflect their own flesh patterns, but they could also reveal a spiritual battle for the mind that Paul warned us about: 'But the Spirit explicitly says that in later times some will fall away from the faith, paying attention to deceitful spirits and doctrines of demons' (1 Tim. 4:1).

Because Satan's primary weapon is the lie, your defense against him is the truth. Dealing with Satan is not a power encounter; it is a truth encounter. When you expose Satan's lie with God's truth, his power is broken. That is why Jesus said, 'You shall know the truth, and the truth shall make you free' (John 8:32). That is why He prayed, 'My prayer is not that you take them out of the world but that you protect them from the evil one. Sanctify them by the truth; your word is truth' (17:15,17, NIV). That is why the first piece of armor Paul mentions for standing against the schemes of the devil is 'the belt of truth' (Eph. 6:14, NIV).

Satan's lie cannot withstand the truth any more than the darkness of night can withstand the light of the rising sun. We are not called to dispel the darkness; we are called to turn on the light. Deceiving spirits are like cockroaches. They come out only at night, and when you turn on the light, they head for the shadows.

Winning the Battle for Our Minds

First, you must 'be transformed by the renewing of your mind' (Rom. 12:2). How do you renew your mind? By filling it with God's Word. To win the battle for your mind you must 'let the peace of Christ rule in your hearts' (Col. 3:15) and 'let the word of Christ richly dwell within you' (v. 16). As you continue to stockpile your mind with God's truth, you will equip yourself to recognize the lie and take it captive.

Think of your mind as a pot full of coffee. Because of what you have put into it, the coffeepot is dark and smelly. You desire your mind to be like clear water again, the way it was before you put the coffee into the pot. There is no way you can filter out the coffee once it has been put inside (no delete button).

Now imagine a bowl of crystal-clear ice, alongside the coffeepot, that says on it 'The Word of God.' There is no way you can dump the whole bowl in at once, but you can put in a cube every day. If you did that long enough, you wouldn't be able to taste, smell or even see the coffee you had originally put inside, even though it is still there. That will work as long as you don't put in a teaspoon of lies and filth along with the cube of ice.

Second, Peter directs us to prepare our 'minds for action' (1 Pet. 1:13). Do away with fruitless fantasy. To imagine yourself doing something without ever doing it is dangerous. You will lose touch with reality. The mind cannot distinguish over a long time period something that has been vividly imagined and something that really happened. If you tell a lie long enough, you may start to think it is true. Scripture always tells us to use our minds actively, never passively, and to direct our thoughts externally, never internally. The devil will seek to bypass your mind, but God works through it.

Third, take 'every thought captive to the obedience of Christ' (2 Cor. 10:5). Practise threshold, first-frame thinking. Evaluate every thought by the truth and don't even consider tempting, accusing or lying thoughts. Should you rebuke every negative thought? No! That is like being in the middle of a pond with 12 corks floating around you, and your entire life's purpose is to tread water and keep the corks submerged. Ignore the stupid corks and swim to shore. Choose the truth and keep choosing it until it becomes the normal pattern of your life.

Fourth, turn to God when you are having anxious thoughts. 'Be anxious for nothing, but in everything by prayer and supplication with thanksgiving let your requests be made known to God' (Phil. 4:6). When your commitment to Plan A is being challenged by Plan B thoughts from the world, the flesh or the devil, bring it to God in prayer. By doing so, you are acknowledging God and exposing your thoughts to His truth. Your double mindedness will dissolve 'and the peace of God...shall guard your hearts and your minds [noema] in Christ Jesus' (v. 7).

Fifth, assume your responsibility to choose the truth and commit yourself to live accordingly.

> Finally, brethren, whatever is true, whatever is honorable, whatever is right, whatever is pure, whatever is lovely, whatever is of good repute, if there is any excellence and if anything worthy of praise, let your mind dwell on these things. The things you have learned and received and heard and seen in me, practice these things; and the God of peace shall be with you (vv. 8,9).

The following story is a wonderful example of what can happen to a Christian when the strongholds of the mind are overthrown by God's truth.

Jeannie is a beautiful and talented woman in her mid--30s. An active Christian for 23 years, she sings in a professional singing group, writes music, leads worship at her church and oversees a discipleship group.

Jeannie attended one of my conferences. She was struggling with bulimia, having been in bondage to the strongholds of food and fear for 11 years. When she was home alone she was held captive by Satan's lies about food, her appearance and sense of worth for hours at a time. She was so fearful that when her husband was gone for a night, she slept on the couch and kept on all the house lights. She had submitted to counseling without success. All the while she believed that the thoughts prompting her to induce vomiting were her own, based on a traumatic experience from her childhood. I happened to be looking at Jeannie — quite unintentionally — when I said, 'Every person I know with an eating disorder has been the victim of a stronghold based on the lies of Satan.'

'You have no idea how that statement impacted my life,' she told me the next morning. 'I have been battling myself all these years, and I suddenly understood that my enemy was not me but Satan. That was the most profound truth I have ever heard. It was like I had been blind for 11 years and could suddenly see. I cried all the way home. When the old thoughts came back last night, I simply rejected them for the truth. For the first night in years I was able to go to sleep without vomiting.'

Two weeks later, Jeannie sent me the following note:

Dear Dr. Anderson,

I can't tell you all the wonderful things the Lord has done for me through the truth you shared at your conference. My relationship with the Lord is so different. Now that I'm aware of the enemy and my victory over him in Christ, my gratitude for our powerful and gracious Savior is *real*. I can't listen to songs about Him without weeping. I can barely lead others in songs of worship without weeping for joy. The truth has set me free in my walk with Christ.

Scripture now leaps off the page, whereas it was so scrambled for me before. I can sleep at night without fear, even when my husband is gone. I can be at home all day with a kitchen full of food and be in peace. When a temptation or lie pops up, I can fend it off quickly with truth. You may not realize the freedom this brings... I used to be in bondage to those lies for hours and hours and hours of my precious time and life, always fearing food.

And here is an incredible change, for the first time in my life I feel like I own my relationship with the Lord. It is no longer the product of my pastor's words or an attempt to reproduce another Christian's walk... it's mine! I'm beginning to understand how very powerful the Holy Spirit is, and how useless I am without prayer. I can't get enough.

Sincerely in Christ,

Jeannie

10
You Must Be
Real to Be Right

I met Judy when I was fresh out of seminary and ministering in the college department of a very large church. She was a 26-year-old university graduate who had a teaching credential, but she looked like a flower child from the '60s. She wore tattered jeans and no shoes, and she carried a well-used Bible.

Judy was a church hopper and attended a women's Bible study class that met in our church. She had sought counseling from the leader of the class several times about her many problems. When the leader learned that Judy had been institutionalized three times in the previous five years as a paranoid schizophrenic, she felt totally inadequate to counsel her. So she asked if I would see Judy. Although I had no formal training in this area of counseling, I agreed to talk to her.

When Judy told me her story, she had difficulty remembering the details of the last several years. I tried to give her a few simple psychological tests, but she couldn't handle them. As we neared the end of our appointment, I felt frustrated because I was clueless about how to help her.

I said, 'I want to meet with you again, but in the meantime I would like you to submit to the authority of this church.'

As soon as I said that, Judy jumped up and headed for the door. 'I've got to get out of here,' she said.

I believe the Lord prompted me to ask, 'Judy, is Jesus your Lord?'

She wheeled around abruptly at the door and snarled

through clenched teeth, 'You ask Jesus who my lord is.' Then she stormed out.

I followed her down the hall and continued to ask her if Jesus was her Lord. Each time she responded by telling me to ask Jesus who her lord was. Finally I caught up with her and asked her again, 'Judy, is Jesus your Lord?'

This time when she faced me her countenance had completely changed. 'Yes,' she said.

'Can we go back to my office and talk about it?' I asked, not really sure what I was going to say.

'Sure,' she responded.

When we were back in my office I said, 'Judy, do you know that there is a battle going on for your mind?' She nodded. 'Has anybody ever talked with you about this before?'

'No one I've talked to has brought it up. Either they didn't know what's going on inside me or they were afraid to deal with it,' she confessed.

'Well, we're going to talk about it and we're going to deal with it,' I assured her. 'Are you willing to do that with me?' Judy agreed.

We began to meet weekly. I assumed that her problems were either the result of a moral failure in her life or a history of exposure to or participation in the occult. So I quizzed her about the moral area and found no basis for her problems. I asked her if she had ever been involved in the occult. She had never even read a book on the subject. By this time I was really scratching my head because I couldn't figure out the source of her severe and obvious spiritual conflict.

Then one day we began talking about her family. She described how her father, a noted paediatrician, had divorced her mother and run off with a nurse. Judy's mother and other family members had vented their hatred and frustration openly. Judy, the only Christian in the family, thought she had to be a good witness. She was determined to be the loving, conciliatory daughter. So she kept silent while her emotions tore her insides to shreds.

'Let's talk about your dad,' I suggested.

'I'm not going to talk about my dad,' she snapped. 'If you talk about my dad, I'm out of here.'

'Wait a minute, Judy. If you can't talk about your father here, where can you talk about him? If you don't deal with those emotional issues here, where will you deal with them?'

I discovered two passages of Scripture that added significant insight to Judy's problem-plagued life. The first one is Ephesians 4:26,27: 'Be angry, and yet do not sin; do not let the sun go down on your anger, and do not give the devil an opportunity.' Judy's unresolved anger toward her father was never confessed, and because she had been repressing her anger instead of confronting it, she had given the devil an opportunity, a 'foothold' (NIV) — literally, a place in her life.

The second passage is 1 Peter 5:7,8 (NIV): 'Cast all your anxiety on him [God] because he cares for you. Be self-controlled and alert. Your enemy the devil prowls around like a roaring lion looking for someone to devour.' Instead of casting her anxieties about her father upon the Lord, Judy tried to be spiritual by covering them up. By not being emotionally honest, Judy became spiritually vulnerable.

Judy began to face her unresolved feelings toward her father and work through the problem of forgiveness, which was the crux of her problem. Within a few months, this young woman, whom psychiatrists had given up as hopeless, made significant progress and became involved in the children's ministry at our church.

Your Emotions Reveal Your Beliefs

Your emotions play a major role in the process of renewing your mind. In a general sense, your emotions are a product of your thought life. If you are not thinking right, if your mind is not being renewed, if you are not perceiving God and His Word properly, it will show up in your emotional life. If you fail to acknowledge your emotions appropriately, you may become spiritually vulnerable.

One of the best scriptural illustrations of the relationship between beliefs and emotions is found in Lamentations 3. Notice Jeremiah's expression of despair as he wrongly perceives that God is against him and that He is the cause of his physical problems:

> I am the man who has seen affliction because of the rod of His wrath. He has driven me and made me walk in darkness and not in light. Surely against me He has turned His hand repeatedly all the day. He has caused my flesh and my skin to waste away, He has broken my bones. He has besieged and encompassed me with bitterness and hardship. In dark places He has made me dwell, like those who have long been dead (vv. 1-6).

Listen to his feelings of entrapment and fear:

> He has walled me in so that I cannot go out; He has made my chain heavy. Even when I cry out and call for help, He shuts out my prayer. He has blocked my ways with hewn stone; He has made my paths crooked. He is to me like a bear lying in wait, like a lion in secret places. He has turned aside my ways and torn me to pieces; He has made me desolate. So I say, 'My strength has perished, and so has my hope from the Lord' (vv. 7-11,18).

If your hope was in God, and these words were a correct portrayal of God, you would be depressed, too. What was Jeremiah's problem? What he believed about God wasn't true. God wasn't the cause of his affliction. God didn't make him walk in darkness. God wasn't a wild beast waiting to devour him. Jeremiah wasn't thinking right or interpreting his circumstances right, so he wasn't feeling or living right.

Then, surprisingly, Jeremiah began to sing a different tune:

> Remember my affliction and my wandering, the wormwood and bitterness. Surely my soul remembers and is bowed down within me. This I recall to my mind, therefore I have hope. The Lord's lovingkindnesses indeed never cease, for His compassions never fail. They are new every morning; great is Thy faithfulness. 'The Lord is my portion,' says my soul, 'therefore I have hope in Him' (vv. 19-24).

What a turnaround! Did God change? Did Jeremiah's circumstances change? No. What he thought about God changed and his emotions followed suit.

You are not shaped as much by your environment as you are by your perception of your environment. Life's events don't determine who you are; God determines who you are, and your interpretation of life's events determines how well you will handle the pressures of life.

We are tempted to say, 'He made me so mad!' or 'I wasn't depressed until she showed up!' That's like saying, 'I have no control over my emotions or my will.' In reality we have very little control over our emotions, but we do have control over our thoughts, and our thoughts determine our feelings and our responses. That is why it is so important that you fill your mind with the knowledge of God and His Word. You need to see life from God's perspective and respond accordingly.

Remember, if what you believe does not reflect truth, then what you feel does not reflect reality. Telling people they shouldn't feel the way they do is a subtle form of rejection. They can do little about how they feel. It would be better to say, 'I can sense your pain and anger, but I'm not sure you understand the whole situation or have all the facts. Let me share my observations and then let's see how you feel.'

For example, suppose your dream of owning your own home was in the hands of a lending institution that was screening your application for financing. All your friends are praying for the loan to be approved. You arrive home one evening to find a message on your phone's answering machine that you didn't qualify. How would you feel? Angry? Depressed? Frustrated?

Now suppose you are getting ready to break the bad news to your spouse that your dream house is still only a dream. Then you listen to the next message on the machine that tells you the first message was a mistake. You actually did qualify! How would you feel now? Elated! What you first believed didn't reflect truth, so what you felt didn't reflect reality.

Imagine the real estate agent, who knows that you qualified, stopping by to congratulate you before you heard the second message on the machine. He expects to find you overjoyed, but instead you are in despair. 'Why are you depressed? You should be happy.' His encouragement is meaningless until he tells you the truth about your loan.

The order of Scripture is to know the truth, believe it, live accordingly by faith, and let your emotions be a product of your trust in God and your obedience to Him. What kind of a life would you live if you believed what you felt instead of the truth? Your life would be as inconsistent as your feelings.

Right after the Fall God said to Cain, 'Why are you angry? And why has your countenance fallen? If you do well, will not your countenance be lifted up?' (Gen. 4:6,7). In the New Testament Jesus said, 'If you know these things, you are blessed if you do them' (John 13:17). In other words, you don't feel your way into good behavior; you behave your way into good feelings.

Don't Ignore the Warning Signs of Your Emotions

I played sports as a young man and I have the scars on my knees to prove it. The incision of my first knee surgery cut across a nerve and I had no feeling around that area of my leg for several months. Sometimes I would sit down to watch TV and, without thinking, rest a cup of hot coffee on my numb knee. I couldn't feel anything, but before long I could sure smell something: my skin burning! For a while I had a neat little brown ring on the top of my knee, the result of not being able to feel anything there.

Your emotions are to your soul what your physical feelings are to your body. Nobody in his or her right mind enjoys pain. If you didn't feel pain, you would be in danger of serious injury and infection. If you didn't feel anger, sorrow or joy, your soul would be in trouble. Emotions are God's indicators to let you know what is going on inside. They are neither good nor bad; they are amoral, just part of your humanity. Just as you respond to the warnings of physical pain, so you need to learn to respond to your emotional indicators.

Someone has likened emotions to the red light on the dashboard of a car indicating an engine problem. You can respond to the red light's warning in several ways. You can cover it with a piece of duct tape. 'I can't see the light now,' you say, 'so I don't have to think about the problem.' You can smash the light with a hammer. 'That'll teach you for glaring in my face!' Or you can respond to the light as the manufacturers intended by looking under the hood and fixing the problem.

You have the same three options in responding to your emotions. You can respond by covering them, ignoring them or stifling them. That is called *suppression*. You can respond by thoughtlessly lashing out, giving someone a piece of your mind or flying off the handle. I call that *indiscriminate expres-*

sion. Or you can peer inside to see what is going on. That is called *acknowledgment.*

The Duct Tape of Suppression

One of the members of our church had a son who went to college to become an architect. During his third year in school, Doug had some kind of a breakdown. His parents brought him home, but Doug wasn't getting better. They didn't know what to do, so they committed him to a mental hospital — against his will — for three weeks of observation. Doug never forgave his parents for putting him into the hospital.

By the time I met him four years later, Doug was an angry, bitter young man. He worked part-time as a draftsman, but he was basically supported by his parents. He heard voices inside his head and he dialogued with them. He spent much of his time outside talking to what nobody else could see. Nobody seemed to be able to help him. His parents asked if I would talk to him, and I agreed.

I spent three months with Doug trying to help him accept himself and own up to his feelings. I asked, 'How do you feel about your parents?'

'I love my parents,' he replied. Doug loathed his parents and his parents could sense it.

'Why do you love your parents?' I pressed.

'Because the Bible says we should love our parents.'

Whenever I suggested the possibility that he hated his parents, Doug would deny it. Finally I asked him, 'Would you agree with me that it's possible for a Christian to feel the emotion of hatred?'

'Well, maybe some could feel that way,' he consented. 'But not me.'

Apparently my probing crowded Doug too closely because he never talked to me again.

Suppression is a conscious denial of feelings (repression is an *un*conscious denial). Those who suppress their emotions ignore their feelings and choose not to confront them. As illustrated by the experiences of Doug and Judy, suppression is an unhealthy response to your emotions.

King David had something to say about the negative effect of suppressing his feelings in his relationship with God:

> When I kept silent, my bones wasted away through my groaning all day long. Therefore let everyone who is godly pray to you while you may be found; surely when the mighty waters rise, they will not reach him (Ps. 32:3,6, NIV).

David is not saying that God takes Himself out of our reach. When extraneous circumstances loom larger to you than God, it will not take long for your emotions to overcome you. When suppressed emotions build up within you like 'mighty waters,' you are less likely to turn to God. You will be driven by your emotions. It is important to be honest with God while you can, because if you bottle up your feelings too long, they will dominate what drives your life.

David also commented on the effect of suppression on relationships with people:

> I said, 'I will guard my ways, that I may not sin with my tongue; I will guard my mouth as with a muzzle, while the wicked are in my presence.' I was dumb and silent, I refrained even from good; and my sorrow grew worse (39:1,2).

Emotional suppression may be one of the major reasons most people are sick for psychosomatic reasons. When David kept quiet about his sins, his 'vitality was drained away as with the fever heat of summer' (32:4). You never bury dead feelings; you bury them alive and they will surface in some way that is not healthy. Suppressing our emotions leads to dishonest communication and is physically unhealthy.

The Hammer of Indiscriminate Expression

Another unhealthy way to respond to emotions is to thoughtlessly express everything you feel. Indiscriminately telling anybody and everybody exactly how you feel is usually unhealthy for the other person. The apostle Peter is a great example. Peter was the John Wayne of the New Testament — a real door slammer. He had no problem telling anyone what was on his mind or how he felt. I like to refer to him as the one-legged apostle because he always had one foot in his mouth.

Peter's indiscriminate expression of his emotions got him into trouble more than once. One minute he makes the greatest confession of all time: 'Thou art the Christ, the Son of the living God' (Matt. 16:16). A few minutes later Peter tells Jesus He doesn't know what He is doing, and Jesus has to rebuke him: 'Get behind Me, Satan!' (vv. 22,23).

It was Peter who missed the point on the Mount of Transfiguration by suggesting they build three tabernacles to honor Moses, Elijah and the Master. It was Peter who impulsively whacked off the ear of Caiaphas's servant during Jesus' arrest in Gethsemane. It was also Peter who promised to follow Jesus anywhere, even to death. Then only hours later Peter swore that he never knew Him. The fact that Peter later became the spokesperson for the Early Church is evidence of the powerful transformation effected by the Holy Spirit.

Indiscriminate expression of emotions may be somewhat healthy for you, but it is usually unhealthy for others around you. 'There, I'm glad I got that off my chest,' you may say after an outburst. In the process though, you just destroyed your wife, husband or children.

James warned: 'But let everyone be quick to hear, slow to speak and slow to anger; for the anger of man does not achieve the righteousness of God' (Jas. 1:19,20). Paul admonished: 'Be angry, and yet do not sin' (Eph. 4:26). If you wish to be angry and not sin, then be angry the way Christ was: be angry at sin. Turn over the tables; don't attack the money changers.

The Openness of Acknowledgment

Nancy was a college student in another city who drove to Los Angeles to talk to me about her difficult relationship with her mother. We ended up talking about Nancy's inability to express the anger and resentment she felt in the relationship. 'My roommate gets to the point sometimes where she just explodes emotionally to let off steam. I have deep feelings, too, but I'm not sure that a Christian is supposed to let off steam.'

I opened my Bible to Psalm 109 and read the following verses to her:

> O God of my praise, do not be silent! For they have opened the wicked and deceitful mouth against me; they have spoken against me with a lying tongue. They have also surrounded me with words of hatred, and fought against me without cause. In return for my love they act as my accusers; but I am in prayer. Thus they have repaid me evil for good, and hatred for my love.
>
> Appoint a wicked man over him; and let an accuser stand at his right hand. When he is judged, let him come forth guilty; and let his prayer become sin. Let his days be few; let another take his office. Let his children be fatherless, and his wife a widow. Let his children wander about and beg; and let them seek sustenance far from their ruined homes. Let the creditor seize all that he has; and let strangers plunder the product of his labor. Let there be none to extend lovingkindness to him, nor any to be gracious to his fatherless children. Let his posterity be cut off; in a following generation let their name be blotted out (vv. 1-13).

'What's that doing in the Bible?' Nancy gasped. 'How could David pray all those evil things about his enemy? How could he talk to God that way? That's pure hatred.'

'David's words didn't surprise God,' I answered. 'God already knew what he was thinking and feeling. David was simply expressing his pain and anger honestly to his God who understood how he felt and accepted him where he was.'

After a couple of thoughtful moments Nancy asked, 'Does that mean it's okay to do what I do?'

'What do you do?'

'Well,' she said, looking slightly embarrassed, 'when the pressure builds up inside me, I get in my car and just drive. I scream and holler and shout and kick. When I get back to the dorm, I usually feel much better.'

I encouraged Nancy that when she is able to dump her hurt and hatred before God, she probably won't dump it on her roommate or her mother in a destructive way. I also reminded her that David was as honest about his need for God as he was about expressing his feelings. He closed the psalm by praying, 'Help me, O Lord my God…. With my mouth I will give thanks abundantly to the Lord' (vv. 26,30).

I think the way David and Nancy acknowledged their feelings is healthy. Perhaps your prayers at times of emotional stress are not very noble, but they are real and honest before God. If you come to your prayer time feeling angry, depressed or frustrated and then mouth a bunch of pious platitudes as if God doesn't know how you feel, do you think He is pleased? Not unless He has changed His opinion about hypocrisy since the time of the Pharisees. The Pharisees tried to look right on the outside while they were far from right on the inside. They weren't real; they were phonies.

Jesus told His disciples, 'Unless your righteousness surpasses that of the scribes and Pharisees, you shall not enter the kingdom of heaven' (Matt. 5:20). In God's eyes, if you are not real, you are not right. If necessary, God may have to make you real to make you right with Him.

Acknowledging your emotions as a real person is essential for intimate relationships. You shouldn't let off steam just anywhere in front of just anybody. That is indiscriminate expression, and you run the risk of hurting others more than you help yourself — and that is wrong. The biblical pattern seems to suggest you have three friends you can share with deeply. During his travels, Paul had Barnabas, Silas or Timothy to share with. In the Garden of Gethsemane, Jesus expressed His grief to His inner circle of Peter, James and John.

Psychologists tell us it is difficult for people to maintain mental health unless they have at least one person with whom they can be emotionally honest. If you have two or three people like this in your life, you are truly blessed.

Emotional Honesty: How to Dish It Out and How to Take It

Early in my pastoral ministry I received one of those middle-of-the-night telephone calls every pastor dreads: 'Pastor, our son has been in an accident. They don't expect him to live. Could you please come to the hospital?'

I arrived at the hospital about one in the morning. I sat with the parents in the waiting room hoping and praying for the best but fearing the worst. About 4:00 A.M. the doctor came into the waiting room and said, 'We lost him.'

We were devastated. I was so tired and emotionally depleted that instead of offering them words of comfort, I just sat there and cried with them. I couldn't think of anything to say. I never felt so stupid in my life. I thought I had failed the family in their darkest hour.

Soon after the accident the young man's parents moved

away. About five years later they stopped by the church for a visit and took me out to lunch. 'Neil, we'll never forget what you did for us when our son died,' they said. 'We didn't need words; we needed love. We knew you loved us because you cried with us.'

Now looking back, I realized I had done what Jesus would have done. I wept with those who wept. When grief-stricken Mary and Martha greeted Jesus with the news of Lazarus's death, He wept (see John 11:35). Paul commanded, 'Rejoice with those who rejoice, and weep with those who weep' (Rom. 12:15). We are not supposed to instruct those who weep.

One of our challenges in life is to learn how to respond to others when they honestly acknowledge their pain. Job was in pain when he said to his three friends who were less than helpful, 'Do you intend to reprove my words, when the words of one in despair belong to the wind?' (Job 6:26). We should not be listening to what people say in the midst of extreme pain. We should be responding to the pain, not the words that express it. In too many cases we ignore the feelings of hurting people, fixate on their words of despair and then react to what they said or how they said it.

For example, let's say a Christian couple you know loses an infant to crib death. Overcome by grief they ask, 'Why did God do this?' Don't answer that question. First, you don't know the answer. Second, their question is an emotional reaction, not an intellectual inquiry. All that their words reveal is the intensity of their pain. Respond to their emotional pain with empathy. There will be ample time to give theological answers later when the emotional pain of their tragic loss has subsided.

Although words should not be the primary focus in emotional acknowledgment, you can guard your intimate relationships by monitoring how you verbally express your emotions to others. For example, you are having a terrible day at the office, so you call home and say to your wife, 'Honey, I'm having a bear of a day. I won't be home until about six o'clock and I have a meeting at church at seven o'clock. Could you have dinner ready when I get home?' She verbally agrees to your schedule.

When you hit the front door you are physically exhausted and emotionally stressed. On an emotional scale from one to ten, you are a nine. Then you discover your wife doesn't have dinner ready as you requested. 'For crying out loud,' you blaze at her, 'I wanted dinner ready at six o'clock! That's why I called you!'

Is your wife really the cause of your emotional outburst? Not really. You had a terrible day and you were tired, hungry and stressed out before you got home. It is not her fault. Anything could have set you off. You could have just as easily kicked the dog. Yet you level your wife and chalk it up to emotional honesty.

Don't forsake love in your eagerness to be honest. Upon learning that dinner is not ready as you asked, you could say, 'Honey, I'm near the end of my rope physically and emotionally.' That kind of nonaccusatory honesty accomplishes two important things.

First, by not blaming your wife, you let her off the hook. She knows you are not mad at her. Second, because she doesn't have to defend herself, she is free to meet your needs. She can say, 'I'll have dinner ready in about 10 minutes. Go to the bedroom and relax; I'll keep the kids off your back. I'll get you to your meeting on time.'

Suppose you are the wife and you have had a terrible day at home. Your husband comes home whistling a happy tune and asks if dinner is ready. 'What do you mean, "Is dinner ready?"' you explode. 'Do you think all I have to do is cook for you? The kids have been on my back all afternoon and...'

That is emotional honesty, all right, but you are going down in flames and you are taking your husband with you.

Rather, you can say, 'Honey, I've had it. The washing machine broke and the kids were little terrors today. I'm right at the edge.' Your nonaccusatory honesty keeps your husband from needing to defend himself and opens the way for him to say, 'Hey, everybody, it's McDonald's time!'

When it comes to acknowledging emotions with your inner circle, honesty is the best policy, but be sure to speak 'the truth in love' (Eph. 4:15).

Another important guideline for acknowledging and expressing your emotions is to know your limitations. Be aware that if you are at a seven or eight on the emotional scale — angry, tense, anxious, depressed — it is not a good time to make decisions about important matters. Your emotions may push you to resolve what you are struggling against, but you may regret your resolution if you push too hard. You will say things you will later regret. Somebody will get hurt. You are far better off if you recognize your emotional limits and say, 'If we keep talking, I'm going to get angry. May we continue this discussion at another time?'

Realize also that a lot of physical factors will affect your emotional limits. If you are hungry, postpone a potentially emotion-charged discussion until after dinner. If you are tired, get a good night's sleep. Women, be alert that certain times of the month are more conducive to positive emotional expression than others. Husbands, you will be wise to understand your wife's monthly menstrual cycle for the same reason.

The important process of renewing your mind includes managing your emotions by managing your thoughts and acknowledging your feelings honestly and lovingly in your relationships with others. Responding to your emotions properly is an important step in keeping the devil from gaining a foothold in your life.

11

Healing Emotional Wounds from Your Past

Dan and Cindy were a fine, young Christian couple preparing for ministry on the mission field. Then tragedy struck. Cindy was raped by an ugly stranger in the parking lot at night after work. The police were unable to find the rapist, and Cindy had a hard time bringing any closure to the nightmare experience. The trauma was so severe that they moved away from the community where it happened. As hard as she tried to get back to normal life, Cindy couldn't shake the horrible memories and feelings from her experience.

Six months after the rape Dan and Cindy attended a church conference where I was speaking. During the conference, Cindy was in tears as she called me. 'Neil, I just can't get over this thing. I know "God causes all things to work together for good to those who love God" (Rom. 8:28), but how is He going to make rape a good thing? Every time I think about what happened I start to cry.'

'Cindy, I think you are misunderstanding the verse,' I said. 'God will work this out for your good, but He doesn't do it by making a bad thing good. What happened to you was sick and evil. God will enable you to come through this crisis a better person.'

'But I just can't separate myself from my experience and let it go,' she sobbed. 'I've been raped, Neil, and I'll be a victim of that all my life.'

'Cindy, the rape was a terrible tragedy and it has temporarily altered your plans, but it hasn't changed who you are, nor does it have to control your life. But if you only see yourself as a rape victim for the rest of your life, you will never get over your tragedy. You're a child of God. No event or person, good or bad, can rob you of that.

'Cindy, let me share an illustration. Suppose you were sitting in your home when someone drove by and threw something at your house. It did some damage to the siding of the house, and you could never find out who did it. How long would you let that incident bother you?' I asked.

'Well, not very long,' Cindy responded.

'Suppose the object went through the window and damaged some good furniture, and you couldn't find out who did it. How long would you let that bother you?' I asked.

'Probably not very long.'

'Suppose the object also hit you and broke your arm. How long would you let that bother you?'

If I kept making the tragedy a little worse each time, is there a point when one can say, 'That did it! That stepped over the line and that will bother me the rest of my life?' I don't think there is such a point from God's perspective. I don't believe God wants anything in our past to have that kind of control over His children. God doesn't fix our past, but He does set us free from it.

Bad Things Do Happen to Good People

Your story may not be as severe as Cindy's, but all of us have some hurtful, traumatic experiences in our past that have scarred us emotionally. You may have grown up with a physically, emotionally or sexually abusive parent. You may have been severely frightened as a child. You may have suffered through a painful relationship in the past: a broken friendship, the untimely death of a loved one, a divorce. Any number of traumatic events in your past can leave you holding a lot of emotional baggage. Those experiences are buried in our memories and available for instant recall.

For example, you reacted emotionally to the topic of rape when you read Cindy's story at the start of this chapter. If you or a close loved one have been recently raped, just reading the story sent you soaring to an eight or nine on an emotional scale of ten. You immediately felt a surge of anger, hatred, fear or righteous indignation. However, if you have only read about rape victims but have never been one, met one or counseled one, your response would be more like a two or three on the emotional scale.

Something as simple as a name can prompt an emotional response. If your kind, loving grandfather was named Bill, you probably have a favorable emotional reaction to other people named Bill. However, if you had a teacher named Bill who was a tyrant or if the school bully was named Bill, your initial reaction to the Bills in your life is probably negative. If your spouse suggests, 'Let's name our first child Bill,' you might react, 'Over my dead body!'

I call the residual effect of past traumas *primary emotions*. The intensity of your primary emotions is determined by your previous life history. The more traumatic your experience, the more intense will be your primary emotion. Notice the sequence of events:

Previous Life History
(Determines the intensity of primary emotions)

Present Event
(Triggers the primary emotion)

Primary Emotion

Mental Evaluation
(The management stage)

Secondary Emotion
(The result of your thought process
and primary emotion)

Many of these primary emotions will lie dormant within you and have little effect on your life until something triggers them. Have you ever started a topic of conversation that upset someone and sent him storming out of the room? *What set him off?* you wondered. He was set off by the topic of your conversation. You touched the 'button' that connected him to his past. Just touching the emotional core may bring tears to a person's eyes. The trigger is any present event that can be associated with past conflicts.

For instance, a lady once told me, 'Every time I hear a siren, I freak out!'

'How long has that been going on?' I asked.

'About 10 years,' she responded.

'What happened 10 years ago?' I asked.

'I was raped,' she said.

Obviously, she heard a siren when she was victimized and 10 years later the sound of a siren triggers an emotional response.

Most people try to control their primary emotions by avoiding any people or events that trigger them. 'I'm not going to go there if he is going to be there.' 'I can't watch that kind of a movie because it comes too close to home.' 'I don't want to talk about that subject.'

The problem is, you can't isolate yourself completely from everything that may set off an emotional response. You are bound to see something on TV or hear something in a conversation that will bring to mind your unpleasant experience. Something in your past is unresolved and therefore still has a hold on you.

Learning to Resolve Primary Emotions

You have no control over a primary emotion when it is triggered in the present, because it is rooted in the past.

Therefore, it doesn't do any good to feel guilty about something you can't control. You can, however, stabilize the primary emotion by evaluating it in light of present circumstances. For example, suppose you meet a man named Bill. He looks like the Bill who used to beat you up as a child. Although he is not the same person, your primary emotion will be triggered. So you quickly tell yourself, 'This is not the same Bill; give him the benefit of the doubt.' This mental evaluation produces a *secondary emotion* that is a combination of the past and the present.

You have done this thousands of times, and you have also helped others do the same. When people fly off the handle, you try to help them cool down by talking to them. You are helping them gain control of themselves by making them think, by putting the present situation in perspective.

Notice how this works the next time you are watching a football game and tempers explode on the field. One player grabs an enraged teammate and says, 'Listen, Meathead, you're going to cost us a 15-yard penalty and perhaps the game if you don't simmer down.' He wants his teammate to play under control.

Some Christians assert that the past doesn't have any effect on them because they are new creations in Christ. I would have to disagree. Either they are extremely fortunate to have a conflict-free past or they are living in denial. Those who have had major traumas and have learned to resolve them in Christ know how devastating past experiences can be.

Most people I counsel have had major traumas in their past. Some have been abused to such an extent that they have no conscious memory of their experiences. Others constantly avoid anything that will stimulate those painful memories. Most don't know how to resolve those past experiences, so they have developed myriad defense mechanisms to cope.

Some live in denial, others rationalize their problems or try to suppress the pain by an excess of food, drugs or sex.

A major role of psychotherapy is to determine the root of primary emotions. Sometimes psychotherapists resort to hypnosis or drug therapy to get at the sources of their clients' problems. I am personally against drug-induced programs or the use of hypnosis to restore a repressed memory. Such methods bypass the mind of the client and ignore the presence of God. Only God can set a captive free and bind up the brokenhearted. He is the Wonderful Counselor.

The answer for repressed memories is found in Psalm 139:23,24: 'Search me, O God, and know my heart; try me and know my anxious thoughts; and see if there be any hurtful way in me, and lead me in the everlasting way.' God knows about the hidden hurts within you that you may not be able to see. When you ask God to search your heart, He will expose those dark areas of your past and bring them to light at the right time. The Holy Spirit 'will guide you into all the truth' (John 16:13), and that truth will set you free (see John 8:31,32).

See Your Past in the Light of Who You Are in Christ

How does God intend you to resolve past experiences? In two ways. First, understand that you are no longer a product of your past. You are a new creation in Christ: a product of Christ's work on the cross. You have the privilege of evaluating your past experience in the light of who you are today, as opposed to who you were then. The intensity of the primary emotion was established by how you perceived the event at the time it happened. People are not in bondage to past traumas. They are in bondage to the lies they believed about themselves, God and how to live as a result of the trauma. That is why truth sets you free.

As a Christian, you are literally a new creature in Christ. Old things, including the traumas of your past, 'passed away' (2 Cor. 5:17). The old you in Adam is gone; the new you in Christ is here to stay. We have all been victimized, but whether we remain victims is up to us. Those primary emotions are rooted in the lies we believed in the past. Now we can be transformed by the renewing of our minds (see Rom. 12:2). The flesh patterns are still imbedded in our minds when we become new creations in Christ, but we can crucify the flesh and choose to walk by the Spirit (see Gal. 5:22-25).

Now that you are in Christ, you can look at those events from the perspective of who you are today. You may be struggling with the question 'Where was God when all this was going on?' The omnipresent God was there and He sent His own Son to redeem you from your past. The truth is, He is in your life right now desiring to set you free from your past. That is the gospel, the good news that Christ has come to set the captives free. Perceiving those events from the perspective of your new identity in Christ is what starts the process of healing those damaged emotions.

One dear Christian missionary I know was struggling with her past because she discovered to her horror that her father was a practising homosexual.

I asked her, 'Knowing that about your father, how does that affect your heritage?'

She started to respond in reference to her natural heritage, but then stopped abruptly. She suddenly realized nothing had changed in her true heritage in Christ. Knowing this, she could face the problems of her earthly family without being emotionally devastated by them. She was relieved when she realized the degree of security she enjoyed in her relationship with God, her true Father. The resulting emotions reflected reality because what she believed about herself corresponded to truth.

Forgive Those Who Have Hurt You in the Past

The second step in resolving past conflicts is to forgive those who have offended you. After encouraging Cindy to deal with the emotional trauma of her rape, I said, 'Cindy, you also need to forgive the man who raped you.'

Cindy's response was typical of many believers who have suffered physical, sexual or emotional pain at the hands of others: 'Why should I forgive him? You don't seem to understand how bad he hurt me.'

Perhaps you have asked the same question. Why should you forgive those who have hurt you in the past?

First, forgiveness is required by God. As soon as Jesus spoke the amen to His model prayer — which included a petition for God's forgiveness — He commented: 'For if you forgive men for their transgressions, your heavenly Father will also forgive you. But if you do not forgive men, then your Father will not forgive your transgressions' (Matt. 6:14,15). We must base our relationships with others on the same criteria on which God bases His relationship with us: love, acceptance and forgiveness (see Matt. 18:21-35).

Second, forgiveness is necessary to avoid entrapment by Satan. I have discovered from my counseling that unforgiveness is the number one avenue Satan uses to gain entrance to believers' lives. Paul encouraged us to forgive 'in order that no advantage be taken of us by Satan; for we are not ignorant of his schemes' (2 Cor. 2:11). I have had the privilege to help people around the world find their freedom in Christ. In every case, forgiveness was an issue and in many cases it was *the* issue that needed to be resolved.

Third, forgiveness is required of all believers who desire to be like Christ. Paul wrote: 'Let all bitterness and wrath and anger and clamor and slander be put away from you, along with all malice. And be kind to one another, tender-hearted, forgiving each other, just as God in Christ also has forgiven you' (Eph. 4:31,32).

What Is Forgiveness?

Forgiving is not forgetting. Forgetting may be a long-term by-product of forgiving, but it is never a means to forgiveness. When God says He will remember our sins no more (see Heb. 10:17), He is not saying 'I will forget them.' God is omniscient; He cannot forget. Rather, He will never use the past against us. He will remove it as far from us as 'the east is from the west' (Ps. 103:12).

Forgiveness does not mean you must tolerate sin. A young wife and mother, attending one of my conferences, told me of her struggle to forgive her mother for continual manipulation and condemnation. She tearfully continued, 'I suppose I can forgive her tonight, but what am I supposed to do when I see her next week? She will be no different. She will undoubtedly try to crowd between me and my family as she always does. Am I supposed to let her keep ruining my life?' No, forgiving someone doesn't mean you must be a doormat to the person's continual sin. I encouraged her to confront her mother lovingly but firmly and to tell her she would no longer tolerate destructive manipulation. It is okay to forgive another's past sins and, at the same time, take a stand against future sins.

Forgiveness does not seek revenge or demand repayment for offenses suffered. 'You mean I'm just supposed to let them off the hook?' you may argue. Yes, you let them off *your* hook realizing that God does not let them off *His* hook. You may feel like exacting justice, but you are not an impartial judge. God is the just Judge who will make everything right in the end. '"Vengeance is Mine, I will repay," says the Lord' (Rom. 12:19). 'But where is the justice?' ask the victims. It is in the crucifixion of Christ. Christ died 'once for all' (Rom. 6:10). He died for his sins, her sins, your sins, my sins.

Forgiveness means resolving to live with the consequences of another person's sin. In reality, you will have to live with the consequences of the offender's sin whether you forgive that person or not. For example, imagine someone in your church says, 'I have gossiped about you all over town. Will you forgive me?' You can't retract gossip any easier than you can put toothpaste back into the tube. You will have to live with the consequences of that person's gossip no matter how you respond. We are all living with the consequences of someone else's sin. We are all living with the consequences of Adam's sin. The only real choice is to live with those consequences in the bondage of bitterness or in the freedom of forgiveness.

Twelve Steps to Forgiveness

The victim may say, 'I can't forgive these people. You don't know how bad they hurt me.' The problem is, they are still hurting you. How do you stop the pain? Forgiveness is what sets us free from the past. What is to be gained in forgiving is freedom. You don't heal in order to forgive. You forgive in order to heal. Forgiveness is to set a captive free and then to realize you were the captive. You don't forgive others for their sake; you do it for your sake. Those you need to forgive may never be aware of your choice to let them off your hook. Forgiveness is the fragrance that is left on the heel that crushed the violet.

Following are 12 steps you can use to walk through the process of forgiving others from your heart. Following these steps will help you unchain yourself from the past and get on with your life:

1. Ask the Lord to reveal to your mind the people you need to forgive. Then write on a sheet of paper the names of those who offended you. Of the hundreds of people who have completed this list in my counseling office, 95 percent put

father and mother as numbers one and two. Three out of the first four names on most lists are close relatives. When making a list, the two most overlooked people are God and yourself. Concerning your relationship with God, only He can forgive your sins, and He has never sinned. We haven't always appropriated that forgiveness, and sometimes we are bitter toward God because we hold false expectations of Him. We need to release God from those false expectations and appropriate God's forgiveness.

2. Acknowledge the hurt and the hate. As you work through the list of people you need to forgive, state specifically for what you are forgiving them (e.g., rejection; deprivation of love; injustice; unfairness; physical, verbal, sexual or emotional abuse; betrayal; neglect and so on). Also state how their offenses made you feel. Remember: It is not a sin to acknowledge the reality of your emotions. God knows exactly how you feel, whether you admit it or not. If you bury your feelings, you will bypass the possibility of forgiveness. You must forgive from your heart.

3. Understand the significance of the Cross. The cross of Christ makes forgiveness legally and morally right. Jesus took upon Himself all the sins of the world — including yours and those of the persons who have offended you — and He died 'once for all' (Heb. 10:10). The heart cries, 'It isn't fair! Where's the justice?' It is in the Cross.

4. Decide you will bear the burden of each person's sin (see Gal. 6:1,2). This means you will not retaliate in the future by using the information about their sin against them (see Prov. 17:9; Luke 6:27-34). All true forgiveness is substitutionary, as was Christ's forgiveness of us. That doesn't mean you tolerate sin or refuse to testify in a court of law. You may have to do that for justice to prevail. Just make sure you have forgiven that person from your heart first.

5. Decide to forgive. Forgiveness is a crisis of the will, a

conscious choice to let the other person off the hook and to free yourself from the past. You may not feel like doing it, but it is necessary for your sake. If God tells you to forgive from your heart, be assured He will enable you to do it. The other person may truly be in the wrong and subject to church discipline or legal action. That is not your primary concern. Your first concern is to receive freedom from your past and stop the pain. Make that decision now; your feelings of forgiveness will follow in time.

6. Take your list to God and pray the following: 'I forgive (*name*) for (*list all the offenses and how they made you feel*).' Stay with each person on the list until every remembered pain has been specifically addressed. That includes every sin of commission as well as omission. If you have felt bitter toward this person for some time, you may want to find a Christian counselor or trusted friend to assist you in the process. Don't say, 'I want to forgive so and so,' or 'Lord, help me to forgive so and so.' That is bypassing your responsibility and choice to forgive.

7. Destroy the list. You are now free. Do not tell the offenders what you have done. Your need to forgive others is between you and God only! The person you may need to forgive could be dead. Forgiveness may lead you to be reconciled to others, but whether or not that happens is not totally dependent upon you. Your freedom in Christ cannot be dependent upon others whom you have no right or ability to control.

8. Do not expect that your decision to forgive will result in major changes in the other persons. Instead, pray for them (see Matt. 5:44) so they, too, may find the freedom of forgiveness (see 2 Cor. 2:7).

9. Try to understand the people you have forgiven, but don't rationalize their behavior. It could lead to incomplete forgiveness. For instance, don't say, 'I forgive my father

because I know he really didn't mean it.' That would be excusing him and bypassing your pain and the need to forgive from the heart.

10. Expect positive results of forgiveness in you. In time you will be able to think about the people without triggering primary emotions. That doesn't mean you will like those who are abusive. It means you are free from them. Old feelings may try to recycle themselves. When that happens, stop and thank God for His provision and don't pick up those old offenses again. You dealt with it; now let it go.

11. Thank God for the lessons you have learned and the maturity you have gained as a result of the offenses and your decision to forgive the offenders (see Rom. 8:28,29).

12. Be sure to accept your part of the blame for the offenses you suffered. Confess your failure to God (see 1 John 1:9) and to others (see Jas. 5:16) and realize that if someone has something against you, you must go to that person and be reconciled (see Matt. 5:23-26).

A Second Touch

One of the greatest personal crises I have faced in the ministry revolved around the problem of forgiveness and a board member I will call Calvin. I struggled to relate to this man, so I asked if he would meet with me weekly. I had only one goal: trying to establish a meaningful relationship with him.

About four months after Calvin and I started meeting, I asked the board if I could lead a tour group from the church to Israel. Calvin's hand shot up. 'I'm against it because, as the tour leader, the pastor will go free, and that's like giving him a bonus.' After assuring Calvin and the board I would pay my own way and use my vacation time for the trip, they agreed.

Despite the burden I carried in my heart about my conflict with Calvin, the trip to Israel was a tremendous spiritual

experience for me. On one of my free days in Jerusalem, I
spent several hours alone in the Church of All Nations pour-
ing out my heart to God about Calvin. I sat there staring at
the rock where Christ reportedly had sweat great drops of
blood as He anticipated taking upon Himself the sins of the
world. I concluded by telling God that if Jesus could take all
the world's sins upon Himself, I could surely endure the sins
of one difficult person. I left that historical monument thinking I had let it go.

Two weeks after I returned, Calvin shifted his attack to
our youth pastor. That did it. I could handle Calvin's resistance to me, but when he started blasting my youth pastor, I
reached the end of my patience. I confronted the board and
demanded they do something about Calvin. If they didn't, I
would resign. Although they agreed with me in private, they
wouldn't stand with me in public, so I decided to resign.

The week before I was going to read my resignation to the
congregation, I got sick. I was flat on my back with a 103.5
temperature and I totally lost my voice. I had never been so
sick before; nor have I since. It doesn't take a genius to recognize that God was not pleased with my decision. When you
are flat on your back, you have nowhere to look but up. So I
began reading the Gospels and came to Mark 8:22-26 where
some people led a blind man to Jesus. After Jesus touched
him, the blind man said, 'I see men... like trees' (v. 24). I got
the message. I was seeing Calvin like a tree, an obstacle in my
path. He was blocking my goal! Oh no he wasn't. I was. I am
the only person on planet Earth who can keep me from being
the person God created me to be. God used that man more
than any other man to make me the pastor God wanted me
to be.

Then Jesus touched the blind man again and he began to
see people as people, not trees. 'Lord, I don't love that man,
but I know you do and I want to. I need a second touch from

You.' God did touch me, and I chose at that moment to forgive Calvin completely.

The next Sunday I went to church, not to resign, but to preach. My voice was still so husky that I almost couldn't speak. I croaked out a message from Mark 8:22-26 about our tendency to be independent in the face of our great need for God and for each other. I confessed to the congregation my own independence and my desire for the Lord to touch me, to help me see people as people and not as obstacles in my path. I explained that there are three kinds of people. Some are blind and need to be led to Jesus. Others see people like trees. They scratch one another or compare their leaves with one another. But we are not trees. We are children of God who are created in His image. Finally, there are those who have been touched by God and consequently see others for who they really are.

At the end of the sermon, I invited anyone who needed a touch from the Lord to join me at the altar. We sang a hymn and people streamed forward. Soon the altar area and the aisles in the front were packed with people. They were going across the aisles to ask forgiveness and to be forgiven. We opened the side doors and people spilled out onto the lawn. Eventually, all but a few people had come forward. It was a revival!

Would you care to guess who was one of the few who did not go forward? To my knowledge Calvin never changed, but I did. I continued to take a stand against what I believed was wrong because I was not about to tolerate sin. I no longer responded in bitterness though. I also learned a hard lesson in life. God is fully capable of cleaning His own fish. My responsibility is to catch them and love them the way Christ loves me. I thank God to this day that God put me flat on my back to make me the pastor He wanted me to be.

12
Dealing with Rejection in Your Relationships

Ruby had experienced more rejection in her 40 years of life than anyone I have ever heard about. She was rejected by her unmarried mother before she was born, miraculously surviving an abortion six months into her mother's pregnancy. Ruby's mother then abandoned her to her father, who in turn gave her to his mother. Ruby's grandmother was involved in a bizarre mixture of religious and occultic practices. So Ruby was raised in an atmosphere of seances and other weird, demonic experiences.

Ruby married at 14 to escape her grandmother's home. By the time she was 21 she had five children, all of whom were convinced by their father that Ruby was no good. Eventually her husband and five children all deserted her. Feeling totally rejected, Ruby unsuccessfully attempted suicide several times. She received Christ during this time, but those who knew her were afraid she would take her own life. 'Don't commit suicide,' they encouraged her. 'Hang on; life will get better.' Yet voices inside her head still taunted Ruby, and an eerie, dark spiritual presence infested her home.

In this condition Ruby came to a weeklong conference I was conducting at her church. On Wednesday night I spoke about forgiveness, encouraging people to list the names of people they needed to forgive. In the middle of the session, Ruby left the room with what appeared to be an asthma attack. In reality it was a spiritual attack.

The next afternoon one of the pastors and I met privately with Ruby to counsel and pray with her. When we began to talk about forgiveness, Ruby brought out the list of names she had compiled — four pages of people who had hurt her and rejected her through the years! No wonder Satan was having a field day in her life. Virtually everyone else had turned her away.

We led her through the steps to forgiveness, and she walked out of the office free in Christ. She realized for the first time that God loves her and will never reject her. She went home thrilled and excited. The evil voices in her head were gone.

Most of us haven't suffered the pervasive rejection Ruby experienced. Everyone knows, however, what it feels like to be criticized and rejected, even by the very people in our lives we want to please. We were born and raised in a worldly environment that chooses favorites and rejects seconds. Because nobody can be the best at everything, we all were ignored, overlooked or rejected at times by parents, teachers, coaches and friends.

Furthermore, because we were born in sin, God also rejected us until we were accepted by Him in Christ at salvation (see Rom. 15:7). Since then, we have been the target of Satan, the accuser of the brethren (see Rev. 12:10), who never ceases to lie to us about how worthless we are to God and others. In this life we all have to live with the pain and pressure of rejection.

When You Are Criticized or Rejected

The thoughts and feelings of rejection that often plague us can be major deterrents to our maturity in Christ. Apart from Christ, we all learned early in life to respond to rejection by taking one of three defensive postures (see Figure 12-A). Even as Christians we can be influenced to react defensively to rejection.

UNDERSTANDING REJECTION
Romans 15:7

**Think or feel
rejected and unloved**

↓

**Determined to please the significant others
to gain their approval**

↓

**More rejection comes resulting in
choosing one of three defense postures**

↓   ↓   ↓

Beat the System*	**Give In to the System***	**Rebel Against the System***
This person basically buys the system and learns to compete or scheme to get ahead and becomes the significant other	Continues the efforts to satisfy others but begins to believe that he or she is rejectable and unlovable	This person fights the system and says, 'I don't need or want your love,' and often behaves or dresses in an objectionable way
Eventually results in more rejection because the ability to perform eventually diminishes	Results in more rejection because acceptance comes less to a person who rejects himself or herself	Results in more rejection because a rebel causes others to be more defensive of the system the rebel rejects

Emotional Results

inability to express feelings emotional insulation perfectionism worries	feelings of worthlessness and inferiority subjectivity introspection self-condemnation	wishing he or she had never been born undisciplined irresponsibility self-hatred bitterness

Attitudes and Reactions Toward God

Refuses to come under God's authority and has little real fellowship with God	Projects earthly father's behavior onto God, unable to trust God	Views God as a tyrant and rebels against Him

*Note: The family system is the most significant, followed by school and society in general.

Figure 12-A

Beat the System

A small percentage of people defend against rejection by buying into the dog-eat-dog world system and learning to compete and scheme to get ahead of the pack. These are the movers and shakers, people who seek to earn their acceptance and strive for significance through their performance. They feel driven to get on top of every situation because winning is their passport to acceptance and significance. They are characterized by perfectionism and emotional insulation and are plagued by anxiety and stress.

Spiritually, the beat-the-system people struggle with the idea of coming under God's authority and have little fellowship with Him. They are prone to controlling and manipulating others and circumstances for their own end, so it is difficult for them to yield control in their lives to God. In our churches, these people jockey to be chairman of the board or the most influential member on a committee. Their motivation may not always be to serve God in this position, however, but to control their world because their sense of worth is dependent upon it. Beat-the-system controllers are often very insecure.

Controlling people's defensive strategy only delays inevitable rejection. Eventually, their ability to control their families, their employees and their churches diminishes, and they are replaced by younger, stronger or more capable controllers. Some survive this midlife crisis, but many who make it to retirement don't enjoy much of it. Studies show that high-powered executives live an average of nine months after they retire. They no longer have any purpose for living.

Give In to the System

'Pastor, I'm a loser,' a high-school boy told me dejectedly. He explained that he wanted to be a star football player but had been cut from the team. Instead of being in the spotlight as an athlete, he had to settle for being a member of the pep band. Compared to star quarterbacks, clarinet players were losers. What a sad commentary on American culture!

The largest group of people respond to rejection as this boy did: by simply giving in to the system. They continue their efforts to try to satisfy others, but their failures prompt them to believe they really are unlovable and unacceptable. The system says the best, the strongest, the most beautiful and the most talented are 'in.' Those who don't fit those categories — which includes most of us — are 'out,' and we succumb to society's false judgment of our worth. As a result, a large segment of the population is plagued by feelings of worthlessness, inferiority and self-condemnation.

These people also have trouble relating to God. They often blame God for their sad state and find it difficult to trust Him. 'You made me a lowly clarinet player instead of a star quarterback,' they complain. '*If* I allow you access to other areas of my life, how do I know you won't make me a loser there, too?'

By giving in to the system's false judgment, these people can only look forward to more and more rejection. The system has rejected them and therefore they find it easy to reject themselves. Any success or acceptance that comes their way will be questioned or doubted on the basis of what they already believe about themselves.

Rebel Against the System

Since the 1960s, this segment of society seems to be growing. These are the rebels and the dropouts who respond to rejection by saying, 'I don't need you or your love.' Deep inside they still crave acceptance, but they refuse to acknowledge their need. They will often underscore their defiance and rebellion by dressing and behaving in ways that are objectionable to the general population.

Rebels are marked by self-hatred and bitterness. They wish they had never been born. They are irresponsible and undisciplined. They see God as just another tyrant, someone else trying to squeeze them into a socially acceptable mold. They rebel against God just as they rebel against everyone else.

These people's rebellious attitudes and behaviors tend to alienate others and push them to defend the system they reject. Therefore rebels' responses to those who reject them just breed more rejection.

In the final analysis, nobody wins in the world's system, but everybody wins in the kingdom of God. God loves each of His children the same. We are not in competition with one another. Paul says, 'We do not dare to classify or compare ourselves with some who commend themselves. When they measure themselves by themselves and compare themselves with themselves, they are not wise' (2 Cor. 10:12, NIV). We are loved and accepted unconditionally by God. There is a necessary place in the Body of Christ for each one of us. Helping another person succeed only results in our succeeding as well. The more we build up one another, the more we help ourselves.

Defensiveness Is Defenseless

No matter how well you live your life, somebody won't like it. How should we respond to those who can't or won't accept us? Should we be defensive? There are two reasons you never need to respond defensively to the world's critical, negative evaluation of you.

First, if you are in the wrong, you don't *have* a defense. If you are criticized for saying something out of order or doing something wrong and if the criticism is valid, any defensiveness on your part would be a rationalization at best and a lie at worst. You must simply respond, 'You're right; I was wrong,' and then take steps to improve your character and change your behavior.

Second, if you are right, you don't *need* a defense. Peter encouraged us to follow in the footsteps of Jesus who, 'while being reviled, He did not revile in return; while suffering, He uttered no threats, but kept entrusting Himself to Him who judges righteously' (1 Pet. 2:21-23). If you are in the right, you don't need to defend yourself. The Righteous Judge, who knows who you are and what you have done, will exonerate you.

In the beginning of my pastoral ministry I was responsible for several volunteers in the youth ministry of our church, including a woman named Alice. Alice was a fine Christian who had been placed in charge of a girls' program at the church. Unfortunately, although gifted in many areas, Alice didn't have the administrative skills to do the job. She struggled with her ministry, feeling frustrated and out of place. Because things weren't going well, Alice must have thought she needed a scapegoat, so she picked me. 'I need to see you,' she fumed at me one day. So we set up an appointment.

When we sat down together, she laid a sheet of paper on the table. 'Neil, I have listed all your good points and all your bad points.' I glanced at her paper and saw two columns. One point was listed in the good column, and the bad points went all the way to the bottom of the sheet and over to the other side. I invited her to read the good point first and then read every bad point on the list.

The part of me made of earth wanted to respond defensively to each of her accusations. The part of me made of the Spirit kept saying, 'Keep your mouth shut, Anderson.' So I just sat and listened attentively until she had emptied both barrels.

Finally I said, 'Alice, it must have taken a lot of courage to come in and share that list with me. What do you suggest I do?'

My question took her completely off guard and she began to cry. 'Oh, Neil, it's not you; it's me,' she sobbed. Well, that wasn't completely right either. There was a kernel of truth in each of the criticisms she had leveled at me. If I had defended myself on any of those points, however, Alice would have been even more determined to convince me that I was not yet qualified to be a member of the Trinity. As it turned out, my openness to her criticism prepared the way for us to discuss her frustration with her ministry. Two weeks later she resigned from the girls' program, and now she is having a great time serving the Lord in a ministry that fits her gifts.

If you can learn not to be defensive when someone exposes your character defects or attacks your performance, you may have an opportunity to turn the situation around and minister to that person. Christians who put down others are hurting people. Mature Christians don't behave that way because they know believers are not supposed to do that.

You are not obligated to respond to rejection by beating the system, giving in to the system or rebelling against the system. The world's system for determining your value as a person is not what determines your value. Peter wrote, 'And coming to Him as to a living stone, rejected by men, but choice and precious in the sight of God' (1 Pet. 2:4). Your allegiance is to Christ your Lord, not to the world.

Paul said, 'See to it that no one takes you captive through philosophy and empty deception, according to the tradition of men, according to the elementary principles of the world, rather than according to Christ' (Col. 2:8). The world's system is very influential, but you don't need to respond to that system because you are not of this world. You are *in* the world but you are not *of* the world (see John 17:14-16). You are in Christ. If you find yourself responding to rejection defensively, turn your attention to those things that will build you up and establish you in your faith.

When You Are Tempted to Criticize or Reject Others

Rejection is a two-way street: you can receive it, and you can give it. We have talked about how to respond to the rejection

You are responsible for. . .

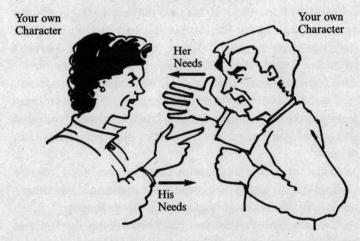

Your own
Character

Her
Needs

Your own
Character

His
Needs

Figure 12-B

we receive within the world's system. Now let's see if we can find the 'way of escape' (1 Cor. 10:13) for when we are tempted to level others with criticism or rejection.

When I was pastoring, I got the kind of distress call to which even policemen don't like to respond. 'Pastor, you'd better get over here,' said the husband over the phone, 'or we're liable to kill each other.' I could hear his wife screaming at him in the background.

When I arrived at the house, I persuaded Fred and Sue to sit down across the table from each other to talk through their problem. I sat at the end of the table. They wailed away at each other for several minutes, slamming each other with accusations and insults.

Finally, I interrupted. 'Time out! Sue, why don't you put on the coffee? Fred, bring me a sheet of paper and a pencil. Each of you get your Bible.' When we sat down together again at the table, I sketched a simple diagram (see Figure 12-B) and shared with them from God's Word.

I asked Fred to read Romans 14:4: 'Who are you to judge the servant of another? To his own master he stands or falls; and stand he will, for the Lord is able to make him stand.'

'That verse is talking about judging another person's character,' I said. 'Before God, each of you is responsible for your own character.' Fred and Sue nodded their agreement.

Then I asked Sue to read Philippians 2:3: 'Do nothing from selfishness or empty conceit, but with humility of mind let each of you regard one another as more important than himself.'

'That verse is talking about needs,' I continued. 'Before God, each of you is responsible for meeting each other's needs.' Again the couple agreed with my statement.

'Do you realize what you have been doing the last two hours? Instead of assuming responsibility for your own character, you've been ripping apart your partner's character. Instead of looking out for your partner's needs, you've been selfishly absorbed with your own needs. No wonder your marriage isn't functioning. You've turned God's Plan A for relationships into a Plan B disaster!' Before I left that day, Fred and Sue had prayerfully committed to assume their responsibilities according to the Word of God.

What kind of families and churches would we have if we all assumed responsibility for our own character and sought to meet the needs of those with whom we live? They would be almost heavenly. Instead of devoting ourselves to develop our own character and to meet each other's needs, we often yield to Satan's prodding to criticize each other's character and selfishly focus on our own needs. That is a prescription for disaster.

Focus on Responsibilities

Satan will also tempt us to focus on our rights instead of our responsibilities. For example, a husband may chip at his wife because he thinks he has a right to expect her to be submissive. A wife may nag her husband because she expects him to be the spiritual leader. Parents harass their children because they think it is their right to demand obedience. Members raise a stink in the local church when they think their rights have been violated by pastors, boards or other church members.

Anytime a nation, a group of people, or even individuals focus on their rights at the exclusion of their responsibilities, they are going down. No culture can withstand that kind of self-centered orientation. Husbands, having a submissive wife is not your right; but being a loving, caring husband is your responsibility. Headship is not a right to be demanded but an awesome responsibility to be fulfilled.

Similarly, wives, having a spiritual husband is not your right; but being a submissive, supportive wife is your responsibility. Parents, expecting your children to obey you is not your right; but disciplining your children in the nurture and instruction of the Lord is your responsibility. Being a member of the Body of Christ and of a local church is an incredible privilege, not a right. This privilege comes with the awesome responsibility to behave as God's children and become a lover of God and people. When we stand before Christ, He will not ask us if we received everything we had coming to us. He will reward us for how well we fulfilled our responsibilities.

Don't Play the Role of Conscience

I grew up having a good, moral background and going to church, but I wasn't a Christian. In those days I really enjoyed beer, especially on a hot day after mowing the lawn. When I received Christ as a young man, I joined a church that preached total abstinence from alcoholic beverages. I didn't drink enough to be a drunk, so I decided to scratch that rule and have my occasional beer. Two years later the Lord brought a sense of conviction about my beer drinking. Along with the conviction came the power to obey, so I gave it up.

Sometimes we are tempted to play the role of the Holy Spirit or the conscience in someone else's life in areas where the Scriptures are not crystal clear: 'Christians don't drink or smoke'; 'You should spend at least 30 minutes a day in prayer and Bible study'; 'Buying lottery tickets is not good steward-ship.'

I am convinced the Holy Spirit knows exactly when to bring conviction in matters of conscience. It is part of the process of sanctification that He superintends. When we attempt to play the role of the Holy Spirit in someone else's life, we misdirect their battle with God onto ourselves; and we are unqualified for the task. In doing so, we often do little more than convey criticism and rejection.

Discipline Yes, Judgment No

Are there any occasions when Christians should confront each other on matters of behavior? Yes. We are required by God to confront and restore those who have clearly violated the boundaries of Scripture. Jesus instructed: 'And if your brother sins, go and reprove him in private; if he listens to you, you have won your brother. But if he does not listen to you, take one or two more with you, so that by the mouth of two or three witnesses every fact may be confirmed' (Matt. 18:15,16).

Let me alert you to an important distinction: discipline is an issue of confronting observed behavior — that which you have personally witnessed (see Gal. 6:1); judgment is an issue of attacking character. We are instructed to confront others concerning sins we have observed, but we are not supposed to judge their character (see Matt. 7:1; Rom. 14:13). Disciplining others is a part of our ministry; judging character is God's responsibility.

For example, imagine you just caught your child telling a lie. 'You're a liar,' you say to him. That is judgment, an attack on his character. However, if you say, 'Son, you just told a lie,' that is discipline. You are holding him accountable for an observed behavior.

Let's say a Christian friend admits to you that he cheated on his income tax return. If you call him a thief, you are judging his character. You can only confront him on the basis of what you see: 'By cheating on your taxes you are stealing from the government, and that's wrong.'

When you discipline others, it must be based on something you have seen or heard personally, not on something you suspect or have heard through the grapevine. If you confront their behavior and they do not respond to you, next time you are to bring two or three witnesses — other eyewitnesses of their sin. If you are the only eyewitness, you confront them alone and leave it at that. It is their word against your word, and that won't stand up in a court of law. If they won't own up to their sin and repent, do we just let them get away with it? Yes, but God isn't finished with them. Imagine the conviction every time they see you.

Much of what we call discipline is nothing less than character assassination. We say to our disobedient children: 'You dumb kid'; 'You're a bad boy'; 'You're worthless.' We say to falling Christian brothers and sisters: 'You're not a good Christian'; 'You're a thief'; 'You're a lustful dirtbag.' Such judgmental statements don't correct or edify. Your children are not liars; they are children of God who have told a lie. Your Christian friends are not thieves; they are children of God who have taken something that doesn't belong to them. Believers caught in moral failures are not perverts; they are children of God who compromised their purity. We must hold people accountable for their sinful behavior, but we are never allowed to denigrate their character.

Express Your Needs Without Judging

If you have legitimate needs *in* a relationship that are not being met, should you risk conveying criticism and rejection by expressing your needs? Yes, but express them in such a way that you don't impugn the other person's character.

For example, you may feel unloved in a relationship, so you say, 'You don't love me anymore.' Or you think your spouse doesn't value you, so you say, 'You make me feel worthless.' Or you feel a distance developing between you and your friend, so you say, 'You never write or call.' You haven't really expressed your need. You criticized the other person. You are usurping the role of the other person's conscience. By pushing off your need as that person's problem, the person will probably respond by getting defensive, further straining the relationship.

What if you expressed your needs this way: 'I don't feel loved anymore'; 'I feel like a worthless, unimportant person'; 'I miss it when we don't communicate regularly'? By changing the 'you' accusation to an 'I' message, you express your need without blaming anyone. Your nonjudgmental approach allows God to deal with the person's conscience and turns a potential conflict into an opportunity for ministry. The other person is free to respond to your need instead of being defensive against your attack.

We all need to be loved, accepted and affirmed. When

these needs go unmet, it is very important that we express them to our family members and fellow Christians in a positive way and allow others to minister to those needs. I believe that a basis for temptation are unmet, legitimate needs. When you are too proud to say, 'I don't feel loved,' or when you push others away by saying, 'You don't love me anymore,' your need for love goes unmet. So Satan comes along with a tempting alternative: 'Your wife doesn't love you like you deserve. But have you noticed the affectionate gleam in your secretary's eye?'

God's primary resources for meeting your needs and keeping you pure are other believers. The problem is that many go to Sunday School, church and Bible study wearing a sanctimonious mask. Wanting to appear strong and together, they rob themselves of the opportunity of having their needs met in the warmth and safety of the Christian community. In the process, they rob the community of the opportunity to minister to their needs — one of the primary reasons God gathered us into churches. By denying other believers the privilege of meeting your legitimate needs, you are acting independently of God and you are vulnerable to getting your needs met by the world, the flesh and the devil.

A pastor once humorously quipped, 'The ministry would be a great career if it wasn't for people.' Perhaps you have said something similar, such as 'Growing in Christ would be easy if it wasn't for the people.' We all know that following Christ involves both the vertical and the horizontal — loving God and loving people. It is important to know that God works in our lives through committed relationships. Where better to learn patience, kindness, forgiveness and team spirit than in the close quarters of working relationships? Committed relationships can be extremely difficult unless we accept our responsibilities to grow and to love others. You can make that commitment. Remember, you are the only one who can keep you from becoming the person God wants you to be.

One of my students brought me the following poem that he insisted was a description of me. I hope he is right. I share it with you because I believe it provides a helpful perspective for our sometimes prickly relationships as Christians:

> People are unreasonable, illogical and self-centered.
>> Love them anyway.
> If you do good, people will accuse you of selfish, ulterior motives.
>> Do good anyway.
> If you are successful, you will win false friends and true enemies.
>> Succeed anyway.
> The good you do today will be forgotten tomorrow.
>> Do good anyway.
> Honesty and frankness make you vulnerable.
>> Be honest and frank anyway.
> The biggest people with the biggest ideas can be shot down by the smallest people with the smallest minds.
>> Think big anyway.
> People favor underdogs but follow only top dogs.
>> Fight for the underdog anyway.
> What you spend years building may be destroyed overnight.
>> Build anyway.
> People really need help, but may attack you if you help them.
>> Help people anyway.
> Give the world the best you've got and you'll get kicked in the teeth.
>> Give the world the best you've got anyway.[1]

Anybody can find character defects and performance flaws in another Christian. It takes the grace of God to look beyond an impulsive Peter to see in him the rock of the Jerusalem church. It takes the grace of God to look beyond Saul the persecutor to see in him Paul the apostle. So as you live day to day with people who are sometimes less than saintly in their behavior — and who see you the same way — may I simply say, 'Grace and peace be multiplied to you' (2 Pet. 1:2).

Note

1. Source and author unknown.

13
People Grow
Better Together

One January I had the privilege of taking 24 seminary students to the Julian Center near San Diego, California, where we lived and studied together for four weeks. My friend Dick Day founded the Julian Center with the vision to educate Christians in a relational context. In the past he had brought together groups for 12 weeks of live-in study, but that January he joined me in teaching seminary students for an abbreviated session.

To introduce the relational dimension of the retreat, I began the January session by dividing the students into groups of three for a relatively nonthreatening get-acquainted exercise. I concluded the exercise by asking students to identify one emotion they had experienced. The typical responses were 'happy,' 'accepted,' 'peace,' 'anticipation' and so on, although a few admitted they were a little scared.

A young man named Danny surprised me when he responded, 'bored.' Danny had come to learn, not to relate. He wanted content, not community. He considered my attempts to build rapport and relationship among the students a waste of his time. Day by day the other students grew closer together, but Danny stayed cool and aloof.

After two weeks, Danny's resistance finally wore down. He began to see that spiritual growth and maturity happen best in a community of people who know and accept each other. When Danny finally opened himself to his fellow students, he really began to get something out of the content of the session.

Following his month at the Julian Center, Danny had a new vision when he went back to the small group of businessmen he was discipling. 'Men,' he told them, 'we've been meeting for a year now, but I don't know what makes you tick, what turns you on or what your family life is like. And you don't know much about me either. We need to move beyond sharing information and start sharing our lives.'

Danny had learned Paul's secret of discipleship: 'Having thus a fond affection for you, we were well-pleased to impart to you not only the gospel of God but also our own lives, because you had become very dear to us' (1 Thess. 2:8).

Relationship: The Heartbeat of Growth and Maturity

The two most common questions I am asked about the ministry of discipling others to spiritual growth and maturity are, 'What curriculum do you use?' and 'What program do you follow?' If your curriculum isn't based on the Word of God and your program isn't relational, then what you are doing isn't discipleship.

The curriculum of discipleship is not the problem. Bible-based studies on spiritual growth abound. The missing link in discipleship is usually the personal interaction. It takes very little commitment to say, 'This book will tell you what you need to do to grow in Christ.' It takes a lot of commitment to say, 'Let's share with each other what Christ is doing in our lives and help each other grow in the grace and knowledge of our Lord Jesus Christ.'

Discipleship is an intensely personal ministry between two or more persons who help each other experience a growing relationship with God. Discipleship is not 'building my life into yours.' Discipleship is a process of building the life of

Christ in one another. The life of Christ does not refer to the 30-plus years Jesus physically lived on planet Earth 2,000 years ago. The life of Christ is the presence of God within us. Discipleship is practising that presence.

Jesus said, 'Come to Me' (Matt. 11:28) and 'Follow Me' (4:19). Mark records, 'He appointed twelve, that they might be with Him, and that He might send them out to preach, and to have authority to cast out the demons' (Mark 3:14,15). Notice that Jesus' relationship with His disciples preceded His assignment to them. Discipleship is being before doing, maturity before ministry, character before career.

Every Christian, including you, is both a disciple and a discipler in the context of his or her Christian relationships. You have the awesome privilege and responsibility both to be a teacher and a learner of what it means to be in Christ, walk by the Spirit and live by faith.

You may have a role in your family, church or Christian community that gives you specific responsibility for discipling others, such as husband, father, pastor, Sunday School teacher, discipleship group leader and so on. As a discipler, you are always a disciple who is learning and growing in Christ. You may not have an official responsibility to disciple anyone, but you have the opportunity to help your children, your friends and other believers grow in Christ through these caring and committed relationships.

In this final chapter, I want to roughly sketch the ministry of discipling one another which we in the Christian community all share. Keep in mind that a good discipler is a good counselor, and a good Christian counselor is a good discipler. Whether you are a professional discipler and/or counselor or are a growing Christian who is committed to helping others grow in Christ, the following designs for discipleship and concepts for counseling will give you some basic practical guidelines for your ministry.

Designs for Discipleship

Paul refers to three levels of maturity in Colossians 2:6-10:

> As you therefore have received Christ Jesus the Lord, so walk in Him, having been firmly rooted and now being built up in Him and established in your faith, just as you were instructed, and overflowing with gratitude.
>
> See to it that no one takes you captive through philosophy and empty deception, according to the tradition of men, according to the elementary principles of the world, rather than according to Christ. For in Him all the fullness of Deity dwells in bodily form, and in Him you have been made complete, and He is the head over all rule and authority.

According to Paul, believers are to be firmly rooted in Christ and then built up to walk, or to live, in Him. This defines three levels of maturity. Each level of maturity has specific conflicts that need to be resolved as illustrated in Figure 13-A. Figure 13-B illustrates the growth at the same three levels. Notice also the five dimensions of application for each level: spiritual, rational, emotional, volitional and relational. Please understand that there are no clear boundaries separating the three levels of maturity or the five dimensions of application as the figures would seem to imply. We are not diced up into little squares.

Level I relates to being firmly *rooted in Christ*. These foundational issues are based on the fact that 'in Him you have been made complete' (Col. 2:10).

Level II relates to being *built up in Christ*, which is how Paul describes our maturity in Christ (see v. 7).

Level III relates to daily *walking in Christ*, which is based on our identity and maturity in Christ. Paul instructed, 'As you therefore have received Christ Jesus the Lord, so walk in Him' (v. 6).

Each level of maturity is dependent on the previous level.

DISCIPLING IN CHRIST
LEVELS OF CONFLICT

	Level I Rooted in Christ (Col. 2:10)	Level II Built Up in Christ (Col. 2:7)	Level III Walking in Christ (Col. 2:6)
Spiritual	Lack of salvation or assurance (Eph. 2:1–3)	Walking according to the flesh (Gal. 5:19–21)	Insensitive to the Spirit's leading (Heb. 5:11–14)
Rational	Darkened understanding and pride (Eph. 4:18; 1 Cor. 8:1)	Wrong beliefs and philosophy of life (Col. 2:8)	Lack of knowledge (Hos. 4:6)
Emotional	Fear, guilt and shame (Matt. 10:28–33; Rom. 8:1,2)	Anger (Eph. 4:31), anxiety (1 Pet. 5:7), depression (2 Cor. 4:1–18)	Discouragement and sorrow (Gal. 6:9)
Volitional	Rebellion (1 Tim. 1:9)	Lack of self-control impulsive (1 Cor. 3:1–3)	Undisciplined (2 Thess. 3:7,11)
Relational	Rejection (1 Pet. 2:4)	Bitterness and unforgiveness (Heb. 12:15)	Selfishness (Phil. 2:1–5; 1 Cor. 10:24)

Figure 13-A

Christians cannot have an effective walk (Level III) if they are not growing in Christ (Level II), and they cannot mature if they are not firmly rooted in Christ (Level I).

DISCIPLING IN CHRIST
LEVELS OF GROWTH

	Level I Rooted in Christ (Col. 2:10)	**Level II** Built Up in Christ (Col. 2:7)	**Level III** Walking in Christ (Col. 2:6)
Spiritual	Child of God (Rom. 8:16; 1 John 5:13)	Walking according to the Spirit (Gal. 5:19–21)	Led by the Spirit (Rom. 8:14)
Rational	Desire to know the truth (John 8:32,33)	Handling accurately the Word of God (2 Tim. 2:15)	Adequate and equipped for every good work (2 Tim. 3:16,17)
Emotional	Free in Christ (Gal. 5:1)	Joy, peace and patience (Gal. 5:22)	Contentment (Phil. 4:11)
Volitional	Submissive (Rom. 13:1,2)	Self-control (Gal. 5:23)	Disciplined (1 Tim. 4:7,8)
Relational	Accepted and affirmed (Rom. 5:8; 15:7)	Forgiving and accepting (Eph. 4:32)	Brotherly love (Rom. 12:10; Phil. 2:1–5)

Figure 13-B

Level I: Rooted in Christ (Colossians 2:10)

The Level I spiritual conflict is the lack of salvation or the lack of assurance of salvation. God wants us to know that we 'have eternal life' (1 John 5:13). To disciple people, we have to first lead them to Christ so the Holy Spirit can bear witness with their spirits that they 'are children of God' (Rom. 8:16).

The Level I rational conflict is intellectual pride. Prideful people are self-sufficient. They don't want anybody to tell them what to do or how to do it. Prideful people don't need God or anyone else. We have to come to the end of our resources to discover God's resources. We are ready to receive from God and others when our prideful spirits are broken.

The emotional conflicts at Level I are fear, guilt and shame. Fear compels people to do what they should not do and inhibits them from doing what they should do. People who are motivated by fear are not experiencing their freedom in Christ. Fear of anyone or anything other than God is mutually exclusive to faith in God. Satan wants to be feared because he wants to be worshiped, but the fear of the Lord expels all other fears (see Ps. 34:4,7). Guilt and shame also need to be overcome by the grace of God because, 'There is therefore now no condemnation for those who are in Christ Jesus' (Rom. 8:1).

The Level I volitional conflict is rebellion. It is very difficult to disciple rebels because they won't submit to authority. Growth at this level involves understanding biblical submission to God and others.

The Level I relational conflict to overcome is rejection. The discipleship process is based on God's unconditional love and acceptance (see Titus 3:5). Building up one another does not start with authoritarian rule that demands accountability; it begins with acceptance and affirmation. When people know they are accepted and affirmed, they will voluntarily be accountable to authority. When authority figures demand accountability without acceptance and affirmation, however, they will never get it.

The first goal of discipleship is to help those you disciple become firmly rooted in Christ. This entails the following:

- Leading individuals to Christ and to the assurance of salvation

- Guiding them to a true knowledge of God and who they are in Christ, and starting them down the path of knowing God's ways

- Changing their basic motivation from irrational fears to the fear of God and helping them overcome guilt and shame

- Helping them see the ways they are still playing God or rebelling against God's authority

- Breaking down their defenses against rejection by accepting and affirming them

Level II: Built Up in Christ (Colossians 2:7)

Building up people in Christ begins in the spiritual dimension by helping them distinguish between walking according to the flesh and walking according to the Spirit. The more they choose to walk according to the flesh, the longer they will remain immature. The more they choose to walk according to the Spirit, the faster they will grow. Fundamental to this truth is the believers' understanding that outside circumstances do not determine who they are, how they walk or what they will someday become. Only God and our response to Him determine that.

Rationally, when Christians buy into Satan's lies or worldly philosophies, they will not be able to grow (see Col. 2:8,18,19). The battle is for the mind, and we must learn to take 'every thought captive to the obedience of Christ' (2 Cor. 10:5). Discipleship requires mental discipline. People who will not assume responsibility for their thoughts cannot be discipled.

Emotions are a product of our thoughts. If our thoughts and beliefs are wrong, we will struggle with negative emotions. Persistent anger, anxiety and depression reveal a faulty belief system. The greatest determinants of mental and emotional health are a true knowledge of God, an acceptance of His ways and the assurance of His forgiveness.

Volitionally, Christians need to exercise the spiritual fruit of self-control instead of succumbing to the fleshly impulses.

Relationally, forgiveness is the key to freedom in Christ. It is the glue that holds families and churches together. Satan uses unforgiveness more than any other human deficiency to stop the growth of individuals and ministries. The unforgiving person is yoked to the past and is not free to move on in Christ.

The second goal of discipleship is to accept God's goal of sanctification and grow in the likeness of Christ. This entails the following:

- Helping people learn to walk by faith in the power of the Holy Spirit

- Guiding them to discipline their minds to believe the truth

- Helping them get off the emotional roller coaster by focusing their thoughts on God instead of on their circumstances

- Encouraging them to develop self-control

- Challenging them to resolve personal problems by forgiving others and seeking forgiveness

Level III: Walking in Christ (Colossians 2:6)

Spiritually mature people are identified as those whose senses are 'trained to discern good and evil' (Heb. 5:14). Discernment is not just a function of the mind; it is also a function of the Spirit. Through His Spirit, God will identify to the spiritually mature believer a compatible spirit and warn against an incompatible spirit. Spiritual discernment is the first line of defense in spiritual warfare.

Rationally, people are perishing 'for lack of knowledge' (Hos. 4:6). Mature people can live productive lives if they know what to do or how to do it. Counseling at this level is just good, biblical common sense.

Emotionally, the mature believer learns to be content in all circumstances (see Phil. 4:11). This life is full of discouragements, and many of the believer's desires will go unmet. None of the believer's goals will go unfulfilled as long as it is a godly goal. In the midst of life's trials, Christians need encouragement. To encourage means to give people the courage to carry on. Every discipler should be an encourager.

Someone has said the successful Christian life hinges on the exercise of the will. The undisciplined person is incapable of living a productive life, but the disciplined Christian is a Spirit-filled person who has no unresolved conflicts of which he or she is aware.

Relationally, mature believers no longer live for themselves but for others. Perhaps the greatest test of the believer's maturity is found in the call, 'Be devoted to one another in brotherly love' (Rom. 12:10). 'By this all men will know that you are My disciples, if you have love for one another' (John 13:35).

Simply stated, the third goal of discipleship is to help others function as believers in their homes, on their jobs and in society. The effective Christian walk involves the proper exercise of intellect, talents and spiritual gifts in serving others and being a positive witness in the world.

Too many Christians are stuck on Level I, locked into the past, immobilized by fear and isolated by rejection. They have no idea who they are in Christ, so they are making very little progress in becoming like Him. Rather than telling immature believers what they should do, let's help them celebrate what Christ has already done and help them become who they already are in Him.

Concepts for Counseling

When I taught pastoral counseling, I asked the students to describe on a sheet of paper the personal problem they would have the greatest difficulty sharing with another individual. When I sensed the anxiety level in the students had peaked, I told them to stop. They were relieved to learn I didn't really want them to share with someone else what they wrote. I seriously doubt if they would have written down their worst offense. I only wanted them to experience what it would feel like to disclose potentially damaging or embarrassing information about themselves. I am sure you understand how hard that would be.

Then I asked the students to describe the kind of person with whom they could share that intimate information. What kind of person would he or she have to be or not be, do or not do. Then I had every student share the number one criterion for sharing with another individual, while I wrote their responses on the board. The list usually included compassion, confidentiality, love, maturity, trust, lack of criticism, competence, ability to help, as well as others. Then I asked who that list described and they always answered, 'God.'

Finally I completed the exercise by asking, 'If you haven't before, would you now commit yourself to become that kind of person?' If you are not that kind of person, nobody will be willing to share anything with you. If others won't share their real problem, you can't help them.

Allow me to ask you the same question: Would you be willing to commit yourself to becoming the kind of person in whom someone could confide? In other words, would you commit yourself to being like Christ? Whether you sit on the platform or in the pew, whether you sit at a desk in a counseling office or at a dining-room table, God can use you to minister to people if you are willing to be a compassionate, caring confidant.

Christian counseling seeks to help people resolve personal and spiritual conflicts through genuine repentance and faith in God. The goal of Christian counseling — whether done by a pastor, a professional counselor or a friend — is to help people experience their freedom in Christ so they can move on to maturity and fruitfulness in their walk with Him. Allow me to give you five practical tips for the formal or informal counseling you may do within your Christian relationships.

1. Help People Identify and Resolve Root Issues

Psalm 1:1-3 compares the mature Christian to a fruitful tree (see Figure 13-C). The fruitfulness of the branches above the ground is the result of the fertility of the soil and the health of the root system. The growing Christian is firmly rooted in Christ.

People usually seek counseling because something is wrong with their daily walk. Instead of being fruitful, their lives are barren. As with a tree, the presenting problem is seldom the root cause for their barren lives. They are not bearing any fruit because something is wrong with the root system.

I have developed 'Steps to Freedom in Christ' designed to help Christians resolve their personal and spiritual conflicts. They are available in most Christian bookstores and can be obtained from the office of Freedom in Christ Ministries. The theological basis and practical use of these steps is explained in my book *Helping Others Find Freedom in Christ* (Regal Books).

2. Encourage Emotional Honesty

Counselees are generally willing to share what has happened to them but are less willing to share their failure or complicity in the problem and are very reticent to share how they feel about it. Unless you model and encourage emotional hon-

COLOSSIANS 2:6–7

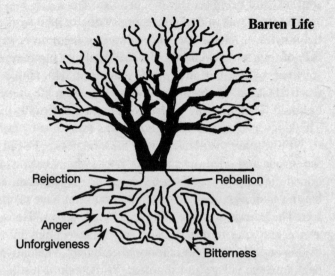

Barren Life

Rejection → ← Rebellion

Anger

Unforgiveness

Bitterness

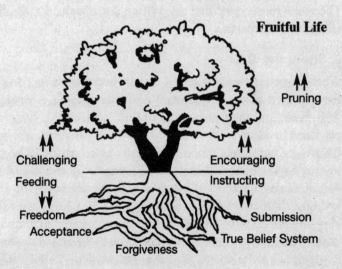

Fruitful Life

Pruning

Challenging

Encouraging

Feeding

Instructing

Freedom

Submission

Acceptance

True Belief System

Forgiveness

Figure 13-C

(The diagram of the trees is adapted from Neues Leben International.)

esty, the chances of your counselees' resolving their inner conflicts and being set free in Christ are slim.

The story was told of a missionary doctor who worked in the jungles of Africa. He labored among the natives, taking care of their physical needs. His real desire was to meet their spiritual needs, but after two years not one native had received Christ. He had modeled the Christian life as well as he could. Then one day his only child was accidentally killed. The loss was overwhelming and he was overcome by grief.

Not wanting the natives to see his weaknesses, he ran into the woods and cried out to God. 'Lord, why have you abandoned me here? I sacrificed my career for evangelism, and I haven't had even one convert. And now You have taken my son. The pain is overwhelming and I can't go on.' He wasn't aware that one of the natives had followed him into the woods and observed his emotional catharsis. The native ran back into the village and shouted, 'White man is just like us. The white man is just like us!' Within six months the whole village was Christian.

3. Share the Truth

When Christians seek help, it is usually because life has dealt them a hard blow. They usually think something is wrong with them, and their perception of God is distorted. What a privilege to share with them the truth of who they are in Christ and help them repair their faulty belief system! I keep several copies of the 'Who Am I?' (chapter 2) and 'Since I Am in Christ' (chapter 3) lists handy in my office. When we lovingly share with people who they are in Christ, we are applying the truth of God's Word to the ailing root system of faulty beliefs. Too often counseling starts by finding out what is wrong with the client. We have the privilege to tell them what is right about them in Christ. This gives them the assurance of victory.

4. Call for a Response

Your role is to share the truth in love and to pray that the counselees will choose to believe it, but you cannot choose it for them. Christian counseling is dependent on the faith responses of the counselees. Our Lord said to those seeking His healing touch, 'Your faith has made you well' (Mark 5:34); 'Let it be done to you as you have believed' (Matt. 8:13). If those you share with will not repent and choose to believe the truth, you can't do much for them.

5. Help Them Be a Part of the Christian Community

Finally, we need to help people move from conflict to growth by encouraging them to develop healthy, supportive relationships. Progressive sanctification is a process that cannot be accomplished apart from the Christian community. The Christian life was never intended to be lived alone. We absolutely need God and we necessarily need each other.

It will take us the rest of our lives to renew our minds and to conform to the image of God. We are what we are by the grace of God. All we have and can hope for — as disciplers and disciples, as counselors and counselees — is based on who we are in Christ. May your life and your ministry to others be shaped by your devotion to Him and the conviction that He is the way, the truth and the life (see John 14:6).

Biblical References

Topic	Scripture
Alive	
physically	Gen. 1:26,27; 2:7;
	2 Cor. 5:1-4,8
spiritually	2 Cor. 4:16
Anger	
unresolved	Eph. 4:26,27;
	1 Pet. 5:7,8
Anxiety	1 Pet. 5:7
Battles	
consideration and choice	Prov. 23:7
environmental stimulation	Rom. 12:2; Eph. 2:1-3
God's way versus man's way	Prov. 3:5,6; Isa. 55:9;
	Hos. 4:6; Jas. 1:8;
	2 Cor. 2:11
sin	Rom. 6:5-7,11; 8:1,2;
	2 Cor. 10:5; Gal. 5:17;
	Col. 3:3,10; Jas. 4:1
strongholds	2 Cor. 10:3-5
temptation	1 Cor. 10:13
win, expose the lie	John 8:32,44; 17:15,17;
	Rom. 12:2; 2 Cor. 10:5;
	Eph. 6:14; Phil. 4:6-9;
	Col. 3:15,16;
	1 Tim. 4:1; 1 Pet. 1:13;
	Rev. 12:9
win, renew your mind	1 Chron. 21:1;
	John 13:2; Act 5:3;
	Rom. 12:2; 2 Cor. 2:11;
	3:14; 4:3,4; 10:5; 11:3

new life

2 Cor. 5:17; Eph. 2:10;
1 Pet. 2:9,10;
1 John 3:1,2

'Who Am I?'

See **'Who Am I?'**

'Who I Am in Christ'

See **'Who I Am in Christ'**

Inheritance

from creation

Gen. 1:26-29; 2:7,18;
2 Cor. 4:16; 5:1-4,8;
Phil. 4:19

from the Fall, negative

Gen. 3

Knowledge of God, lost

Gen. 3:7,8; 4:1;
John 1:14;
Eph. 4:18

Lie, expose

See **Battles**, win,
expose the lie

Life

difference that Christ makes

1 Cor. 4:17; 15:22

new birth

John 3:3,36;
Rev. 21:27

new identity

See **Identity**, new life

spiritual, uninterrupted

John 1:4; 6:48; 10:10;
11:25; 14:6; Luke 23:46

Maturity

See **Built Up in Christ**

growth and relationship

See **Relationship**,
growth and maturity

Nature

grafted in

Matt. 7:20;
2 Cor. 5:16,17;
Eph. 5:8; Col. 2:6,7

new heart and new spirit

Prov. 4:23; Jer. 17:9;
Ezek. 36:26; John 15:3;
Gal. 2:20; Col. 3:1-3;
Heb. 10:16

new man

Rom. 12:2;
Col. 1:13; 3:10

'Twenty Cans of Success'
Ps. 27:1; Lam. 3:21-23;
Dan. 11:32;
Matt. 28:20;
John 16:33;
Rom. 8:1,31,37; 12:3;
1 Cor. 1:30; 2:12;
14:33; 2 Cor. 2:14;
3:17; 5:21;
Gal. 3:13,14; 5:1;
Phil. 4:11,13,
19; 2 Tim. 1:7;
Heb. 13:5; Jas. 1:5;
1 Pet. 5:7; 1 John 4:4

Walking in Christ
  designs for discipleship, Level Three Hos. 4:6; John 13:35;
Rom. 12:10; Phil. 4:11;
Heb. 5:14

'Who Am I?'
Exod. 3:14;
Matt. 5:13,14;
John 1:12; 8:24,28,58;
15:1,5,15,16;
Rom. 6:18,22;
8:14,15,17; 1 Cor. 1:2;
3:16; 6:17-19; 12:27;
15:10; 2 Cor. 5:17-19;
Gal. 3:26,28; 4:6,7;
Eph. 1:1,17; 2:6,10,19;
3:1; 4:1,24; 5:30;
Phil. 1:1; 3:20;
Col. 1:2; 3:3,4,12;
1 Thess. 1:4; 5:5;
Heb. 3:1,14;
1 Pet 2:5,9-11; 5:8;
1 John 3:1,2; 5:18

'Who I Am in Christ'

John 1:12; 15:15;
Rom. 5:1;
8:1,2,28,31-39;
1 Cor. 3:16; 6:17,20;
12:27; 2 Cor. 1:21,22;
5:17-20; 6:1;
Eph. 1:1,5; 2:6,10,18;
3:12; Col. 1:14; 2:10;
3:3; Phil. 1:6; 3:20;
4:13; 2 Tim. 1:7;
Heb. 4:16; 1 John 5:18

STUDY
GUIDE

CONTENTS

A NOTE FROM NEIL ANDERSON

Luke 5:1-11 is my favorite account of how the Lord taught. Jesus was instructing the multitudes from Peter's boat. 'And when He had finished speaking, He said to Simon, "Put out into the deep water and let down your nets for a catch"' (v. 4). Jesus had stopped talking, but He had not stopped teaching. Peter heard what Jesus said, but he hadn't learned until he got into the boat and put out the nets.

This study guide gives you an opportunity to get into the boat and put out the nets. You can do it alone, but I recommend that you do it with other faithful learners. It provides an opportunity for more collective wisdom, and greater learning always takes place in the context of committed relationships. Developing trusting relationships and being devoted to one another in prayer are what make group study so enriching.

I am thankful for the tremendous work that Lisa Guest did in putting together the first edition of this study guide. Another helpful resource is *Breaking Through to Spiritual Maturity* (Gospel Light, 1992, revised 2000), a curriculum for teaching these truths in a Sunday School class or small group. Since all this material has been professionally videotaped, you may want to consider an hour of video instruction each week and then use this study guide for group interaction. Contact details for the British branch of Freedom in Christ Ministries are given at the end of this study guide. The British branch has access to all FICM resources, and runs regular seminars in local UK churches.

It is my prayer that you will fully realize who you are in Christ and learn to live as a child of God. If this study guide helps make that possible, I will be thankful. May the grace and love of our heavenly Father bless you with all the riches of your inheritance in Christ.

Neil T. Anderson

1. Who Are You?

Jesus promises His people that 'You shall know the truth, and the truth shall make you free' (John 8:32). Our identity in Jesus Christ is a fundamental truth that we believers need to understand if we are to experience this promised freedom and to grow to Christian maturity.

Who Are You?
(pages 21-22)

'Who are you?' It sounds like a simple question, but attempting to answer it soon reveals the complexity of the issue. How would you answer the question if someone asked you, 'Who are you?'

We tend to identify ourselves and each other by what we look like, what we do, and perhaps even by our theological position, our denominational preference or our role in the church. But is who you are determined by what you do, look like and believe in? Or is what you do, look like and believe in determined by who you are? That's an important question, especially as it relates to Christian maturity.

● Neil Anderson believes that your hope for growth, meaning and fulfillment as a Christian is based on understanding who you are, specifically, your identity in Christ as a child of God. Your understanding of who God is and who you are in relationship to Him is the critical foundation for your belief system and your behavior patterns as a Christian.

Do you naturally identify yourself as a child of God as

you think about who you are? Why or why not?

Where in your own life do you see a connection between your belief system and your behavior patterns? Give an example or two of how your beliefs about yourself influence your behavior.

What changes in your behavior might result if you were able to clearly see yourself as the much-loved child of God that you are?

False Equations in the Search for Identity
(pages 22-25)

● Neil tells of an attractive 17-year-old girl who, from the outside, seemed to have everything going for her: excellent grades, musical talent, a full-ride university scholarship, a wonderful wardrobe and a brand new car.

Upon talking with Mary, Neil quickly realized that what was on the inside didn't match the outside. He asked Mary, 'Have you ever cried yourself to sleep at night because you felt inadequate and wished you were somebody else?' Through her tears, she asked, 'How did you know?'

What does your appearance suggest about you? What do you think people see as they look at you?

Perhaps, like Mary, you have felt inadequate and wished you were somebody else. How does what is inside you differ from your outward appearance? Comment on any discrepancy between your outward appearance and your inner reality.

Shame, fear, insecurity, loneliness, past hurts — there are many reasons why people, intentionally or otherwise, hide their real selves from others. Why do you hide your real self under an outside appearance that is so different from what is inside?

● Often what we show on the outside is a false front arising from our belief that if we appear attractive, perform well or enjoy a certain amount of status, then we will have it all together inside as well. But such is not the case. You plus attractiveness, you plus good performance and you plus status do not equal wholeness and significance. The only identity equation that works in God's kingdom is you plus Christ. Only you plus Christ equal wholeness and meaning.

How did you learn that being attractive, performing well or earning status does not mean wholeness or does not win you love?

In what area(s) of your life has Christ given you the wholeness and meaning you once were seeking?

In what area(s) of your life would you like Jesus to give you wholeness and meaning?

In God's kingdom, everyone has the same opportunity for a meaningful life. Why? Because wholeness and meaning in life are not products of what you have or don't have, what you've done or haven't done. In Christ you are already a whole person positionally and you already possess a life of infinite meaning and purpose because of who you are — a child of God.

● Although a Christian's identity in Christ is the key to wholeness, many believers have difficulty with their identity, security, significance, spiritual maturity and sense of worth. Ignorance is probably the primary reason (see Hosea 4:6). For others it is carnality, or the lack of repentance and faith in God, and for some it is deception by the father of lies (see John 8:44).

What false ideas might you have about who you are?

Asking a person about false ideas about him- or herself may be like asking fish about the water they swim in. The individual can't see what is so much a part of his or her reality. If you're not sure which ideas about yourself are false, ask someone you trust to help you see yourself as God sees you. Also, spend some time in prayer asking God to help you see yourself through His eyes.

- Neil tells of a young woman convinced that she was evil. While she may have done some evil things, at the core of her being she wasn't evil, as evidenced by the deep remorse she felt after sinning. She did, however, let Satan's accusations about her behavior influence her perception of herself instead of believing the truth.

In what ways are you trapped in this same downward spiral? Have you, for instance, failed at something and therefore see yourself as a failure? Are you basing your identity on something you've done rather than on who you are as a child of God? Be specific, and then, as you pray about this downward spiral, thank God that He sees you as His child.

Why would it be to your disadvantage to focus on the missteps you've taken in your life?

When we swallow Satan's lie and believe that what we do determines who we are, that false belief sends us into a tailspin of hopelessness and more defeat.

The Original Creation
(pages 26-30)

Genesis 1 and 2 tell how God created Adam and Eve in His image which gives us the capacity to fully think, feel and choose. After God breathed life into his nostrils, Adam was both physically and spiritually alive (see Genesis 1:26,27). For the Christian, to be spiritually alive is to be in union with God by being in Christ. And that union with God means three important things for believers.

Significance — In the original creation, humankind was given a divine purpose — dominion over all the other creatures. As a restored child of God, you have important work to do for your Lord.

Safety and Security — In the garden of Eden, Adam and Eve's needs were cared for. Likewise, we who follow Christ lack nothing. Safety and security is another facet of our inheritance in Christ.

Belonging — A true sense of belonging comes not only from knowing that we belong to God but also from belonging to each other just as God created Eve to provide a meaningful, open, sharing relationship for Adam.

Which of these is most appealing to you right now? Why?

Which of these seems most unreachable to you? Why?

Significance, safety and security, and belonging were no longer human attributes once sin entered the world.

The Effects of the Fall
(pages 30-39)

The effects of man's fall were dramatic, immediate and far-reaching, infecting every subsequent member of the human race — infecting you. We'll look at five effects of the Fall.

Spiritual Death

● With the Fall, Adam and Eve's union with God was severed. They were separated from God.

When did you first become aware of your separation from God? What circumstances brought you to the realization that you needed God?

Maybe you're just now realizing your need for God. In a brief prayer, tell Him of your need and how you have fallen short of being the person He wants you to be. Read 1 John 1:9 and thank God for the gift of His forgiveness. Cleansed and forgiven because of Jesus' death on your behalf, accept Jesus as your Savior and ask Him to help you live with Him as Lord of your life. (Note: It is important to find a church body that will help you grow in your knowledge of and commitment to God.)

Lost Knowledge of God

● The Fall affected the way Adam and Eve (and you and I) think. The fact that Adam and Eve tried to hide from God (see Genesis 3:7,8) clearly indicates a faulty understanding of who God is.

When have you tried to hide from God? What prompted that attempt?

Are you trying to hide from God right now? If so, what is causing you to do this? Read Psalm 23. Hear God's words of love for you. Believe the truth that you have no reason to hide from a loving and forgiving God.

● In God's original design, knowledge was relational. When

Adam and Eve lost their relationship with God, they lost the knowledge of God that was intrinsic to that relationship. In our unregenerate state, we know something about God, but we don't know God because we have a broken relationship with Him. When we enter God's family, however, we can know God as Adam and Eve did.

Describe the differences in your life once you took the step from knowing *about* God to *knowing* Him. How is the after picture different from the before picture? How are you a different person now that you know God personally?

In Christ we are able to know God personally because we have received the mind of Christ in our inner selves at salvation (see 1 Corinthians 2:16).

Dominant Negative Emotions

● Not only did the Fall affect humankind's thinking, it also affected us emotionally.

For one thing, we have become fearful and anxious. What fears dominated your life before you realized that you are a child of God? (The fact that these fears may continue to intrude doesn't make you less of a Christian.)

Another emotional by-product of sin is shame and guilt. What have been some sources of shame and guilt in your life?

Humankind also became depressed and angry after the Fall. What events and circumstances trigger your feelings of depression and/or anger?

Fear and anxiety, shame and guilt, depression and anger: what would God have you do with these powerful and destructive emotions?

In Genesis 4, God talks to an angry Cain about his feelings and says, 'If you do what is right, will you not be accepted?' (Genesis 4:7, *NIV*). In other words, if you do what is right, you won't feel angry and depressed. When have you noticed that bad feelings follow wrong behavior and/or good feelings follow right behavior? Be specific.

Think about your life right now. What changes in your actions need to be made in light of the truth about the relationship between feelings and behavior?

Too Many Choices

- The Fall affected our wills to choose as well as our thinking and our emotions. In the garden, everything that Adam and Eve wanted to do was okay except eating from the tree of the knowledge of good and evil (see Genesis 2:16,17). One result of their bad choice to eat from that tree is the myriad of good and bad choices you and I face every day.

Which choices that you face bring into clearest focus the sharp contrast between your will and what God would have you do?

What can you do to insure that your choices are the choices God would have you make?

Attributes Become Needs

- Another long-term effect of sin is that humankind's glowing attributes before the Fall became glaring needs after the Fall. Acceptance was replaced by rejection, so we feel the need to belong.

When you have felt the need to be accepted by God and/or by people, what steps have you taken to meet that need?

How has God met this need in your life? How can you help meet the needs of others?

● Innocence was replaced by guilt and shame, so we need our legitimate sense of worth restored.

If you have a low sense of worth, if you are your own harshest critic or if you have a hard time liking yourself, what have you done (or what could you do) to overcome this?

How is your identity as a child of God — or how might your identity in Christ be — the means to overcome a negative self-image?

● Dominion was replaced by weakness and helplessness, so we strive for strength and self-control.

How have you, during times of weakness and helplessness, found strength and peace in the Lord? Be specific about the circumstances.

Neil Anderson observed that 'the human soul was not designed to function as a master. You cannot serve God and wealth' (see Matthew 6:24). Consider how you spend your time, your talents and your money. Who or what are you serving and, if you can figure that out, why?

● We human beings have several basic needs. Since the Fall, we've had the need to belong, the need to have our legitimate sense of worth restored and the need to have strength and self-control.

As Neil Anderson observes, 'Every temptation is an attempt by the devil to get us to live our lives independently of God. Satan tempts us as he did Jesus by appealing to our most basic and legitimate needs.' What evidence from your own life supports this observation? In other words, when have your attempts to meet basic needs led you to sin? Know that, as one who calls Jesus 'Lord,' you are forgiven for the sins you confess (see 1 John 1:9).

As God's unique creation, you have significance. As a child of God, you can find safety and security. As a member of God's family, you can experience a sense of belonging.

Living What You Learn

Guided by the truths of this chapter, answer the question, 'Who are you?' Through the week, use some of the answers to who you are to counter any negative thoughts you have about yourself.

A Word of Prayer

Father God,

It is a privilege to be Your child. It is a gift of grace I don't fully comprehend. I thank You for Your wondrous love for me, and I ask that You would help me lead a life that honors You. Help me live according to the truth that my identity is based on who I am in Christ. May I see myself through Your eyes. May I understand more clearly how much You love me and let that love empower and guide me. I pray in the name of Jesus Christ through whom You graciously demonstrated Your amazing love for sinful me. Amen.

LOOKING AHEAD

As a believer, your true identity is not based on what you do or what you possess but on who you are in Christ. You will better understand who you are in Christ when you see how Jesus won back for you the identity that was lost when man was expelled from the garden. Christ's triumph and what it has gained for you are the themes of the next chapter.

2. The Whole Gospel

As we've seen, many Christians are not living free and productive lives because they don't understand their identities and positions in Christ. Until they see themselves the way God sees them, they can't fully understand the gospel and the dramatic change that occurred the moment they trusted in Christ.

The Whole Gospel
(pages 41-44)

- Remember the story of Bill and the example of Eric Liddell?

  What does the story of Bill say to you about the race you are running for the Lord, your focus and your fitness?

  Olympic runner Eric Liddell withdrew from a race scheduled on Sunday — a race he might have won — in honor of his heavenly Father. When has your commitment to the Lord caused you to take a stand that many people around you didn't understand?

  We Christians are salt and light in a dying and dark world because of the dramatic change that occurs in us the moment we trust in Jesus.

The Example of Christ

Too many Christians identify with the first Adam — with the Adam who sinned and was exiled from the presence of God. In reality, however, Christians are identified with Jesus Christ, the last Adam. As a result, the difference in your history is eternally profound. You need to be sure you're identifying with the right Adam, with Jesus your Savior.

- What we notice about Jesus is His complete dependence on God the Father.

    Where do you struggle and, like the first Adam, even fail to depend completely on God? What areas of your life (attitudes, responsibilities, etc.) are you reluctant to surrender to God?

    What keeps you from trusting God and depending on Him completely? Confess those barriers that keep you from trusting and ask God to help your lack of faith (see Mark 9:24).

    When have you taken a step of faith and found God faithful beyond your greatest expectations? Describe that experience in detail and let it serve as a touchstone the next time you need to step out in faith.

    Where do you have the opportunity to take a step of faith today? What might happen, best- and worst-case scenarios, if you took that step? Share your concerns, fears and hopes with God and ask for His guidance and courage as you take the step.

Jesus Came to Give Us Life

- Both Jesus and Adam were born spiritually alive. Adam died spiritually when he sinned. But Jesus, unlike Adam, stayed spiritually alive.

    Where do you, like the first Adam, fall short of God's will for you? Confess areas of persistent sin in your life and ask God to help you find strength in Him when Satan attacks and offers temptations to which he knows you are especially susceptible.

Now read Matthew 4:1-11. What does this scene from Jesus' life show you about how to resist sin?

What specific step would you like to take this week to become better acquainted with God's Word so that, like Jesus, you can better resist sin? Start with a realistic goal such as reading a passage of Scripture each day, attending a Bible study or taking your Bible to church so that you can follow the sermon more closely. Let reaching this goal be the first step toward wielding the sword of the Spirit when Satan attacks (see Ephesians 6:17).

What difference does it make to a Christian — to you and me — that Jesus was totally dependent on God and that He did not forfeit His spiritual life by sinning? It's the difference between life and death.

The Whole Gospel
(pages 44-45)

- Many Christians are living under half a gospel. Consequently, we are ending up with forgiven sinners instead of redeemed saints.

What two important points might be missing from most gospel presentations?

Which, if either of these two points, was a surprise to you? Why?

Write out in a simple statement how you would present the whole gospel, including all of the points mentioned in this section.

What a Difference Christ's Difference Makes in Us!
(pages 45-51)

The difference between the first and last Adams spells the difference between life and death for us.

- In 1 Corinthians 15:22, Paul writes, 'As in Adam all die, so also in Christ all shall be made alive.'

  What does the phrase 'in Christ' mean to you personally as you live out your life day by day?

- New life in Christ begins when you first trust Jesus as your Lord and Savior, and that new life means a new identity. In turn, that new identity means a new way of living as you live out who you are as a child of God.

  How does (or how would) seeing yourself as a much-loved child of God enable you to better live the Christian life?

  Satan can do nothing to damage your position and identity in Christ, but if he can deceive you into believing that you are not acceptable to God and that you'll never amount to anything as a Christian, then you will live according to those debilitating thoughts rather than in the freedom and wholeness available to you in Christ.

  What thoughts about yourself may be deceptions generated by Satan?

  God calls you a saint, and that glorious truth should overshadow the deceptions about yourself that Satan would have you believe.

What truths about your identity in Christ can you use to counter Satan's deceptions about who you are? (If you're not sure, keep working through this lesson!)

Often we have to act as if we love someone before we find ourselves loving that person. That principle of acting first and letting feelings follow may need to function in your life if you are to live out your identity in Christ.

What can you do today to live like a saint, a person loved and called by God, rather than like a sinner, a person hunched over by a sense of unworthiness and failure?

Remember that what you do doesn't determine who you are (for instance, failing at something doesn't make you a failure). Rather, who you are — a child of God — determines what you do if you let yourself believe the truth that God loves you. After all, you can't consistently behave in a way that's inconsistent with the way you perceive yourself.

What Is True of Christ Is True of You
(page 51)

One way to perceive yourself as God does is to reaffirm who you are in Christ.

● In the *Victory over the Darkness* text, you were invited to read aloud the list of answers to the question 'Who Am I?' found on pages 52-53. Whether or not you accepted that invitation then, do so now. Slowly read the list of answers aloud. Let yourself *hear* the words and be amazed by God's grace to you.

If you hesitate to read aloud these wonderful words of God's love, what are your reasons?

Which statements of fact are especially meaningful to you right now?

Why do these two or three truths you just listed mean so much to you?

How would believing the truths you listed above make your life different?

You can make the truths you listed more meaningful and productive in your life by simply choosing to believe what God has said about you. That sounds simple enough, but why isn't that step easy for you to take?

Lay before God your answer to the previous question. Ask God to heal those places where you've been hurt, to strengthen you where you've been crippled and to free you where you have been in chains and unable to know His love for you.

One of the greatest ways to help yourself grow into maturity in Christ is to continually remind yourself of who you are in Him. The more you reaffirm who you are in Christ, the more your behavior will begin to reflect your true identity.

The Bright Hope of Being a Child of God
(pages 55-56)

● If you're beginning to think you are someone special as a Christian, you're right! You are special not because of anything you've done but because of God's gracious invitation to be His child. Read again the words of 1 John 3:1-3 and hear the wonder in the apostle's voice.

What hope for today do you find in these verses?

What hope for the future do you find in 1 John 3:1-3?

The hope you, as a believer, have in God is a present hope as well as a future hope. As a child of God, you are being conformed to the image of God and you can begin living according to who you really are — a child of God.

LIVING WHAT YOU LEARN

On 3x5-inch cards, write out the most meaningful answers to the question 'Who Am I?' (one per card) and pray through those truths each day this week. Ask God to help you believe these words — words He has spoken *about* you and *to* you — so that you may experience freedom and wholeness in Him.

A WORD OF PRAYER

Father in heaven,
    What a privilege to address You as such! I marvel that You name me Your child, and I ask that You would help me believe that I am. Help me to believe who I am in Christ that I may better live out the Christian life as Your witness and as a vessel of Your love and grace. And, Lord God, keep me focused on the race I have to run as Your child. Give me boldness to take a stand for You, unafraid of being different from the people, the culture, the society around me. May I, almighty and all-loving God, depend completely on You, just as Jesus did. In His name I pray. Amen.

LOOKING AHEAD

If you take nothing else away from this lesson, take this truth: You cannot consistently live in a manner that is inconsistent with how you perceive yourself. You must believe you are a child of God in order to live like a child of God.

3. See Yourself for Who You Really Are

Every born-again believer is a child of God. Consider how that fact can affect your life now.

See Yourself for Who You Really Are
(pages 59-61)

- Reconsider the stories of Claire and Derek. As a college student, Claire simply believed what she perceived herself to be — a child of God — and so was committed to being transformed into His image and to loving people and growing in Christ.

  How did you react to the description of Claire when you first read it in the *Victory over the Darkness* text? What aspect of Claire's journey revealed an important truth to you?

- Derek was well into his 30s before he learned that God is not a perfectionistic, impossible-to-please heavenly Father. He also realized that he already was pleasing God by who he is in Christ.

  How did you react to Derek's story? What aspect of Derek's journey revealed an important truth to you?

  With whom do you identify more closely: Claire who is confident about her identity in the Lord or Derek who had to learn the truth about his heavenly Father?

Comment on the similarity you've noted.

Theology Before Practicality
(pages 61-65)

The experiences of Claire and Derek illustrate the importance of establishing our Christian lives on right beliefs about God and ourselves. We need to understand who we are as a result of who God is and what He has done (i.e., theology) before we can live out our faith (i.e., practical Christianity).

- Many Christians struggle to live out their faith because they try to base their spiritual growth and maturity on practical sections of the Scriptures (what we need to do to live out our faith) and spend too little time internalizing the doctrinal sections (what we need to know about God, ourselves, sin and salvation).

    Consider your own Bible-reading patterns. What do you tend to focus on? Why?

    In light of what you've read so far in *Victory over the Darkness*, what value would internalizing doctrinal sections of Scripture have for someone struggling with the question 'Who am I?'

- When you don't understand the biblical truths pertaining to your position in Christ, you have no ground for success in the practical arena. How can you hope, for instance, to 'stand firm against the schemes of the devil' (Ephesians 6:11) if you have not internalized the truth that you are already victoriously 'raised . . . up with Him, and seated . . . with Him in the heavenly places, in Christ Jesus' (Ephesians 2:6)? How can you rejoice in hope and persevere in tribulation (see Romans 12:12) without the confidence of knowing that you have been justified by faith and have peace with God through the Lord Jesus Christ (see Romans 5:1)?

When has God's truth served you well in the practical arena? Perhaps the truth that you are already victorious over Satan through Christ (see Ephesians 2:6) has helped you stand strong against his temptations. Also, perhaps knowing that you have been justified by faith through Jesus (see Romans 5:1) has helped you persevere in difficult times. Describe in detail such a time.

In what area(s) of your life are you struggling to live out your faith right now? Outline the situation and then spend some time with your Bible. Find a doctrinal truth that can help you live out your faith in the circumstances you just described.

When your basic belief system about God and yourself is shaky, your day-to-day behavior will be shaky. But, as experiences from your own life may have reminded you, when your belief system is intact and your relationship with God is based on truth, you'll have very little trouble working out the practical aspects of daily Christianity.

● The music director and his wife whose marriage was failing found that, when each of them got right with God, they were able to work out their problems. Getting right with each other began with getting right with God. But what does 'getting right with God' mean? Getting right with God always begins with settling once and for all the issue that God is your loving Father and you are His accepted child.

Why would wholehearted acceptance of this truth help two individuals through the problems of their marriage?

What problems would be alleviated by your wholehearted acceptance of the truth that God loves you?

● As long as you believe that God is your loving Father and you are His accepted child, your faith will permeate your daily experience. If you question the finished work of Christ, you will continue to struggle to earn the acceptance that is already yours in Christ.

In what ways have you tried to earn God's acceptance?

What lesson did you learn from the experience?

● Hear these freeing words: We don't serve God to gain His acceptance; we are accepted, so we serve God. We don't follow Him in order to be loved; we are loved, so we follow Him.

What tends to motivate your worship and your service?

Think about your relationship to your spouse, a favorite family member or a special friend. What is it about the relationship that frees you to give and receive?

Thank God for placing people in your life who accept you as you are, thus helping you learn about His gracious and unconditional love.

In order to live the victorious Christian life, you have to believe what is already true about you. Will you have opposition to believing this truth? Of course!

The father of lies (see John 8:44) has deceived the whole

world (see Revelation 12:9). If that isn't enough, others will put you down. We have to keep reminding ourselves of these positional truths.

● As you read in the previous chapter, one way to learn to perceive yourself as God does is to reaffirm who you are in Christ. The 'Who Am I?' list was designed to help you do just that. Here in chapter 3 you find a supplement to that list.

In the *Victory over the Darkness* text, you were invited to read aloud the truths listed on pages 66-67. Whether or not you accepted the invitation then, consider doing so now. Read slowly the list of statements that describes your identity in Christ; do this regularly until these truths become a part of you.

Which statements are especially meaningful to you right now?

Why do you think the truths you just listed mean so much?

If you could believe the truths you listed above, how would your life be different?

Ask God to help these truths about the effects of God's grace enter your heart, not just your mind. Also, as before, ask Him to heal those places where you've been hurt, to strengthen you where you've been crippled and to free you where you have been in chains and unable to know His love for you.

Your perception of your identity makes a big difference in how well you live out your faith and deal with the challenges and conflicts of life. And the only basis for an accurate identity is God's unfailing Word.

Relationship versus Harmony
(pages 68-70)

Perhaps this emphasis on God's complete acceptance of you in Christ has raised the question 'What happens to this relationship when I sin?' The grace-filled answer is that your relationship with God is based on the blood of the Lord Jesus Christ. You are a born-again child of God in spiritual union with Him by His grace, which you received through faith. Your relationship with God was settled when you were born into His family.

- Just as you will always be related to your biological father and mother, you will always be related to your spiritual Father. And just as you lived in harmony with your father when you trusted and obeyed him, you will live in harmony with your heavenly Father when you trust and obey Him. (You might consult your church's or pastor's view on this point.)

  Consider a time when you failed to take God at His word or when you chose to walk by the flesh — a time of distrust, disobedience or disharmony with God. What did you learn from that experience?

  Have you ever worried that you had forfeited your relationship with your heavenly Father? If not, why not? If so, what reassurance did you find that, even in your sin, you hadn't forfeited your status as His child? If you are worried right now, review the truths of John 10:27,28; Romans 8:35-39; and 1 Peter 1:18,19.

  Right now are you living in harmony with your heavenly Father or taking advantage of your gracious relationship with your heavenly Father? Explain why you answer as you do.

What can you do to enrich your fellowship with your heavenly Father?

Think about your life right now. What decision or situation, if any, becomes clear in light of this call to obey God?

Know that there is nothing you can do to improve upon your relationship with God other than believing that it is true. You are a child of God, period. The only thing you can do to improve the harmony of your relationship with God is to believe the truth and live in submissive obedience to Him.

Believing the Truth About Others
(pages 70-71)

● As important as it is that you believe in your true identity as a child of God, it is equally important that you perceive other Christians as children of God as well and treat them accordingly.

The statistics are frightening: for every positive statement a child hears, he or she receives 10 negative statements. What kinds of statements are the children in your life hearing from you? Let your answer prompt a minute or two of prayer.

What kinds of statements are fellow Christians in your life hearing from you? Again, let your answer prompt a minute or two of prayer.

Who in your life has been a vessel of God's grace with his or her words of edification and encouragement? Thank God for that person and perhaps thank him or her in a note or with a phone call!

Relating to God
(pages 72-74)

- Many Christians live their lives as though they were walking on glass. They are afraid to make mistakes because if they do, the hammer of God will fall on them. Dear Christian, the hammer has already fallen. It fell on Christ. He died once for all our sin (see Romans 6:10).

  How does your behavior show that you might be living in fear of the hammer of God falling on you? Where do you feel — as the missionary did — that you are a failure in your Christian walk?

  Do you relate to the missionary who wrote to Neil Anderson? In what ways? How does what he declares in his last paragraph affect you personally?

- Review the list in chapter 3 (pp. 66-67) that describes your identity in Christ.

  What most astounds you about what God says about you and your relationship with Him? How will that change how you relate to your loving God from now on?

  Read the truths about yourself listed in chapters 2 and 3 (pp. 52-53, 66-67) often; believe them and walk in them. When you walk by faith, your behavior as a Christian will conform to what you believe.

LIVING WHAT YOU LEARN

What is one thing you can do this week to bring more harmony to your relationship with your heavenly Father? Consider persistent or habitual sins that He can help you resist (see 1 Corinthians 10:13).

Who is one person you can ask God to help you see through His eyes so that you can offer him or her words of grace rather than thoughts of criticism, dislike or anger? Pray and then consider extending an act of grace, trusting that your feelings will follow.

A WORD OF PRAYER

God of grace,

I thank You that my ability to serve You is not what gains Your acceptance, that my ability to follow You is not what determines whether I am loved. Thank You for Your acceptance that frees me to serve You and Your love that frees me to follow You. And I thank You for the security of my relationship with You. May I believe these truths and base my life on them. Help me, Lord, to trust and obey You so that our relationship may be harmonious. And, God, so that there may be greater harmony within Your Body, help me see Your people through Your eyes. And help me control my tongue so that I speak only words that build up, not words that hurt and tear down. I pray in Jesus' name and for His sake. Amen.

LOOKING AHEAD

The Bible teaches that you are a child of God. Nevertheless, you are still less than perfect in your behavior. You are a saint who sins, and that is the great Christian dilemma that the next chapter addresses.

4. Something Old, Something New

Being a saint who is alive and free in Christ does not mean being spiritually mature or sinless, but it does provide hope and future growth. Despite God's provision for us in Christ, we are still far less than perfect. We are saints who sin. Our positions in Christ are settled, but our daily performances are often marked by personal failures and disobedience, which disappoint us and disrupt the harmony of our relationships with God.

Something Old, Something New
(pages 75-76)

● In Romans 7, Paul groans, 'The good that I wish, I do not do; but I practice the very evil that I do not wish' (v. 19).

What is 'the good' that you wish to do but somehow don't or can't manage to do?

What is 'the very evil' that you do not wish to do but somehow don't or can't avoid?

If you can answer either of these two questions truthfully, you have personally experienced the struggle that believers have with their old patterns of behavior. A better understanding of this sinful side of your sainthood will help you see your identity in Christ more clearly and enable your further Christian growth.

The Nature of the Problem
(pages 76-77)

Fallen humanity lives 'in the flesh,' and 'those who are in the flesh cannot please God' (Romans 8:8). Since birth we have learned to live our lives independently of God. This learned independence is one of the chief characteristics of the flesh. The flesh is self-reliant rather than God-dependent; it is self-centered rather than Christ-centered.

Until now, what have you understood about the relationship between your old nature, old self and sinful flesh, and your new nature as a child of God?

What have been the consequences — emotional as well as behavioral — of your understanding about the relationship between your old nature and your new nature?

● Positionally, several things changed at salvation. First, God transferred us from the domain of darkness to the kingdom of His beloved Son (see Colossians 1:13). Second, sin's dominion through the flesh has been broken (see Romans 8:9).

How do these truths about your position in Christ affect you? How will you choose to live your life?

Christians are no longer in the flesh, but since the characteristics of the flesh remain in believers, they have a choice. They can walk or live according to the flesh (see Galatians 5:19-21) or they can walk or live according to the Spirit (see Galatians 5:22,23).

We Have Been Grafted In
(pages 78-79)

Concerning your nature, 'you were formerly darkness, but now you are light in the Lord' (Ephesians 5:8). Are we both light and darkness? Paul also wrote, 'If any man is in Christ, he is a new creature; the old things passed away; behold, new things have come' (2 Corinthians 5:17). Are we partly new creatures and partly old creatures?

Why is it significant that you weren't merely in the dark but were darkness and that you haven't simply moved into the light but are light?

- Neil Anderson used the illustration of grafting navel oranges onto ornamental orange tree stocks to explain what happened when we became new creatures in Christ.

What fruit have you seen in your new life as evidence of having the new nature grafted onto your old root stock?

What encouragement do you receive from this illustration?

In order to grow and bear fruit, Christians must all be organically centered in Christ. This firm rooting is our positional sanctification, and growing and bearing fruit is our progressive sanctification.

A New Heart and a New Spirit
(pages 80-82)

One of the greatest prophecies concerning our salvation is given in Ezekiel 36:26 (*NIV*): 'I will give you a new heart and put a new spirit in you; I will remove from you your heart of stone and give you a heart of flesh.'

In what ways have you experienced that you have a new heart and a new spirit?

What changes occurred in you the moment you were grafted into the vine?

'You are already clean' (John 15:3), and you will continue to be sanctified as He prunes you so that you may grow and bear fruit.

New Things Have Come
(pages 82-84)

• The New Testament teaches that when you came into spiritual union with God through your new birth, you didn't add a new divine nature to your old sinful nature. Instead, you exchanged natures.

Why is this fact a source of hope and encouragement?

• Your new identity is already determined because the nature of Christ is within you, enabling you to be like Christ, not just act like Him. God knows that you can't solve the problem of your old sinful self by simply improving your behavior (acting like Christ). He knows He must change who you are and give you an entirely new self, which is made possible by the life of Christ in you.

What do these truths teach you about your heavenly Father? Praise Him for His wisdom and love!

Only after God makes you a partaker of Christ's nature are you able to change your behavior. What behavior(s) have you seen change since becoming a Christian?

- You are a spiritual person in Christ. That is your true identity. The issue now is learning to walk in harmony with who you really are.

Since becoming a Christian, when have you chosen to live according to the old way? Give an example or two.

What were the consequences of your choice? Think about feeling or not feeling convicted, and describe any lessons you learned from that experience.

The conviction that comes when we sin is another evidence of the presence of the nature of Christ within us. Sinning is not consistent with who we really are in Christ.

A New Man
(pages 80-81)

What does it mean to be a new man? We still look the same physically, and we still have many of the same thoughts, feelings and experiences. We have to believe that our new identity is in the life of Christ and to commit ourselves to grow accordingly.

If you are a new creation in Christ, have you ever wondered why at times you still think and feel the same way as you did before? That's because everything you learned before is still programmed into your memory. There is no mental Delete button.

- Just as Neil had to learn to react differently to the Navy ship's new skipper after serving two years under a tough old skipper, Christians who have the new life of Jesus Christ implanted within them have some adjusting to do.

Think about your actions, reactions, emotional responses,

thought patterns, memories and habits. Name one or two that are still clearly in opposition to God and centered on yourself.

What does the Bible offer as an alternative to the behaviors and/or thoughts you just named? Ask God to help you live according to these models. Plan the first step you'll take, and take it!

As a child of God, you are no longer under the authority of Satan and dominated by sin and death. The old man is dead and new things have come.

New Things Have Come
(pages 82-84)

Despite the fact that at times believers still live according to their old selves, they are new persons — new in relationship to God and new in themselves. We have a new master. Our old master was the god of this world, Satan. Our new master is our heavenly Father. We also have a new nature that is now oriented toward God rather than toward self and sin.

• The conviction that comes when we sin is evidence of the presence of the nature of Christ within us. Sinning is not consistent with who we really are in Christ.

Describe a time when you have felt this conviction. What happened and what did you do at the time to dispel that conviction?

When have you found the strength in God that you needed to stand strong against the powerful appeal of sin? Be specific about the details and let this incident help you stand strong the next time you are tempted to sin.

- God has not given us the power to imitate Him. He has made us partakers of His nature so that we can actually *be* like Him.

God knows you cannot solve the problem of your old sinful self by simply improving your behavior. He must change your nature and give you an entirely new self — the life of Christ in you — which is the grace you need to measure up to His standards. What is your reaction to these statements? How might it be expressed in your life from this day on?

Only after God changes who you are and makes you a partaker of His divine nature will you be able to change your behavior.

A New Master
(pages 84-85)

- The death of your old self formally ended your relationship with sin, but it did not end sin's existence. Sin is still present, appealing and powerful.

Stating clearly the points where you are particularly vulnerable to sin's enticements may help you stand strong against temptation. In what areas of your life are you especially likely to act independently of God and commit sin?

By virtue of the crucifixion of the old self, sin's power over you is broken (see Romans 6:7,11). You are no longer under any obligation to serve sin, to obey sin or to respond to sin. Write a one- or two-line prayer based on this truth, and use that prayer to help you stand strong in those areas of vulnerability you just identified.

'There is therefore now no condemnation for those who are in Christ Jesus. For the law of the Spirit of life in Christ Jesus has set you free from the law of sin and of death' (Romans 8:1,2). The law of sin and death is still operative, but you can overcome it by a greater law — the law of life in Christ Jesus!

Saved and Sanctified by Faith
(pages 85-86)

Through God's work of atonement, through Christ's death on the cross for your sins, God changed sinners to saints. This change — this regeneration — occurred at the moment of your salvation. The ongoing change in your daily walk — the process of sanctification — continues throughout your life.

• Have you, like the pastor who visited Neil, been struggling because your old self hasn't died? Do you, like the pastor, need to be reminded that your old self died at the point of your salvation (see Colossians 3:3)?

Explain in your own words why you, and this pastor, don't need to be in turmoil over the old self that doesn't seem to have died yet.

What freedom for Christian joy and spiritual growth do you find in the truths of Colossians 3:3 and Galatians 3:2?

Know that sanctification is only fully effective when the radical, inner transformation by regeneration is realized and appropriated by faith. That's one reason why it is so important to understand your identity in Christ.

• A new Christian is like a lump of coal. With time and

pressure, that coal becomes hardened and beautiful. The lump of coal consists of the right substance to become a diamond, and it does so.

Whom have you seen or known who was at first a lump of coal but after giving his or her life over to God, became a shining example and vessel of His love and grace? (Think about the apostle Paul if no one else comes to mind.) Describe what you saw of the process of that person's sanctification.

Let that real-life example encourage you in your journey toward spiritual maturity, toward being a diamondlike light for your God.

Balancing the Indicative and the Imperative
(page 87)

The *indicative* is what God has already done and what is already true about us, and the *imperative* is what remains to be done as we respond to God by faith and obedience in the power of His Holy Spirit.

Where have you experienced the imbalance between the indicative and the imperative in your Christian life?

What have you learned in this chapter that will help you bring a better balance to your life as you grow in spiritual maturity?

You have to know and believe posititional truth in order to successfully progress in your sanctification, or you are going to try doing for yourself what God has already done for you.

In Summary
(pages 87-90)

Our entire beings were morally corrupt before we came to Christ. Our minds were programmed to live independently of God, and the desires of our flesh are in opposition to the Spirit of God. The old flesh has to be crucified by the believer. There is no instant maturity. It will take us the rest of our [earthly] lives to renew our minds and conform to the image of God.

What circumstances in life helped you recognize Satan's deception and brought you to the point of naming Jesus as your Lord and Savior?

Are you presently living your Christian life as though you were still a slave of sin, much as the freed slaves did after the Civil War? What verse(s) can you claim as your Spiritual Emancipation Proclamation?

The seed that was sown in us by God is only a beginning. Being a child of God and being free in Christ are positional truths and are birthrights of every believer.

LIVING WHAT YOU LEARN

What truth in this chapter was most life changing for you as you began to understand it? How will your walk with Christ be changed as a result of this truth?

What is one area in which you have felt conviction as a result of the truths you have learned? What will you do now to make the changes needed to bring your behavior in line with God's truth?

A Word of Prayer

Gracious God,

Thank You that my old self has died — and help me accept that truth on faith even though I continue to struggle with what my old self taught and conditioned me to think and do. Paul's words could easily be mine: 'The good that I wish, I do not do; but I practice the very evil that I do not wish' (Romans 7:19). I'm glad that You understand my struggle. By Your grace I choose to win the battle against sin and stand strong against its appeal. May I find real joy and freedom under my new Skipper. Teach me, Father God, to live so that the new life within — the life of Jesus Christ — can flourish. I pray in His precious name. Amen.

Looking Ahead

Sanctification is the process of becoming in your behavior what you already are in your identity. Spiritual growth and maturity result when you believe the truth about who you are and then do what you are supposed to do to renew your mind and walk in the Spirit.

5. Becoming the Spiritual Person God Wants You to Be

The story of Anne Sullivan and Helen Keller is a moving account of the power of God's love at work in and through His people. What does it take to be such a vessel of your heavenly Father's grace?

Becoming the Spiritual Person God Wants You to Be
(pages 91-93)

What does it take to be the kind of Christian who can love a person whom others call hopeless? What moves us beyond our selfishness to deeds of loving service to God and others?

- First, Christian love and service require a firm understanding of who you are in Christ.

  In your own words, describe who you are in Christ. Begin with 'As a child of God, I am . . .' Then read your words aloud, really hear what you're saying and rejoice!

  You can't love like Jesus loved until you accept the reality that, because you are in Christ, you are a partaker of His divine nature.

- Second, you must begin to crucify daily the old sin-trained flesh, to walk in accordance with who you are in Christ and to be transformed by the renewing of your mind (see Romans 12:2). It requires the grace of God, and to live under grace, we need to learn to walk or live by the Spirit. This process is called 'walking by the Spirit' (see

Galatians 5:16-18), and walking by the Spirit cannot be explained with three steps and a formula.

Is the fact that it is a process reassuring, frightening or both?

Instead of trying so hard to nail down all the details of the spiritual life, focus on trusting Christ and then let Him move you along in the right direction. You must not limit what life in Christ, the One who died for you, is all about.

Three Persons and the Spirit
(pages 93-100)

Although Scripture doesn't outline a simple formula for living the spiritual life, God's Word does give us some guidelines and important information. We'll begin by considering the distinction Paul made between natural persons, spiritual persons and fleshly persons.

The Natural Person

● This person is spiritually dead, separated from God and therefore living completely independently of Him. Consequently, the natural person sins as a matter of course.

What was your reaction when you studied diagram 5-A (p. 94)? What surprises did you find in the description of how living apart from God can affect your mind, body, emotions and will?

At what points — flesh, body, emotions, will or mind — did you see something of yourself before you named Jesus as your Lord and Savior?

Thank God for the wholeness He has brought to your life.

The Spiritual Person

- At the point of conversion, this person's spirit became united with God's Spirit. As a result, this person lives knowing forgiveness for sin, acceptance in God's family and a positive sense of worth.

  The description of the spiritual person in diagram 5-B (p. 96) reflects the ideal. Whom have you known who most closely matches this ideal? What has that person taught you about God? About faith?

  At what points — body, emotions, spirit, will or mind — does Figure 5-B (p. 96) suggest where God has been at work transforming you from the natural 'before' person to the spiritual 'after' person?

  Again, thank God for the wholeness He is bringing to your life.

The Fleshly Person

- Instead of being directed by the Spirit, this believer chooses to follow the impulses of the flesh.

  Review the description of the fleshly person in diagram 5-C (p. 98). What did you learn about your own tendencies to follow the impulses of the flesh rather than the Spirit?

  Which of the following words describe your feelings about yourself and about life: inferiority, insecurity, inadequacy, guilt, worry and doubt?

  According to the text (see p. 99), what does your answer to the preceding question tell you about yourself?

- Believers struggle with the behavior aspect of their growth because they are still struggling with the belief aspect of who they are in Christ.

  Consider how you are feeling about yourself and about life (inferior, insecure, inadequate, guilty, worried or doubtful to some degree). Look up the following Scriptures and choose one of the relevant verses to start memorizing this week.

  Inferiority — Ephesians 2:6
  Insecurity — Hebrews 13:5
  Inadequacy — Philippians 4:13
  Guilt — Romans 8:1
  Worry — Philippians 4:6
  Doubt — James 1:5

Most believers live somewhere between the mountaintop of spiritual maturity (Figure 5-B, p. 96) and the depths of fleshly behavior (Figure 5-C, p. 98). Walking in the Spirit is key to the process of transformation, which makes God's people more spiritual.

- So why are so few Christians enjoying the abundant, productive life we have inherited through Christ? Ignorance, lack of repentance, lack of faith in God and unresolved conflicts keep people from growing. However, the world and the flesh are not the only enemies of our sanctification. We have a living, personal enemy — Satan — who attempts to accuse, tempt and deceive God's children.

  What are your thoughts about Satan and his power? Are you ignorant? Are you looking for him behind every bush? Or are you aware of his existence and relying on the armor of God to protect you (see Ephesians 6:10-18)? Explain and support your answer. Be assured that chapter 9 focuses on this topic.

Satan takes an active role in opposing our spiritual growth, but it's a role we can stand strong against when we understand the parameters of the Spirit-filled walk.

Parameters of the Spirit-Filled Walk
(pages 100-108)

No matter how mature you may feel your faith is, you can never be productive for God's kingdom unless you are walking by faith in the power of the Spirit. Again, there is no magic formula or list of foolproof steps for how to do this, but the Bible does help us see what the Spirit-filled walk is and what it is not.

• Know that walking by the Spirit is relationship not regimentation.

What rules or formula for your faith did you begin with or are you beginning with?

What good purpose did or do these rules serve?

How have you moved beyond (or how do you hope to move beyond) these rules to a personal relationship with God?

What the Spirit-Filled Walk Is Not

• Paul clearly teaches that walking in the Spirit is not license. It is not a disregard for rules and regulation constituting an abuse of privilege. It is not doing anything you want to do. Being led by the Spirit means being free to live a responsible, moral life.

When have you learned that what appears to be an act of freedom can lead to bondage?

How have you found true freedom by walking with Christ? Give an example as Neil did to the questioning high school student on pages 102-103.

Walking by the Spirit is also not legalism. When have you been the victim of legalism — whether other-imposed or self-imposed? When have you been legalistic and judgmental in your attitude toward fellow believers?

What have you learned about the relationship between a person's faith and doing the right, Christian thing? Are daily Bible study, faithful prayer and regular church attendance guarantees of a Spirit-filled walk?

Walking by the Spirit is not legalism or license. The Bible's teachings are not to be used as hammers or ignored as irrelevant. Instead, within the confines of God's law, we are free to nurture a spirit-to-Spirit relationship with God, which is the essence of walking in the Spirit.

What the Spirit-Filled Walk Is

● The Spirit-filled walk is neither license nor legalism. It is liberty. As a believer, you are free to choose to walk according to the Spirit or according to the flesh. Walking according to the Spirit does not mean sitting and waiting for God to do it all; nor does it mean running in an exhaustive round of activities, trying to do everything ourselves.

Which extreme — sitting and waiting or running ahead —

do you tend to lean toward and why? Talk to God about your hesitation to take a step forward or your tendency to be busy in an attempt to be more spiritual.

What was your reaction to the description of the young ox being yoked to an older, seasoned ox (see p. 106)? In what ways do you try to run ahead of Jesus? Thank God for the privilege of being yoked to His Son in a relationship of rest and in service to the Kingdom.

How are you like Buster, the dog who never learned with his master? How are you choking, or exhausting, yourself by rushing ahead? How have you been yanked forward when you strayed off the path?

Our spiritual walk was never meant to be a burden. The key to a restful relationship yoked with Jesus is to learn from Him and to open yourself to His gentleness and humility (see Matthew 11:28-30). That yoke is also key to serving God. Nothing will ever be accomplished if you and the Lord don't walk together.

Being Led by the Spirit

● When Jesus describes Himself as the Good Shepherd (see John 10:14), He is speaking to our need to be led in our walk of faith.

Do you struggle with the thought that you are a sheep in need of a shepherd? Why or why not?

Consider the comparison between the way Neil drove the sheep ahead and the way the shepherd in Israel led his sheep (p. 107). Why is this difference between being driven and being led significant to you personally?

Thank God that He leads! And He leads hoping that you'll choose to follow. God won't make you walk in the Spirit, and the devil can't make you walk in the flesh, although he'll certainly tempt you to do so.

The Proof Is in the Fruit

● How can you know if you're walking according to the Spirit or according to the flesh? Look at your attitudes and actions, which are the fruit of your choices.

According to Galatians 5:22,23, what is the fruit of the Spirit-filled life?

Do the traits you just listed describe your behavior in the last 24 hours? And what does your answer to this question tell you about your relationship with Jesus right now?

● We must learn to have enough self-awareness to know when we are living according to the flesh and assume responsibility for our own attitudes and actions. We need to walk in the light and learn to confess, to consciously agree with God concerning our sins. When a deed of the flesh becomes evident, mentally acknowledge that to God and ask Him to fill you with His Holy Spirit.

Is it hard for you to admit your failures and confess your sins? Why? Talk to God about that and ask Him to be at work in you.

Walking according to the Spirit occurs when you choose to follow the Spirit instead of the temptations of the flesh. When you stray from that path, you can admit your missteps and begin anew in the freedom of God's gracious forgiveness.

LIVING WHAT YOU LEARN

Review the ideals reflected in 'The Spiritual Person' (Figure 5-B, p. 96). Read again the discussion of the young ox yoked to the older ox, which is based on Matthew 11:28-30 (see p. 106). Now consider your life today. In what situation can you live out one of the traits of a spiritual person? What set of circumstances calls you to walk more in tandem with Jesus than you are currently walking? How will you put into action your answers to these two questions?

A WORD OF PRAYER

Heavenly Father,

I thank You for sending Your Son as my Savior and Shepherd, for that gift of immeasurable love and grace. As I consider all You've given me and my attempts to live a life that honors You, I am aware of how I fall short. Show me where I'm guilty of license and guilty of cheapening Your grace. And show me where I am guilty of legalism toward others in a judgmental attitude or toward myself in demanding perfection. Thank You for Your forgiveness when I stumble and stray. And teach me, Father God, the liberty I may experience in You so I may enjoy a richer relationship with You and greater sensitivity to Your Spirit. I pray in Jesus' name. Amen.

LOOKING AHEAD

As a Christian you are free to choose to walk by the Spirit. Satan does not want you to have that freedom and will try to keep you from enjoying the liberty you have in Christ. The more you walk in step with Jesus, however, the better prepared you will be to recognize and resist Satan's deception.

6. The Power of Believing the Truth

Wilma Rudolph was born with major health problems that left her crippled, but after exercising her faith, her courage and her body for years, she became an Olympic medalist and Sullivan Award winner. Can faith do such great things for you?

The Power of Believing the Truth
(pages 109-110)

- Reconsider Wilma Rudolph's account of faith.

  What message does Wilma Rudolph's story have for you personally?

  Give another example of a person you know of, or, better yet, know personally whose faith enabled him or her to rise above incredible odds and achieve things other people haven't.

  When has your faith enabled you to stand strong in a difficult situation? Be specific.

  What current set of circumstances calls for faith that sometimes seems beyond you? Lift that situation before God in prayer, letting Him know what He already knows — that you're struggling to trust Him.

  Faith is indispensable to the Christian life. Believing who God is, what He says and what He does is the key to the kingdom of God.

The Essence of Faith
(pages 111-115)

Faith is the essence of the Christian's day-to-day activity. Faith is the basis for our salvation and the means by which we live.

● First, faith depends on its object. The critical issue is *what* or *whom* you believe in.

What are some of the objects and people that believers and nonbelievers alike put their faith in during the course of a regular day? Start your list with the example of red lights and other drivers mentioned in the text.

Which of the faith objects you listed are valid and trustworthy?

What does it mean to you that 'Jesus Christ is the same yesterday and today, yes and forever' (Hebrews 13:8)?

The fact that Jesus Christ never changes makes Him eminently trustworthy and eternally faithful. Faith that is dependent upon God is faith that can enable you to do great things.

● Second, how much faith you have is dependent on how well you know the object of your faith. When we struggle with our faith in God, it's not because our faith object has failed or is insufficient. It's because we don't have a true knowledge of God and His ways.

Faith in God only fails when we have a faulty understanding of Him. When has your faith wavered because, as you saw later, you had had a faulty understanding of God? Be specific.

If your faith is wavering now with regard to a certain situation, could it be because of a faulty understanding of God? Search the Scriptures. Seek counsel from a trusted and mature Christian. Talk to God about your struggle.

The only way to increase your faith is to increase your knowledge of God. When has learning something about God enabled you to trust Him more?

The only limit to your faith is your knowledge and understanding of God, which grows every time you read your Bible, memorize a Scripture verse, participate in a Bible study or meditate on God's Word.

- Third, faith is an action word. Faith without action isn't faith. If we really believe God and His Word, we will do what He says. What we believe determines what we do. If what we profess to believe doesn't affect our walk or our talk, then we really don't believe.

Reflect on the first time you took a step or made a stand in faith. How did you feel beforehand? What did you learn from the experience? What impact did your active faith have on your relationship with God?

Distortions of Faith
(pages 115-119)

Explain the difference between positive thinking and truth believing. Share your reaction to the distinction. How does the idea of truth believing call you to greater faith?

Read through 'Twenty Cans of Success' once again (see p. 118-119). Which 'can' are you going to open right now? Do so by looking up the Scripture reference given and memorizing it.

Believing that you can live a victorious Christian life takes no more effort than believing you cannot. So why not believe that you can walk by faith and in the power of the Holy Spirit? Let the 'Twenty Cans of Success' expand your knowledge of Almighty God, the object of your faith, and thereby give your faith the opportunity to grow.

What Happens When I Stumble in My Walk of Faith?
(pages 120-124)

Do you worry that God may be ready to give up on you because you stumble and fall instead of walking confidently in Him? Hear the following two wonderful truths:

God Loves You Just the Way You Are

● The primary truth you need to know about God in order for your faith to remain strong is that His love and acceptance are unconditional.

Who in your life was among the first to give you a taste of God's unconditional love? Thank God for that person.

Do you feel that God loves you when your walk of faith is strong but probably loves you less (if at all) when you're weak and inconsistent? If so, why do you think you have those feelings? And if not, why do you think you are able to rest in God's unconditional love?

Who in your life right now needs a taste of God's

unconditional love and acceptance? What will you do to show him or her that kind of love?

Know that, as your loving heavenly Father, God can and does understand your weakness and forgives your sin, and He'll never stop doing so.

God Loves You No Matter What You Do

● Of course God wants His people to do good, but He has made a provision for our failure through His Son, Jesus Christ, so that His love is constant in spite of what we do (see 1 John 2:1,2). Thanks to the powerful advocate you have in Jesus Christ, God will still love you because the love of God is not dependent upon its object. It is dependent on His character.

What have you done that you feel is reason enough for God to stop loving you?

Turn your answer to the preceding question into a prayer of confession and then read aloud this truth: 'No matter what I do in life, God is always going to love me. He may not approve of everything I do, but He's always going to love me.'

Jesus Christ has cancelled the debt of your sins — past, present and future. No matter what you do or how you fail and despite the lies Satan would have you believe, God will still love you.

LIVING WHAT YOU LEARN

As Paul teaches in Romans 10:17, 'Faith comes from hearing, and hearing by the word of Christ.' The only way to increase your faith is to increase your knowledge of God. What will you do to increase your knowledge of God? Set some goals

— long-range and short-range — regarding church attendance, reading the Bible, attending a Bible study, meditating on God's Word and memorizing passages from Scripture. Find someone who will encourage you, hold you accountable and, even better, join you in your efforts. Then identify the step you will take this week.

A Word of Prayer

God of love and faithfulness,

I've been reminded of some wonderful truths in this chapter, and I offer my thanksgiving and praise! It's exciting to think that the only limit to my faith is my knowledge and understanding of You, and it's also very convicting. Forgive me for my laziness, for not making time to study the Bible and get to know You better, for not being willing to spend time reading Your Word — for it is Your Word, God, that will teach me more about who You are. Despite all I have yet to learn about You, God, even now I praise You for being eminently trustworthy and eternally faithful and for extending to me Your unconditional and eternal love and acceptance. What a privilege and joy to be Your loved child! May I share the love You give to me with others so that they, too, may come to know You better. I pray in Jesus' name. Amen.

Looking Ahead

God wants you to accept your identity in Him and live as a child of God should. But even when you forget who you are, He still loves you. He wants you to walk in the Spirit, but even when you stumble and stray, He still loves you. That unconditional, unending love enables you to live out what you believe, to walk in the Spirit, and by your life, to invite others to come along.

7. You Can't Live Beyond What You Believe

A basic truth about your spiritual life — and an underlying premise of this book — is that your Christian walk is the direct result of what you believe. And, as the title of this chapter says, you can't live beyond what you believe.

You Can't Live Beyond What You Believe
(pages 125-127)

- The story of Karl's tee shot that opens chapter 7 in the text (see p. 125) illustrates an important aspect of the life of faith: If your faith is off, your walk will be off. If your walk is off, you need to take a good look at what you believe.

  When have you experienced 'if your faith is off, your walk will be off'? Describe that experience and how your faith got back on track.

- Walking by faith simply means that you function in daily life on the basis of what you believe.

  Think about a typical day. How does what you believe guide what you do as a spouse, friend, parent, homemaker and/or worker? Be as specific as possible.

  Was the preceding question difficult for you to answer? If so, what does that suggest about your faith and your walk of faith?

  What difference does walking by faith make in your life as

a believer? Compare, for instance, how you make decisions, choose a profession, deal with newspaper headlines or cope with personal loss to how nonbelievers do those things.

● If you haven't done so already, complete the eight questions that comprise the 'Faith Appraisal' form (see pp. 126-127).

Look at how you completed the eight sentences. What do your answers show you about yourself?

How well does what you think about these eight values line up with what God says? In other words, what do your answers show you about your walk of faith?

If you do not have the same definitions for success, significance, fulfillment, satisfaction, happiness, fun, security and peace that God does, your walk of faith will be faulty.

Feelings Are God's Red Flag of Warning
(pages 127-133)

But how can you know if what you believe is right? You can know because God has designed human beings with a feedback system so that we can know on a moment-by-moment basis if our beliefs are properly aligned with His truth. There are emotional signposts that may alert you when a goal is based on a wrong belief.

Anger Signals a Blocked Goal

● Anger is the first emotional signpost that can alert you that you may be cherishing a faulty goal based on a wrong belief.

Think about times when you have felt angry and evaluate the preceding statement. Were you angry because one of your goals was blocked? If so, what was that goal?

Was your goal faulty? If so, what wrong belief (counter to what God teaches) was it based on?

Now evaluate your main two or three goals in life. Are they healthy? Why or why not?

Feelings of anger should prompt us to reexamine what we believe and the goals we have formulated to live out those beliefs.

Anxiety Signals an Uncertain Goal

- When you feel anxious in a task or relationship, your anxiety may be signaling that achieving your goal may be uncertain.

When has your anxiety indeed signaled a goal that you later realized you shouldn't have been pursuing? Be specific about the situation and the lesson you learned.

Depression Signals an Impossible Goal

- When there is no physical cause for it, depression can be a signal that your goal, no matter how spiritual or noble, may never be reached.

When, if ever, have you experienced feelings of depression because you were working toward an impossible goal? Be specific about the goal and how you resolved your depression.

Sometimes depression reveals a faulty concept of God (see King David's words in Psalm 13:1,2). When, if ever, has your depression been linked to a wrong idea about God?

David moved away from his wrong concept of God and its accompanying depression (see Psalm 13:5,6; 43:5). What does David's example teach you? What hope does it give you?

Again, depression often signals that you are desperately clinging to a goal you have little or no chance of achieving, and that's not a healthy goal.

Wrong Responses to Those Who Frustrate Goals

● If your goal can be blocked or is uncertain, how do you respond to someone or something that threatens your success? You may attempt to control or manipulate people or circumstances who stand between you and the achievement of your goals.

When have you attempted to control or manipulate certain circumstances or people who were keeping you from reaching certain goals? Consider the experiences you've already shared in this lesson.

What happened as a result of your attempts to control and/or manipulate?

What lessons did you learn from these experiences?

Why do people try to control others? Because they believe (falsely) that their self-worth is dependent on other people and circumstances. But when they are unable to control, they become bitter, angry, resentful or martyred. The solution for this, and the lesson for you, is to adjust your goals and learn who you are in Christ.

How Can I Turn Bad Goals into Good Goals?

(pages 133-136)

- A faith-stretching question: If God wants something done, can it be done? In other words, if God has a goal for your life, can it be blocked? Is its fulfillment uncertain or impossible?

  Why does it make sense that the goal your Creator God has for your life cannot be blocked?

  No goal God has for your life is impossible or uncertain. Nor can it be blocked. For what area of your life does this fact give you hope?

  Just as you wouldn't give your child a task he or she couldn't accomplish, God doesn't assign you goals you can't achieve. His goals for you are possible, certain and achievable. You need to understand what His goal for your life is, and then say, with Mary: 'Behold, the bondslave of the Lord; be it done to me according to your word' (Luke 1:38).

Goals versus Desires

- In order to live a successful life you need to distinguish a godly goal from a godly desire.

  A godly goal reflects God's purposes for your life and doesn't depend on people or circumstances beyond your ability or right to control. The only person who can block a godly goal or render it uncertain or impossible is you. What godly goal(s) do you have for your life?

  A godly desire depends on the cooperation of other people, the success of events and/or the existence of favorable circumstances that you have no right or ability to control. (You cannot base your success or sense of worth on these desires, no matter how godly they are, because you cannot control their fulfillment.) What is a godly desire or are some godly desires that you have for your life?

You will struggle with anger, anxiety and depression when you elevate a desire to a goal in your mind. When has that happened to you? (Perhaps you didn't recognize the situation as such at the time, but now looking back through this lens you can see what was happening.) What did you learn from the situation(s)?

It's important to be sure that goals are goals, not elevated desires. One reason is that dealing with the disappointment of unmet desires is a lot easier than dealing with the anger, anxiety and depression caused by unreached goals that are based on wrong beliefs.

The Goal Is to Become the Person God Called You to Be
(pages 136-139)

When you align your goals with God's goals and your desires with God's desires, you will rid your life of a lot of anger, anxiety and depression. Such alignment will be easier when you acknowledge that God's basic goal for your life is character development: becoming the person God wants you to be.

- Becoming the person God wants you to be is clearly a godly goal. Nobody and nothing can keep you from being the person God called you to be. But along the way you can be sure to encounter distractions, diversions, disappointments, trials, temptations and traumas that will disrupt the process.

Life's distractions, diversions, disappointments, trials, temptations and traumas are a means of achieving your supreme goal of Christian maturity (see Romans 5:3-5; James 1:2-4). How have these difficulties in your life helped your faith mature? Give three or four examples.

What current difficulty can you look at as a means of growing in your faith? What do you think God would have you learn in this situation?

Trials and tribulations can reveal wrong goals, and they can actually be the catalyst for achieving God's goals for our lives — which is our sanctification. When has this proved true in your own life? When have life's hard times revealed to you the wrongness of your goals? Be specific about the circumstances and the goal(s) you were able to adjust after the experience.

Is there an easier way to become God's person than to endure trials and persevere through hard times? Believers who have gone before you will tell you that trials and hard times serve as fertile soil for spiritual growth. God may have already taught you that fact firsthand.

LIVING WHAT YOU LEARN

Review the important distinctions between godly desires and godly goals (see pp. 134-136, especially p. 135). With that fresh in your mind, evaluate your goals. Are they goals or, more accurately, are they desires? If you've never really set goals for yourself, let this be the opportunity to do so. Godly goals and desires help guide our growth in faith. What two or three goals can you establish and align with God's goals for you? Having written down a few goals — be they long-held ones or newly formulated ones in light of the points in this chapter — determine which one you will begin to work toward and what your first step will be, and then take that step!

A Word of Prayer

Almighty and gracious God,
   I've read that if my faith is off, my walk will be off and that if my walk is off, I need to take a good look at what I believe. Show me in these quiet moments where my walk is not what You would have it be and where my beliefs are not accurate. I've also read that anger, anxiety and depression can alert me to faulty goals. Again I ask that You would open my eyes and show me which goals I'm pursuing are in line with Yours. May my goals be the goals You would have for me. And, heavenly Father, may my sense of self-worth be based on the value You give me as Your child in Christ. Finally, God, may the overarching goal of my life be to become the person You want me to be. Teach me, guide me, mold me. I pray in Jesus' name. Amen.

Looking Ahead

God's basic goal for your life is character development: becoming the person He wants you to be. And, in the Bible, He offers some basic guidelines for your walk of faith — the walk that will help you reach that goal.

8. God's Guidelines for the Walk of Faith

How do you become the person God wants you to be? By walking the walk of faith. The Bible offers important guidelines for doing just that.

God's Guidelines for the Walk of Faith
(pages 141-142)

- Neil's special breakfast of eggs, sausage and muffins never materialized when his admirable goal was blocked.

  When has one of your goals been blocked? Give two or three examples and let them range in importance from your child deciding to be the lead guitarist in a rock band instead of a doctor, to getting to work late because of traffic.

  How did you respond emotionally to your foiled plans and blocked goals? What thoughts went through your mind?

  Often our sense of worth is tied up with reaching the goals we set for ourselves. When that's the case, life can be a real roller coaster ride. The only way to get off the roller coaster is to walk by faith according to the truth of God's Word.

Proper Guidelines Lead to a Proper Walk
(pages 142-153)

As we've seen, our walk of faith will be off to the same degree that our beliefs about success, significance, fulfillment, satisfaction, happiness, fun, security and peace are off. So let's see what the Bible teaches about these areas of belief. These lessons from God's Word may help you make some vital adjustments to your walk of faith.

Success. Key Concept: Goals

- Success is related to goals. If you're having trouble reaching your goals, it's probably because you're working on the wrong goals.

  A good summary of God's goal for you, His child, is found in 2 Peter 1:3-10, and that goal begins with who you are, based on what God has already done for you. God has given you 'life and godliness,' and now your job is to diligently adopt God's character goals and apply them to your life. List the seven goals mentioned in 2 Peter 1:5-7. Next to each, give an example from your life where you can work toward that goal (for instance, your income tax return may give you the opportunity to work toward moral excellence).

  Remember Joshua? His success hinged entirely on his obedience even when God's plan to march around Jericho for seven days sounded quite foolish (see Joshua 6). What lesson does Joshua offer you and to what current situation in your life can you apply that lesson?

  Focusing on God's goals — moral excellence, knowledge, self-control, perseverance, godliness, brotherly kindness and Christian love — will lead to ultimate success, success on God's terms.

Significance. Key Concept: Time

- Time is the true test of significance. What is forgotten in time is of little significance. What is remembered for eternity is of great significance.

When has a brother or sister in the Lord done something for you that he or she said was nothing but was in fact instrumental in your walk of faith? Be specific, and then reflect on the definition of significance given above.

What activities are you involved in that will be remembered for eternity? Answer that question knowing that there is no such thing as a lowly child of God!

What we do and say for Christ, no matter how insignificant it seems in this world, will last forever. And that is significance.

Fulfillment. Key Concept: Role Preference

- Fulfillment in life comes when you discover uniqueness in Christ and use your gifts and talents to edify others and glorify the Lord.

What does the world promise as the means to fulfillment? Which of these things have you realized, from personal experience, doesn't make good on that promise?

God has a unique place of ministry for each of us, and your greatest fulfillment will come from accepting and occupying, to the best of your ability, God's unique place for you. What can you do today to be God's representative in the following settings?

Your home
Your workplace
Your neighborhood
Your church

Your community
The places you run errands

Find fulfillment in life by deciding to be an ambassador for Christ in the world, in *your* world — and that means at home, in your neighborhood, at work, at school, in your community, wherever you encounter people who don't yet know the Lord and fellow believers whom you can encourage and support.

Satisfaction. Key Concept: Quality

- Satisfaction comes from living righteously and seeking to improve the quality of relationships, projects, products and activities with which you're involved. Satisfaction is a quality issue, not a quantity issue.

When have you experienced the truth that greater satisfaction comes with doing a few things well rather than from doing many things hastily?

Look at your life through the lens of the statement 'Satisfaction is a quality issue, not a quantity issue.' What does this suggest about how to eliminate some of the dissatisfaction you may currently be feeling?

The key to personal satisfaction is not found in broadening the scope of your activities but in deepening them through a commitment to quality.

Happiness. Key Concept: Wanting What You Have

- The world says that happiness is having what we want. God, in essence, says, 'Happy is the person who wants what he or she has' (see Matthew 6:31-33).

It's tempting to believe that things we don't have will bring us happiness. This faulty thinking results in discontentment. Change your focus and spend a few minutes now counting your blessings. List some of the many blessings God has given you.

Was Christ on your list of blessings? Explain in your own words why you already have everything you need to make you happy forever when you have Christ. Read the explanation aloud and allow it to be a prayer of thanksgiving.

If you really want to be happy, learn to be content with life and thankful for what you already have in Christ.

Fun. Key Concept: Uninhibited Spontaneity

- Simply put, fun is uninhibited spontaneity, and the secret to enjoying uninhibited spontaneity as a Christian is to remove unscriptural inhibitors.

What is your idea of fun?

When has (or does) people pleasing (an inhibitor) interfered with your fun? Be specific about the inhibitor: pride, insecurity, the need to be accepted, a desire to protect your image, etc.

Know that you'll find a lot more fun in pleasing the Lord than in trying to please people, so ask God to help you let go of any need to please others, protect a reputation or maintain a certain form of false decorum.

Security. Key Concept: Relating to the Eternal

- The key to experiencing security in your life is to depend on things eternal, not things temporal over which you have no control.

Think about times when you've felt insecure. What temporal things were you depending on?

Read through Romans 8:35-39 and replace some of the general categories listed (troubles, hardships, persecutions, powers or circumstances of the present [see vv. 35,38]) with some specifics from your life. Consider then the rhetorical question: How much more secure can you get than depending on God's promise that none of these things you listed can separate you from the love of Christ?

Our security can only be found in the eternal life of Christ.

Peace. Key Concept: Establishing Internal Order

• The peace of God is internal not external. Peace *with* God is something you already have (see Romans 5:1). The peace *of* God is something you need to appropriate daily in your inner world.

When you named Jesus as your Lord and Savior, you received the gift of peace with God. The peace of God, however, is something you need to appropriate daily. What does 'the peace of God' mean to you? Give an example or two of when you have experienced it.

You can control the inner world of your thoughts and emotions by allowing the peace of God to rule in your heart on a daily basis. What do you do to access the peace that God gives?

Know that personal worship, prayer and interaction with

God's Word enable you to experience the peace of God, the peace that passes all understanding (see Philippians 4:7).

LIVING WHAT YOU LEARN

As you've read about these eight categories and examined your walk of faith through the lens that they provide, what have you discovered about why you do the things you do? What beliefs do you need to adjust? Which belief will you work on transforming this week?

A WORD OF PRAYER

Heavenly Father,

I know that when You call Your people to do something, You also empower them, and that's what this chapter has done. Thank You for the perspective and encouragement it has given me on my walk of faith and on how You would have me walk. Lord, may Your goals for me be my goals. Help me to develop the moral excellence, knowledge of God, self-control, perseverance, godliness, brotherly kindness and Christian love that You want to characterize Your people.

May I find significance in doing things that touch eternity, fulfillment as I represent You in the situations You have placed me in, satisfaction in doing things for You and doing them well and happiness in my greater awareness of the many blessings You have showered upon me. May I find fun in the gift of life as I stop worrying about my image and other people's thoughts, security in You and You alone and the peace that comes from knowing You.

Help me, Father God, to adjust my beliefs so that

my actions will follow and my walk of faith will indeed bring honor and glory to You. I pray in Jesus' name. Amen.

LOOKING AHEAD

Are you ready to change your belief system so that your walk of faith will be on God's track? Winning the battle for your mind will be an important step in that direction.

9. Winning the Battle for Your Mind

Untold numbers of Christians are ignorant of Satan's schemes. They don't realize that there is a battle going on for their minds. They are being 'destroyed for a lack of knowledge' (Hosea 4:6).

Winning the Battle for Your Mind
(pages 155-159)

What was your reaction — emotional and intellectual — to Shelley's story? How credible do you find her experience?

You may or may not struggle to accept the very real power of Satan and his demons. If you don't accept the power of the demonic realm, why do you hesitate to believe what is taught in Scripture? If you acknowledge Satan and his efforts to trip up believers, how did you come to understand that truth?

What do you do to battle Satan when you recognize his efforts to deceive and debilitate?

When struggling believers resolve their personal and spiritual conflicts through repentance and faith in God, they too will experience their freedom in Christ.

God's Way versus Man's Way
(pages 157-159)

Faith in God is the Christian way to live and humanistic philosophical reasoning is man's way, but they are often in conflict. God is a rational God and He does work through our ability to reason. The problem is that our ability to reason is limited and prone to rationalization (see Isaiah 55:9).

- We can live God's way by faith (Plan A), or we can live our way by humanistic reasoning (Plan B).

The strength of Plan A in your life is determined by your personal conviction that God's way is always right and by how committed you are to believing Him. When has your conviction that God's way is always right wavered? What specific issues have moved you to question God's way?

The strength of Plan B is determined by the amount of time and energy you invest in entertaining thoughts that are contrary to God's Word. Are you, for instance, currently establishing an escape route in case God's plan fails? In other words, are you contemplating your own plans on how to live your life instead of investing time and energy in seeking God's plan and asking Him to help you live it out?

When you vacillate between God's Plan A and your Plan B, your spiritual growth will be stunted, your maturity in Christ will be blocked, and your daily experience as a Christian will be marked by disillusionment, discouragement and defeat.

The moment a Christian wife begins to think that she should get a part-time job in case her marriage doesn't work out, she cannot help but take something away from her wholehearted commitment to Plan A. The more she thinks about Plan B, the better the chances that she's going to need it. Where do such Plan B thoughts come from?

● First, your flesh still generates humanistic thoughts and ideas. You became a new person when you accepted His Son as Lord and Savior, but the old Plan B habits and thought patterns came with you.

On what issues does your flesh speak out most vocally and call you to live independently of God?

● Plan B thoughts come from the flesh, from this fallen world and from the devil and distract you from your walk of faith by establishing negative, worldly patterns of thought in your mind.

What negative thought patterns, past or present, might have been the result of the influences of the world, the flesh and the devil?

The essence of the battle for your mind is the conflict between Plan A, living by faith in God, and Plan B, living by the flesh as it is influenced by the world, your own flesh and the devil. Although you may feel quite helpless, you need to realize that God has provided all you need to win this battle for your mind.

Strongholds of the Mind
(pages 159-165)

● You need weapons of the Lord to overcome the strongholds of your mind — strongholds that were established either through repetition over time or through traumatic experiences.

At this point in the chapter, what strongholds in your mind can you identify for yourself?

Consider now the formation sources of the strongholds of the mind.

Environmental Stimulation

● Everything you learned in the formative years of your life was assimilated from the environment in which you were raised. There are two types of experiences that affect you as you mature — prevailing experiences and traumatic experiences.

What were the prevailing experiences of your home, school and neighborhood environments that are still affecting your walk with Christ today in positive ways? In negative ways?

Was there a traumatic experience in your childhood that has developed into a stronghold?

Evaluate the validity and the morality of the environmental stimulation you have experienced and its impact on you.

We all were conformed to this world, and even as Christians we still can be. We might choose to listen to the wrong music, watch the wrong TV programs, have the wrong friends and think the wrong thoughts. We are still going to be tempted to live our lives independently of God since we are living in a fallen world.

Temptation

● Temptation always comes by way of a thought, and the key to resisting temptation is to take that initial thought captive to the obedience of Christ.

God has provided a way for you to escape every temptation, but that opportunity for escape must be seized the moment you are tempted. When have you, like Cathy in the comic strip, let your unchecked, initial thought carry you away like a runaway freight train, leading you to do exactly what you didn't want to do initially? Give a specific example.

When have you been tempted but have taken that thought captive and acted in obedience to Christ? Explain what occurred. (Did God give you strength at the point you needed it? Did you receive freedom once you decided on God's Plan A course of action? Did you walk away from the temptation?)

If we don't capture the initial tempting thought when it first arises, it will probably capture us!

Consideration and Choice

• If you begin to mull over a tempting thought in your mind, your emotions will be affected and the likelihood of yielding to that temptation is increased. Your emotions are a product of your thought life.

'If what we think does not reflect the truth, then what we feel does not reflect reality.' Have you experienced a situation similar to the example (p. 162) in the book? What did you fear would happen? What actually happened? Were you able to avoid the temptation to sin in this situation?

Considering the experience you just described (or relating to the example in the book), what could you have chosen to think and do in this situation that could have alleviated the negative emotions?

There are many Christians who don't feel saved, who don't feel that God loves them, because of old thoughts raised up against the knowledge of God. When we tear down those strongholds and take every thought captive in obedience to Christ (see 2 Corinthians 10:5), our emotions will begin to conform to the reality of God's love.

Action, Habit and Stronghold

- When you pause to consider a temptation and then make the Plan B choice, you will find yourself acting on that choice and owning that behavior. And you are responsible for that action because you failed to take the tempting thought captive. If you continue to do that action for six weeks, it becomes a habit or, in this context, a stronghold.

  Inferiority, hostility, homosexuality, anorexia and bulimia are examples of strongholds. A stronghold is a mental habit pattern. It is memory traces burned into our minds over time or by the intensity of traumatic experiences. Now, having learned more about strongholds, identify any strongholds that exist in your mind.

- Perhaps it still isn't easy to identify strongholds in your mind. Considering possible sources of strongholds may help.

  A woman who was raped while a siren wailed in the background went into a deep depression every time she heard a siren. Has a similar brief and traumatic encounter resulted in a stronghold in your mind? If so, identify that stronghold.

Three brothers learned their various responses to hostile behavior (fighting, appeasing and running away) growing up in a home with an alcoholic father. What strongholds in your mind are the result of the prevailing atmosphere of your life?

Imagine life without these strongholds you've identified. How would life be different for you?

Any negative thoughts and actions you cannot control spring from a stronghold. Somewhere in the past you consciously or unconsciously formed a pattern of thinking and behaving that now controls you. But you need not remain a victim of these mental strongholds for the rest of your life. You can renew your mind.

Renewing The Mind
(pages 165-168)

If the strongholds in your mind are the result of conditioning, know that you can be reconditioned by the renewing of your mind. Through the preaching of God's Word, Bible study and personal discipleship you can stop being conformed to this world and experience the transformation of the renewing of your mind.

● You face more than just prior negative conditioning. You're also up against the devil who is scheming to fill your mind with thoughts that are opposed to God's plan for you.

In 2 Corinthians 10:5, Paul writes 'We are taking every thought captive to the obedience of Christ.' Thoughts need to be taken captive because they are contrary to God's ways and because they may be the enemy's thoughts. Comment on that fact. What kind of encouragement do you find in this truth? How does it help you as you consider trying to take thoughts captive?

Satan's strategy is to introduce his thoughts and ideas into your mind and to deceive you into believing that they are yours. Comment on the effectiveness of this strategy and identify two or three times when you have realized later that ideas you thought were your own were actually Satan's.

What do these two truths (i.e., taking thoughts captive and Satan's strategy) help you understand about times in the past when you've chosen Plan B?

In light of these truths, what will you do to be better prepared the next time temptation arises?

If you knew Satan had a certain idea planted in your mind, you'd reject that thought, wouldn't you? Disguising his suggestion as your idea is Satan's primary deception. If Satan can get you to believe a lie, you can lose some element of control in your life. If you fail to take every thought captive to the obedience of Christ, you may be allowing Satan to influence your life in a negative direction.

Expose the Lie and You Win the Battle
(pages 168-169)

Satan is a defeated foe; therefore his power is limited, but he still has the power to deceive the whole world (see Revelation 12:9). Satan has no power over you except what you yield to him when you are deceived into believing his lies. What kind of deception are you possibly experiencing due to the enemy? His attacks range from voices in one's mind to mental distractions that negatively affect your personal devotion to God.

Since Satan's primary weapon is the lie, your defense against him is the truth. When you expose Satan's lie with God's truth, his power is broken.

Winning the Battle for Our Minds

● How can you win this battle for your mind?

First, you must be transformed by the renewing of your mind (see Romans 12:2), and that happens when you fill it with God's Word. What are you doing regularly to let 'the word of Christ richly dwell within you' (Colossians 3:16)?

Second, you must prepare your mind for action (see 1 Pet. 1:13). What imaginings would you do well to dispose of?

In what current situation do you need to actively direct your mind to think about God's truth?

Third, take every thought captive in obedience to Christ (see 2 Corinthians 10:5). What can you do to keep alert and be sure to capture a thought when it first arises?

Fourth, when you are having anxious thoughts, turn to God in prayer. Why is this hard to do when Plan B thoughts are challenging your commitment to Plan A?

When you bring Plan B ideas before the Lord in prayer, you are acknowledging God and exposing your thoughts to His truth. That means victory over your enemy, the deceiver.

LIVING WHAT YOU LEARN

What have you learned about yourself in this chapter? What plan of action do these lessons about yourself call for? You may need to talk to a pastor or counselor about the strongholds you seem to be battling. It would be a good course of action to get some suggestions about the kind of further Bible study you can be doing as you work to fill your mind with God's truth. Let this lesson you've just completed empower you as you discover in God's truth the effective weapon you need against Satan and his deceptions.

A WORD OF PRAYER

Heavenly Father,

Your words of truth are like a refreshing wind blowing away the chaff and clearing my mind. Thank You for this perspective on your Plan A versus my too often considered Plan B on strongholds in my mind. Thank You that, with Your truth, I can be victorious over Satan's deceptions. God, my thoughts need to be taken captive because Satan often disguises his suggestions as my ideas. Please show me which negative thoughts and behavior patterns are strongholds that Satan uses against me in my walk of faith. Teach me to be vigilant in the analysis of my ideas and diligent in filling my mind with Your truth and turning to You in prayer. God, I want to stand strong in Your truth so that I may experience freedom in You. I pray in Jesus' name. Amen.

LOOKING AHEAD

Again, when you expose Satan's lies with God's truth, Satan's power is broken and the victory is yours. Such victory in the battle for your mind is the undisputed inheritance of everyone who is in Christ.

10. You Must Be Real to Be Right

Victory in the battle for your mind is the undisputed inheritance of everyone who is in Christ, and recognizing that there is a battle is the first step.

You Must Be Real to Be Right
(pages 175-177)

- Review the story of Judy and then consider these questions.

  How does Judy's story illustrate the chapter title 'You Must Be Real in Order to Be Right'? In light of Judy's experience, explain what that title means.

  Why are anger and anxiety perfect footholds for Satan?

  Where have you not been — or where are you not being — real about your emotions?

  Judy's unresolved feelings toward her father and her efforts to cover up her anxieties kept her from spiritual victory, spiritual growth and freedom in Christ. What's keeping you from experiencing these things?

Your Emotions Reveal Your Beliefs
(pages 177-180)

Your emotions play a major role in the process of renewing your mind. If you fail to appropriately acknowledge your emotions, you become spiritually vulnerable.

● As we see in Lamentations 3, the prophet Jeremiah's despair changed when what he thought about God changed. When Jeremiah recalled God's unceasing loving-kindness and great faithfulness, his emotions followed suit.

When have your emotions clearly been the result of wrong thinking about a situation, a person or God Himself?

How did your thinking get straightened out? What change in emotions did you experience as a result?

● You are not shaped as much by your environment as you are by your perception of your environment. Likewise, life's events don't determine who you are; God determines who you are — your interpretation of life's events determines how well you handle the pressures of life.

What did you learn from the story about the real estate loan (see p. 180)? What did this illustration show you about the connection between events, thoughts and emotions?

● If what you believe does not reflect truth, then what you feel does not reflect reality. Even so, you can't simply change or turn off your emotions. The problem that must be addressed is the wrong perception of the situation that is making you feel the way you do. The solution is to adjust your perception of the situation and base it on truth.

Describe your general state of emotions right now. If you're feeling more negative than positive, consider whether you are thinking wrongly about a certain event. Ask God to give you insight as you adjust your thinking and know that the emotions will follow.

- The order of Scripture is to know the truth, believe it, live accordingly by faith and let your emotions be a product of your trust in God and your obedience to Him.

Why is it so easy to believe what you feel?

What will you do to know the truth better so that you can trust truth rather than emotions?

'If you know these things, you are blessed if you do them' (John 13:17). In other words, you don't feel your way into good behavior, you behave your way into good feelings.

Don't Ignore the Warning Signs of Your Emotions
(pages 181-187)

Your emotions are to your soul what your physical feelings are to your body. If you didn't feel the gamut of emotions from anger to joy, from sorrow to delight, your soul would be in trouble. Emotions let you know what is going on inside you.

- Think about your general attitude and reaction toward emotions.

Are you comfortable with people's expressions of emotions? Why or why not?

Are you comfortable expressing emotions? Why or why not?

Why is it significant that God designed emotions?

Just as you have learned to respond to the warnings of

physical pain and to the red warning lights on you car's dashboard, you need to learn to respond to your emotions. We'll look at three response options.

The Duct Tape of Suppression

● Suppression is a conscious denial of feelings. It is the choice not to deal with them, and it is an unhealthy response to your emotions.

Were you taught to suppress your emotions? Describe how you learned that lesson (through modeling, being reprimanded, environmental influences, etc.).

What have been the unhealthy consequences of suppressing your emotions? How have you suffered because other people suppressed their emotions?

Why are you sometimes or even often tempted to suppress certain emotions? Ask God to help free you from this fear and to teach you a better way to deal with your emotions.

Don't cover over your emotions. Suppression isn't good for you, for others or for your relationship with God.

The Hammer of Indiscriminate Expression

● Another unhealthy way to respond to emotions is to thoughtlessly express everything you feel.

Do you sometimes choose this option? Describe some of the consequences (personal and interpersonal) of indiscriminately expressing your emotions.

Anger is a prime candidate for indiscriminate expression. How do you deal with anger? Talk to God about how you would like to deal with anger and any other emotions you tend to share indiscriminately. Open your heart to His way.

If you wish to be angry and not sin, then be angry the way Christ was: be angry *at* sin. Turn over the tables; don't attack the money changers (see Matthew 21:12,13).

The Openness of Acknowledgment

- If you come to your prayer time feeling angry, depressed or frustrated and then mouth a bunch of pious platitudes as if God doesn't know how you feel, do you think He is pleased? Not unless He's changed His opinion about hypocrisy since the times of the Pharisees!

Acknowledging your feelings is healthy. Not acknowledging them is unhealthy and hypocritical. What keeps you from acknowledging your feelings?

Acknowledging your emotions as a real person is essential for intimate relationship. In fact, it is difficult to maintain mental health unless you have at least one person with whom you can be emotionally honest. With whom can you be emotionally honest? Thank God for that person. If there is no one in your life right now with whom you can be emotionally honest, ask God to give you that important friend and, in the meantime, work on being emotionally honest with God.

So now you understand the importance of emotional honesty and you want to be emotionally honest, but it's unfamiliar territory for you. How do you start? The following guidelines will help.

Emotional Honesty: How to Dish It Out and How to Take It

(pages 187-190)

One of the challenges in the area of emotions is learning how to respond to others when they honestly acknowledge their pain.

- Tired and emotionally depleted, Neil had no words of comfort for the parents whose son had died. Instead, he sat there and cried with them. Later, they told him that his tears had let them know of his love.

Why do you think we (or, more specifically, you) always feel the need to respond to someone's emotions with words?

When has someone shown you that he or she understands what you're feeling by crying with you? How did you react to that person's tears?

What people say in the midst of extreme pain is not what we should be listening to. We should be responding to the pain, not the words that express it. In too many cases we ignore the feelings of hurting people and fixate on their words of despair, reacting to what they said or how they said it. Your Savior wept, for instance, when grief-stricken Mary and Martha told Him of Lazarus's death.

- It's important to respond to the feelings of someone in pain. It's also important to not take too seriously the words of someone who is expressing his or her emotions honestly.

Why is this a good rule to follow?

How do you want people to respond to you when you're dealing with some intense emotions and needing to talk them out? (Your answer may be a good guideline for you to follow the next time you're with a person who is hurting.)

You weep with those who weep. You don't offer lectures in response to the rhetorical questions asked out of the depth of their pain.

- Another important point about dealing with emotions is this: Don't forsake love in your eagerness to be honest.

Remember the husband, the wife, the six o'clock dinner and the seven o'clock meeting? How would you like to respond if you were the husband? If you were the wife?

What do you do to try to control your tongue so that, when emotions are high, you don't sacrifice love in the name of honesty?

When it comes to acknowledging emotions with your inner circle, honesty is the best policy. But be sure to speak the truth in love (see Ephesians 4:15).

- When you're dealing with emotions, know your limitations. Be aware that times of high emotions are not times for good decision making. Also, be ready to continue a discussion at a later time before you say something you'll regret.

What emotions tend to push you to make decisions that aren't always the best? Are those emotions signals to you to put off decisions until your emotions have subsided?

Is 'May we continue this discussion at another time?' part of your vocabulary when you've reached your emotional limits? If so, how has it served you? If not, what can you do to add it to your repertoire?

As human beings, we have limitations, and emotions can push us to those limits. We need to give ourselves permission to acknowledge our limits and stay within the bounds of love and patience when emotions are running high.

● Finally, realize that various physical factors affect your emotional limits.

What physical factors tend to affect your emotional limits?

Which of those factors are you dealing with right now? What are you doing to cope with them?

The important process of renewing your mind includes managing your emotions by managing your thoughts and perceptions. The process also involves acknowledging your feelings honestly and lovingly in your relationships with others.

LIVING WHAT YOU LEARN

Review the guidelines for emotional honesty and choose which guideline you need to work on the most. Then read through the guidelines for emotional honesty with a person who is affected by your ability to be emotionally honest (a spouse, child, parent, close friend, coworker, roommate, etc.). Let that person know what you will be working on and ask him or her to work with you and hold you accountable. That person may also want to choose a guideline on which to work.

A Word of Prayer

Creator God,

You gave me my emotions so that I can know what is going on inside. Thank You for that gift. Too often though, I listen to and believe my emotions rather than the truth. At moments when that happens, please bring me back to Your truth so that I can believe it, live accordingly by faith and let my emotions follow. And, Father God, please free me from emotions I have suppressed and/or my tendency to suppress my emotions. Forgive me for times I have indiscriminately expressed my emotions and show me whom I've hurt and need to ask forgiveness of. Give me the courage and sensitivity I need in order to acknowledge my emotions and to support those I care about when they are sharing their emotions. May I reflect Your love as I learn to follow the guidelines for emotional honesty that I've been reading about. And Father, enable me to be emotionally honest with You, as You already know what I'm feeling anyway. I pray in Jesus' name. Amen.

Looking Ahead

Responding to your emotions properly is an important step in keeping the devil from gaining a foothold in your life. Sometimes you also need to respond to emotions and emotional wounds left over from the past.

11. Healing Emotional Wounds from Your Past

All of us have an emotional history. We've all been hurt along the way, and the emotions from these life experiences can interfere with our spiritual growth.

Healing Emotional Wounds from Your Past
(pages 191-192)

● Reread the story of Cindy and Dan.

What misunderstanding of God's truth was keeping Cindy from leaving behind her identity as a rape victim? (See Romans 8:28.)

Neil explained to Cindy that God works everything for good but that He doesn't make a bad thing good. How might this truth affect Cindy's emotions?

Where can you apply Neil's explanation of Romans 8:28 to your life? And how can this truth affect your emotions?

Cindy needed to be reminded that she is a child of God and encouraged to see herself as His much-loved daughter instead of as a rape victim. You, too, are a child of God. Remember that as you consider hurts from your past.

Bad Things Do Happen to Good People
(pages 192-194)

Any number of traumatic events in your past can leave you

holding a lot of emotional baggage. Consider how emotions from the past may be affecting you today.

● As the next two questions will illustrate, those traumatic experiences are buried in your memory and available for instant recall.

How did you react to the story of Cindy's rape? What events from your past determined your reaction?

What names evoke a positive emotional reaction from you? What names bring forth negative emotions? Give a few examples of each and say, if you can, why you react as you do.

The residual effects of past traumas are primary emotions. The intensity of your primary emotions is determined by your previous life history.

● Review the path from 'Previous Life History' to 'Secondary Emotion' (see p. 193) and then answer these questions.

When have you experienced the process outlined here? When has a present event triggered a primary emotion? Be specific.

What did you do to deal with the primary emotion? In other words, what did you do at the Mental Evaluation stage?

What secondary emotion did you then deal with?

If you handled well the primary and secondary emotions you felt in the experience you just outlined, you may have learned how to resolve conflicts from your past. It's important to learn how to do that so you can deal with the primary and secondary emotions they prompt. Also, resolving previous conflicts keeps emotional baggage from accumulating, weighing you down and even controlling your life.

Learning to Resolve Primary Emotions
(pages 194-196)

Some Christians assert that the past doesn't have any effect on them since they are new creations in Christ, but those who have experienced major traumas and learned to resolve them in Christ know how devastating past experiences can be.

- When you ask God to search your heart, He will expose those dark areas of your past and bring them to light — into His healing light — at the right time.

  Which of the ideas in this chapter are new to you? What are your thoughts about the possibility of memories being buried deep within one's subconscious, the past holding a person in bondage, or primary emotions being rooted in events of long ago?

  Perhaps these ideas are not unfamiliar to you. You may have even seen God, the Wonderful Counselor, work in your life or in the life of someone close to you. If so, comment on God's timing. How did His revelation of the past correspond with your (or the person's) level of maturity?

  Consider praying with David the words of Psalm 139: 'Search me, O God, and know my heart; try me and know my anxious thoughts; and see if there be any hurtful way in me, and lead me in the everlasting way' (vv. 23,24). God knows about the hidden hurts within you that you may not be able to see. You can trust Him to be by your side as you feel the emotions from the past and to free you from their effect on your life.

The Holy Spirit will guide you into all the truth (John 16:13), and the truth will set you free (see John 8:32).

See Your Past in the Light of Who You Are in Christ
(pages 196-197)

How does God intend for you to resolve those past traumas?

● Understand that you are no longer a product of your past. You are a product of Christ's work on the cross — a new creation. You have the privilege of evaluating your past experience in light of who you are today.

If the hurts happened before you were a believer, you can find hope in the fact that, as a Christian, you are a new creation in Christ. Old things, including the traumas of your past, are passed away. Spend some time now praying about this powerful truth. Ask that God would help you believe in that newness as you deal with emotions and hurts from the past.

If you were a believer when the trauma(s) occurred, what hope do you find in the promise of Romans 8:28 and the perspective that offered Cindy hope at the beginning of this chapter?

● Remember the relationship between emotions and beliefs? Keep in mind that the intensity of the primary emotion was determined by how you perceived the event at the time it happened.

Explain how this truth can help you deal with the primary emotions rooted in your past.

● People who have been verbally abused by their parents struggle to believe that they are loved unconditionally by Father God. Their primary emotions argue that they are unlovable to a parent figure. They find it hard to believe that they are of great value in Christ.

What did you learn from this example of primary emotions, rooted in the past, that contradict today's reality?

If the verbally abused (and maybe you're one of them) began to believe their value in Christ, how would life be different?

Perceiving painful events of the past from the perspective of your new identity in Christ (or of your renewed appreciation of that identity) is what starts the process of healing damaged emotions.

Forgive Those Who Have Hurt You in the Past
(pages 198-205)

The first step in resolving past traumas is to evaluate the past in light of who you are in Christ now. The second step is to forgive those who have offended you. And why should you forgive those who have hurt you in the past?

● First, forgiveness is required by God.

Read again Matthew 6:14,15. Comment on the inclusiveness of the command and what it reflects about the One who issued the command.

Like all of God's commands, the command to forgive is given for your benefit. What happens to us when we don't forgive those who have hurt us?

● Second, forgiveness is necessary to avoid entrapment by Satan.

Why is lack of forgiveness the number one avenue Satan uses to gain entrance to believers' lives? What can the deceiver do with that foothold to block someone's relationship with God?

When have you seen a person entrapped by his or her unwillingness to forgive? Describe the effects on that person.

● Third, forgiveness is required of all believers who desire to be like Christ (see Ephesians 4:31,32).

Why is forgiveness important in the community of believers?

Why is forgiveness important to the witness of the community of believers?

There are several reasons why we should forgive those who have hurt us in the past, but first . . .

What Is Forgiveness?

Let's begin to answer that question by saying what forgiveness is *not*.

Forgiveness is *not* forgetting. Respond to this truth. Is this a new perspective for you? What does it mean concerning the forgiveness you've extended to people in the past?

Forgiveness does *not* mean tolerating sin. When has extending forgiveness meant explaining that you won't tolerate the same offense in the future? Describe how you dealt with or would like to deal with that situation.

Forgiveness does *not* seek revenge or demand repayment. You can let the ones who hurt you off your hook because you realize that God does not let them off His hook. Why is it hard to leave justice up to God?

• Forgiveness is not forgetting; it's not tolerating sin; it's not seeking revenge. What then is forgiveness? Forgiveness is resolving to live with the consequences of another person's sin. You can choose to live with those consequences in the bondage of bitterness or in the freedom of forgiveness.

Describe a time when you found peace once you forgave someone who wronged you.

Now consider an opportunity you currently have to forgive someone. What's holding you back? Make this situation a topic of prayer.

Expect positive results when you extend forgiveness to those who have hurt you. In time, you will be able to think about the people who offended you without feeling hurt, angry or resentful.

Twelve Steps to Forgiveness

• Forgiveness is what sets us free from the past. What is to be gained in forgiving is freedom. You don't heal in order to forgive; you forgive in order to heal. You don't forgive others for their sake; you do it for your sake. The text outlines the 12-step process for forgiving someone (see pp. 200-203).

Which steps in the process surprise you?

Which steps in the process are especially hard for you?

Comment on the wisdom of the steps and why this process proves effective and freeing.

As difficult as these steps can be, know that forgiveness really sets you free from past hurts.

A Second Touch

- In Mark 8:22-26, Jesus heals a blind man. At Jesus' first touch, the man says, 'I see men . . . like trees' (v. 24). When Jesus touches the man a second time, he begins to see people as people.

  Why does seeing people as people, not as obstacles, enable us to forgive them when they hurt us?

  Where do you need a second touch from the Lord right now? Think about people who have hurt you. Which of those do you need to see more clearly as people?

In a few quiet moments now, ask for a second touch from the Lord that you might see those who hurt you as people who themselves have been hurt. As you do so, know that this second touch is one way God will help you become more the person He wants you to be.

LIVING WHAT YOU LEARN

You've read through the steps of forgiveness. Now it's time to work through them. After you pray the prayer that follows, get out a blank sheet of paper, list the names of people who have offended and hurt you, and describe the specific wrongs you suffered. With that, you will have taken the first step in the journey toward freedom from past hurts. Then move on to the second step, and don't be afraid to invite a trusted friend or a professional counselor to help you and pray for you at this step or any of the others. What is to be gained by forgiveness is freedom.

A Word of Prayer

All-knowing and all-loving God,

I come before You with David's words on my lips, 'Search me, O God' (Psalm 139:23). Maybe there is something in my past that, brought to light, into Your healing light, can mean freedom for me. Show me, merciful and gentle God, whom I need to forgive and of what I need to forgive them.

Bad things do happen to good people — to Your people, God. Help me to trust Your love and Your power of redemption as I look to You to work good from the pain I've experienced.

And, God, as I confront that pain, I hear Your call to forgive those who have hurt me. I know that Your command to forgive is for my own good, but it's so hard. Yet as Jesus hung from the cross, He asked You to forgive those who crucified Him. May I follow His example. Be with me as I work through the steps of forgiveness. May I be aware of Your love and protection as I deal with harsh truth and deep pain. I pray in the precious name of Your Son and my Savior, the One who forgives and enables me to forgive. Amen.

LOOKING AHEAD

Healing emotional wounds from the past will enable you to find victory over the darkness and freedom in God's light. Dealing with any rejection you've experienced is also essential to realizing victory.

12. Dealing with Rejection in Your Relationships

Everyone knows what it feels like to be criticized and rejected, and often we know criticism and rejection from the very people we so want to please. All of us have experienced the pain of rejection to some degree.

Dealing with Rejection in Your Relationships
(pages 207-208)

- Most of us haven't suffered the pervasive rejection that Ruby experienced, but each of us has been ignored, overlooked or rejected at times by parents, teachers, coaches and friends.

  In chapter 11 you took the first step in the process of forgiveness and listed people who had hurt you. Which of those people inflicted pain, knowingly or unknowingly, by rejecting you?

  How has Satan been using your experiences of being rejected to keep you from believing you are a loved child of God? What lies has Satan taught you and ingrained into your mind?

  Since we all know rejection, we all need to be aware that Satan uses those experiences to keep us down. But God, who Himself rejected us until we were accepted by Him in Christ at salvation, is able to free us from the pain of rejection and the false messages that Satan has etched into our minds.

When You Are Criticized or Rejected
(pages 208-212)

● Rejection, and the accompanying thoughts and feelings, can be a major deterrent to our maturity in Christ.

What thoughts and feelings about yourself do you deal with as a result of the times you've been rejected?

How do you think these thoughts and feelings have blocked your growth — spiritually and otherwise?

There are various ways to respond to rejection, and most of us choose one of the three negative, defensive options rather than the positive approach.

Beat the System

● Some people respond to rejection by learning to compete and scheming to get ahead. Striving to earn acceptance and significance through their performance, these people are characterized by perfectionism, emotional insulation, anxiety and stress. Committed to controlling people and circumstances for their own ends, these beat-the-system people also have a hard time coming under God's authority.

Why is beating the system an appealing option for someone who has been rejected?

Do you know someone who fits the description of a beat-the-system person? Describe the rejection that person experienced and the consequences of this response.

Beat-the-system people are often very insecure. Sadly, their strategy only delays the inevitable rejection.

Give In to the System

- Most people today respond to rejection by simply giving in to the system. They continue to try to satisfy others, but their failures prompt them to believe that they really are unlovable and unacceptable. These people tend to blame God for their situations and find it difficult to trust Him.

Why do many people choose this option in response to the rejection they've experienced?

Do you know someone who fits the above description? Describe the rejection that person experienced and the consequences of this type of response.

People who give in to the system's false judgment can only look forward to more and more rejection. They have bought the lie and therefore find it easy to reject themselves.

Rebel Against the System

- Rebels and dropouts respond to rejection by saying, 'I don't need you or your love.' Deep inside they still crave acceptance, but they refuse to acknowledge their need. Full of self-hatred and bitterness, rebels see God as just another tyrant and they rebel against Him just like they rebel against everyone else.

What is appealing and even understandable about this response to rejection?

Do you know someone who fits the above description? Describe the rejection that person experienced and the consequences of this response.

This person's rebellious attitude and behavior tend to

alienate others, and so the rebel experiences further rejection.

Your Response

Where do you see yourself or traits of yourself in these profiles of negative responses to rejection? Is your approach to beat the system, give in to the system or rebel against the system? Explain, if you can, why you have chosen that option and the consequences of your choice.

Defensiveness Is Defenseless
(pages 212-215)

● There are two reasons why you never need to respond defensively to the world's critical, negative evaluation of you:

First, if you are wrong, you don't *have* a defense. When you're wrong, any defense would be rationalization at best and a lie at worst. Think about times you've been wrong and responded defensively. Was your response a rationalization or a lie?

Why is it so hard to admit when you're wrong instead of being defensive?

Second, if you are right, you don't *need* a defense. The Righteous Judge, who did not revile when He was reviled or make threats when He suffered (see 1 Peter 2:23), will exonerate you. Comment on that fact. How can this truth make a practical difference in your life?

What did you learn from Neil's conversation with Alice (see pp. 213-214)?

As Neil's response to Alice's criticism vividly illustrates, you are not obligated to respond to criticism defensively. After all, the world's system for determining your value as a person is not what determines your value. You are in the world, but you are not of the world. You are in Christ. So if you find yourself responding to rejection defensively, let it remind you to focus your attention on those things that will build up and establish your faith.

When You Are Tempted to Criticize or Reject Others
(pages 215-223)

Rejection is a two-way street: you can receive it and you can give it. We've looked at how to respond when you are criticized and rejected. Let's look now at how to respond to the temptation to criticize and reject others.

● Review the situation of Fred and Sue (see pp. 215-216).

What does it mean to you that you are responsible for your own character?

What does it mean that you are responsible to meet other people's needs in the context of those you live with or any other relationship between believers?

● Relationships don't work when, instead of assuming responsibility for your own character, you attack the other person's character and, instead of looking out for that person's needs, you are selfishly absorbed in meeting your own needs.

Think about the last time you clashed with your spouse, a friend, a coworker or one of your children. Does the description you just read apply to what was going on? Be specific about how you failed to assume responsibility for your own character and attacked the other person and how you were concerned about your own needs rather than the other person's. An apology and request for forgiveness may be in order.

Answer this somewhat rhetorical question: What kind of families and churches would we have if we all assumed responsibility for our own character and sought to meet the needs of those with whom we live and worship?

Instead of devoting ourselves to developing our own character and to meeting each other's needs, we often yield to Satan's prodding to criticize each other's characters and selfishly focus on our needs.

Focus on Responsibilities

● Another way Satan has deceived us in our interpersonal relationships is by tempting us to focus on our rights instead of our responsibilities.

Describe things you feel you have a right to and therefore tend to demand. (The text gives examples on page 217.)

Now consider the flip side of those rights — your responsibility in the given situation, be it your marriage, your family, your job (see page 217).

What does this discussion about rights versus responsibilities show you about yourself and where you need to be working to become more the person God wants you to be?

What specific step will you take?

When we stand before Christ, He will not ask if we received everything we had coming to us. Instead, He will reward us for how well we fulfilled our responsibilities.

Don't Play the Role of Conscience

● Sometimes we are tempted to play the role of the Holy Spirit or conscience in someone else's life.

How do you respond when someone assumes the role of Holy Spirit or conscience for you? Why do you respond that way?

When have you acted as Holy Spirit or conscience for someone? Be specific about the issue, the person and that person's reaction.

What good came from your self-appointed role as Holy Spirit or conscience? Take note!

The Holy Spirit knows exactly when and how to bring conviction to a person. When we attempt to play the role of the Holy Spirit in others' lives, we misdirect their battles with God to ourselves. In doing so, we often do little more than convey criticism and rejection. Your job is to surround people with acceptance and love. Allow the Holy Spirit to bring conviction and change.

Discipline Yes, Judgment No

● But there are times when Christians are called to confront their fellow believers. When someone has clearly violated the boundaries of Scripture, we are to accept the sinner but not the sin. We are to confront that person in an attempt to restore him or her to fellowship with God and His people, and Scripture outlines how such church discipline should be handled (see Matthew 18:15,16).

When have you seen or been a part of the process of church discipline that Jesus describes in Matthew

18:15,16? Describe the process — how easy or difficult it was — and what happened in the person's life as a result of biblical discipline.

- Be aware that discipline is an issue of confronting behavior you have personally witnessed but that judgment is an issue of character. Disciplining others is a part of our ministry; judging character is God's responsibility.

With your choice of words, you can too easily cross the line from discipline to character assassination. For instance, rather than calling your son a liar (which is a brutal attack on his character), you say, 'Son, you just told a lie,' a statement that holds him accountable for observed behavior. Think about what you said when you discovered someone doing something wrong recently. Where did you cross the line from discipline to judgment? Give a specific example. Again, an apology and request for forgiveness may be in order.

We must hold people accountable for their sinful behavior, but we are never allowed to denigrate their character.

Express Your Needs Without Judging

- If you have legitimate needs in a relationship that are not being met, you are to express those needs in such a way that you don't impugn the other person's character.

'You don't love me anymore' has a very different impact from 'I don't feel loved anymore.' How would you react to each of these statements? Why would you be more receptive to one than the other?

- The nonjudgmental approach of an 'I' statement frees the other person to respond to your need instead of defending him- or herself against your attack.

Do you have trouble asking for your needs to be met? To help you understand the importance of doing so, explain in your own words how *not* expressing your needs can give Satan a foothold in your life.

● When you deny fellow believers the privilege of meeting your legitimate needs, you are acting independently of God and you are leaving yourself vulnerable to getting your needs met by the world, the flesh and the devil.

How did you react to the poem on page 222? What points support the truths you've been working with in this lesson?

Anybody can find character defects and performance flaws in another Christian. It takes the grace of God to look beyond people's less-than-saintly behavior to recognize that they are saints in God's eyes. May God give us that grace.

LIVING WHAT YOU LEARN

A good first step in applying the many truths of this lesson is to focus on making 'I' statements rather than 'you' statements when you are expressing your needs. Perhaps there is a recurring situation or two for which you can plan an appropriate 'I' statement. Also, talk with your friends and your family about how to express needs without hurting people. Make this a group effort toward eliminating feelings of criticism and rejection in your home.

A WORD OF PRAYER

Lord Jesus,
    You know what it feels like to be rejected. You know what I have experienced and how I feel inside. Forgive

me for responding so differently from the way You did. Forgive me for trying to beat the system by controlling, manipulating, using and hurting people. Or for giving in to the system and believing Satan's lies. Or for being filled with self-hatred and bitterness, rebelling against the system and against You. Forgive me, too, for finding it hard to trust You to judge those who have rejected me. Help me believe that I don't need to respond to criticism and rejection. Help me to trust You to be my defense.

Then, Lord, there's my criticism of others. Forgive me for such unloving ways. Help me to work on developing my own character rather than attacking someone else's, on meeting another's needs rather than seeking to have my needs met, and on fulfilling my God–given responsibilities in various situations rather than demanding my rights. And help me to control my tongue so that I speak words of discipline, not harsh words of judgment, and offer 'I' messages rather than 'you' messages when I share my needs.

God, give me the grace to forgive those who have rejected and hurt me and the grace to love and accept those whom I am tempted to criticize and reject. I pray in Jesus' name. Amen.

LOOKING AHEAD

For 12 chapters you've studied growth and what can block it. As this study closes, you'll look at one thing that fosters spiritual growth and maturity like nothing else does — and that's community.

13. People Grow Better Together

You've looked at some of the factors in your life that can prevent your spiritual growth. You'll end this call to victory over the darkness by looking at a factor that contributes greatly to your spiritual and personal growth: the community of Christ.

People Grow Better Together
(pages 225-226)

● Danny had gone to the retreat to learn, not to relate. He wanted content, not community. After two weeks, however, he came to see that spiritual growth and maturity happen best in a community of people who know and accept each other.

How did you learn the truth that 'people grow better together'? Describe an experience that made that lesson very clear to you.

Maybe you haven't yet experienced the truth that people grow better together. What do you think about that possibility? If you are skeptical, what will you do to find out whether what was true for Danny will be true for you?

Jesus calls His people to share their lives — not just information about Him — with another. That is the secret to successful discipleship and to spiritual growth.

Relationship: The Heartbeat of Growth and Maturity
(pages 226-227)

• In a ministry of discipleship, your curriculum must be the Bible and your program must be relational. Otherwise, you're not doing discipleship. Lots of Bible-based books can be found, but few are the people who will commit themselves to share what Christ is doing in their lives and to help others grow in the grace and knowledge of our Lord Jesus Christ.

When has someone made the commitment to disciple you? Describe the experience you two shared and how you grew spiritually and personally.

When have you made the commitment to disciple another person? Again, describe the experience and how you both grew spiritually and personally.

Discipleship is an intensely personal ministry between two or more persons helping each other experience a growing relationship with God, and Jesus modeled this with His 12 disciples. In discipleship, being is before doing, maturity before ministry and character before career.

• Earlier questions asked about formal disciple/discipler relationships in your life. Whatever experiences your answers reflected, know that as a Christian you are both a disciple and a discipler, a learner and a teacher in your Christian relationships.

What role do you have in your family, church or Christian community that gives you the specific responsibility of discipling (teaching) others about God?

What opportunities do you have in your family, church or Christian community to be discipled?

As a discipler, you are always a disciple who is learning and growing in Christ. You may not have an official responsibility, but you have the opportunity to help your family members, your friends and other believers grow in Christ through these caring and committed relationships.

Whether you are a professional discipler and/or counselor or simply a growing Christian who is committed to helping others grow in Christ, let these designs for discipleship and concepts for counseling give you some basic practical guidelines for ministry.

Designs for Discipleship
(pages 228-234)

Based on Paul's words in Colossians 2:6-10, the three levels of maturity deal with the issues of being rooted in Christ, being built up in Christ and walking in Christ. Each level is dependent on the previous level(s), and the learning at each level must be experienced in five dimensions: spiritual, rational, emotional, volitional and relational. A point of conflict at each of these five dimensions of application indicates how sin, the world, the flesh and the devil interfere in the discipleship process (see Figures 13-A and 13-B on pp. 229-230). Please remember that there are no clear boundaries between the three levels of maturity or the five dimensions of application as the chart implies.

Level I: Rooted in Christ (Colossians 2:10)

● Being firmly rooted in Christ is based on the fact that 'in Him you have been made complete.'

Review the conflicts of Level I (see Figure 13-A, p. 229).

Which conflicts were especially challenging for you? How did you come to resolve those conflicts for yourself?

If you are a Level I believer now, welcome to God's family! Understand that He wants you to know of His deep love for you and will enable you to work through the conflicts of this stage (and beyond) as you become firmly rooted in Christ. Which conflicts are you experiencing now? What are you doing to work through them? Who is or could be a discipler for you?

If you are mature in your faith and able to be a discipler, review the five points of responsibility listed on pages 231-2. Which one(s) do you need to be better prepared to do? What will you do to become better prepared?

Level II: Built Up in Christ (Colossians 2:7)

- Being 'built up in Him' is how Paul described our maturity in Christ.

Review the conflicts of Level II (see Figure 13-A, pp. 229). Which conflicts were especially challenging for you? How did you come to resolve those conflicts for yourself?

If you are a Level II believer now, be encouraged during this stage of sanctification. God is at work in you as you grow in the likeness of Christ. Which conflicts are you experiencing now? What are you doing to work through them? Who is or could be a discipler for you?

If you are mature in your faith and able to be a discipler, review the five points of responsibility listed on page 233. Which one(s) do you need to be better prepared to do? What will you do to become better prepared?

Level III: Walking in Christ (Colossians 2:6)

● Walking in Christ means living out our faith in day-to-day life.

Review the conflicts of Level III (see Figure 13-A, p. 229). Which conflicts are especially challenging for you right now? What are you doing to resolve those conflicts?

When you are at this level — and you may be here now — you will find yourself being discipled as well as being a discipler to other Level III believers. With which point(s) of conflict do you need to be better prepared in order to help your fellow believers deal with similar points? What will you do to become better prepared?

The effective Christian walk involves the proper exercise of intellect, talents and spiritual gifts in serving others and being a positive witness in the world. Wherever you are on your spiritual journey, you can celebrate what Christ has already done in your life and look forward to what He will continue to do.

Concepts for Counseling
(pages 235-239)

● Are you willing to commit yourself to being the kind of person someone could confide in? In other words, are you willing to commit yourself to being like Christ?

What are your thoughts and feelings about counseling? Are you wary or skeptical? Are you unsure how to counsel or whether or not God uses counseling? Are you confident that one way God heals is through counseling?

Christian counseling seeks to help people resolve personal and spiritual conflicts through genuine repentance and faith in God. The goal of Christian counseling — whether done by a pastor, a professional counselor or a friend — is to help people experience their freedom in Christ so they can move on to maturity and fruitfulness in their walk with Him. Allow me to give you five practical tips for the formal or informal counseling you may do within your Christian relationships.

Help People Identify and Resolve Root Issues

- The first goal in counseling is to help the counselee identify the root cause for an unfruitful Christian walk.

Find Figure 13-C on page 237. When have any of the root causes of a barren life interfered with your Christian walk? What did you do about those blocks?

The fruitfulness of the branches is a result of the fertility of the soil and the health of the root system.

Encourage Emotional Honesty

- Counselees are generally willing to talk about what has happened to them, but they are less willing to admit responsibility and reveal how they feel about the situation. Emotional openness and honesty are key to healing, though.

Why are people so reluctant to talk about their feelings?

Why have you been or are you reluctant to talk about your feelings?

Have you had an experience like the missionary doctor in Africa had (see p. 238), in which you were trying to reach someone for Christ but nothing happened until you were emotionally honest? What occurred?

Unless you model and encourage emotional honesty, the chances of your counselee's resolving his or her inner conflicts and being set free in Christ are slim.

Share the Truth

- Life's hard blows can lead many Christians to wonder what's wrong with them. Their perception of God has been distorted, and they feel that He can't possibly love them.

  When have hard times made you wonder whether God loves you? What did you do to come to terms with those feelings and to come face-to-face with the truth that He loves you unconditionally and always?

  What would you say to someone doubting God's love in the face of life's pain and disappointments? (See 'Who Am I?' pp. 52-53; and 'Since I Am in Christ,' pp. 66-67.) Speak that truth to yourself if you're still trying to accept God's love for you.

  What a privilege to share with hurting believers who they are in Christ and to help them adjust their faulty belief system!

Call for a Response

- Your role is to share the truth in love and pray that the counselee will choose to believe it, but you cannot choose for him or her.

  What role has prayer played when you have been a counselee (whether formally or informally)?

  What struggles have you had to repent of, first changing

your mind and then your ways? Describe one time and let it remind you of what your counselees may be feeling.

Our Lord said to those seeking His touch: 'Your faith has made you well.' (Mark 5:34); 'Let it be done to you as you have believed' (Matthew 8:13). If those you share with will not repent and choose to believe the truth, you can't do much for them.

Help Them Be a Part of the Christian Community

• Help your counselees develop healthy, supportive relationships — family, friends, church. The Christian life was never intended to be lived alone. Progressive sanctification is a process that cannot be accomplished apart from the Christian community.

How has a strong support system helped you stand strong when life was tough? Describe the support system and list specific kinds of help you received from those involved.

How have you dealt with the never-fast-enough process of healing and change? What lessons that you learned along the way can you use to counsel and encourage a fellow believer?

The goal of counseling is to help people experience freedom in Christ so that they can move on to maturity and fruitfulness in their walk in Him.

LIVING WHAT YOU LEARN

If you have begun your spiritual journey relatively recently, pray for someone to disciple you. While you wait for that formal one-on-one relationship with a discipler, begin to work through a Bible-based study of spiritual growth on your own. Also, find a Bible study and experience the joy of Christian community as you learn more about your Lord and Savior and His love.

If you are farther along on your journey, ask God to help you be sensitive to His calling to come alongside someone and disciple him or her in a formal way that will mean mutual growth. In preparation for that discipling, work on those points of conflict that you identified earlier where you see yourself as weak.

A WORD OF PRAYER

Gracious and loving God,

Thank You for being a personal God — for sending Your Son who died for *my* sins, who is *my* Savior and who longs to have a personal relationship with *me*. And thank You that I can learn more about You and Your love through relationships with Your people. Thank You for putting in my life people to disciple and counsel me. Use me, Lord, to be a discipler and counselor for my brothers and sisters in Christ. I pray in Jesus' name. Amen.

LOOKING AHEAD

You are what you are by the grace of God. All you have and can hope for (as a discipler and disciple, as a counselor and counselee) is based on who you are in Christ. May your life and your ministry be shaped by your devotion to Him and the conviction that He is the way, the truth and the life (see John 14:6).

RESOURCES

Books

Anderson, Neil T. *The Bondage Breaker (with Study Guide)*. Rev. ed. London: Monarch Books, 2002.

———. *Breaking Through to Spiritual Maturity*. Ventura, CA: Gospel Light, 1992.

———. *Helping Others Find Freedom in Christ*. Ventura, CA: Regal Books, 1995.

———. *Living Free* (omnibus edition of *Living Free in Christ* and *Walking in the Light*). London: Monarch Books, 1999.

———. *Set Free* (omnibus edition of *Released from Bondage* and *A Way of Escape*). London: Monarch Books, 1998.

———. *Victory over the Darkness (with Study Guide)*. Rev. ed. London: Monarch Books, 2002.

Anderson, Neil T., and Hal Baumchen. *Finding Hope Again*. Ventura, CA: Regal Books, 1999.

Anderson, Neil T., and Tom McGee, Jr. *Helping Others Find Freedom in Christ Training Manual and Study Guide*. Ventura, CA: Gospel Light, 1995.

Anderson, Neil T., and Rich Miller. *Freedom from Fear*. London: Monarch Books, 1999.

———. *Walking in Freedom Devotional*. Ventura, CA: Regal Books, 1999.

Anderson, Neil T., and Charles Mylander. *The Christ-Centered Marriage*. Ventura, CA: Regal Books, 1996.

Anderson, Neil T., with Dave Park. *Radical Image*. London: Monarch Books, 1999.

———. *Higher Ground*. London: Monarch Books, 1999.

———. *Righteous Pursuit*. London: Monarch Books, 1999.

Anderson, Neil T., and Robert Saucy. *God's Power at Work in You*. London: Monarch Books, 2001.

Anderson, Neil T., and Elmer L. Towns. *Rivers of Revival*. Ventura, CA: Regal Books, 1997.

Anderson, Neil T., and Pete and Sue Vander Hook. *Spiritual Protection for Your Children*. Ventura, CA: Regal Books, 1996.

Anderson, Neil T., with Joanne Anderson. *Each New Day with Neil T. Anderson*. London: Monarch Books, 2001.

Warner, Tim. *Spiritual Warfare*. Wheaton, IL: Crossway Books, 1991.

Freedom in Christ is an international ministry which exists to glorify God by equipping churches, Christian organizations and mission groups in obedience to the Great Commandment in order to accomplish the Great Commission.

Freedom in Christ Ministries offers a number of valuable video, audio and print resources that will help both those who are in need and those who minister. Among the topics covered are the following:

Victory over the Darkness
Search for Identity • Walking by Faith • Faith Renewal • Renewing the Mind • Battle for the Mind • Emotions • Relationships • Forgiveness

The Bondage Breaker
Position of the Believer • Authority • Protection • Vulnerability • Temptation • Accusation • Deception and Discernment • Steps to Freedom in Christ

Discipleship Counseling
Biblical Integration • Theological Basis • Walking by the Spirit • Surviving the Crisis • The Process of Growth • Counseling and Christ

The Christ-Centered Marriage
God's Perfect Design • Disappointment with Marriage • Resolving Conflicts • Love Language • Sexual Freedom • The Snakebite of Adultery • Forgive Seventy Times Seven • When Only One Will Try • Steps to Setting Your Marriage Free

Freedom from Addiction
Programmed for Addiction • Who Will Set Me Free? •
Strongholds of Addiction — The Lies that Keep us in
Bondage • Our Greatest Needs • The Battle for the Body •
The Battle for the Mind

Setting Your Church Free
Protected from the Evil One • Prayer for Unity • Balance of
Power • Situational Leadership • Servant Leadership • The
Pastor as Saint • The Church in Communion • Looking at
Your Church's Strengths and Weaknesses • Dealing with the
Power of Memories • Dealing with Corporate Sins • The
Prayer Action Plan • Leadership Strategy

For a Resources Catalogue or further details of how
Freedom in Christ can help your church please contact:
Freedom in Christ Ministries (UK)
PO Box 2842
Reading
RG2 9RT

E-mail: ukoffice@ficm.org

Freedom In Christ
In The UK

Church Leaders - can we help you?

Many churches use Neil Anderson's material to help Christians find
their freedom in Christ - often with results that amaze them. If you
are a church leader and would like to establish your own "freedom
ministry", Freedom In Christ is here to help: we run a programme
of conferences and training; we can provide opportunities for
church leaders to see freedom appointments in action; and we are
always more than happy to offer advice.

Send for our Resource Catalogue

Send for our full colour catalogue of Neil Anderson books, videos
and audiocassettes. It includes resources for individuals, for
churches, and for local freedom ministries as well as for specialist
freedom areas such as fear, depression and addiction. It's also
crammed with hints and tips.

Join the UK Freedom Fellowship

If you are ministering to your community using Neil Anderson's
materials, join our network of like-minded Christians and receive
regular news, encouragement and affirmation. Open to anyone
involved in a local freedom ministry or considering setting one up.

For details of any of the above write to us at:

Freedom In Christ Ministries (UK), PO Box 2842, READING RG2 9RT

Or e-mail us: ukoffice@ficm.org

You can find the Freedom In Christ worldwide web site at www.ficm.org

"It is for FREEDOM that Christ has set us FREE"
Galatians 5:1

*Freedom in Christ is an international, interdenominational ministry whose objective is to
"free Christ's body to advance His kingdom".*

Please note that Freedom In Christ Ministries does not generally arrange
personal freedom appointments but works by equipping local churches.
We may be able to refer you to a local freedom ministry.